# PUBLIC LIBRARIES

PURCHASED AT PUBLIC SALE
OUT OF DATE MATERIAL FROM THE SLCLS

# PUBLIC LIBRARIES

---

*Travel Treasures of the West*

Marty and Anna Rabkin

NORTH AMERICAN PRESS
Golden, Colorado

Copyright © 1994 Marty and Anna Rabkin

Book design by Richard Firmage

All interior photos by the authors unless otherwise indicated.

*Front Cover Photos:*
  (top) Exterior, Wilkinson Public Library, Telluride, Colorado;
  Photo by David Marlow Studios, courtesy Gibson and Reno Architects
  (bottom left) Exterior, Green Valley Library, Henderson, Nevada;
  Photo courtesy Las Vegas–Clark County Library District
  (bottom right) Exterior, Linda Vista Branch Library, San Diego, California; Photo
  by Frank Domin, courtesy Rob Wellington Quigley, AIA

*Back Cover Photo:*
  Interior, Flagstaff City–Coconino County Library, Flagstaff, Arizona; Photo copyright © Timothy Hursley, courtesy Snowdon and Hopkins Architects

All rights reserved. No part of this publication may be reproduced, stored in a retrieval system or transmitted in any form or by any means, electronic, mechanical, photocopying, recording or otherwise without the prior written permission of the publisher.

Library of Congress Cataloging-in-Publication Data

Rabkin, Marty.
    Public libraries : travel treasures of the West / Marty and Anna Rabkin.
        p.    cm.
    Includes index.
    ISBN 1-55591-915-4 (pbk.)
    1. Public libraries—West (U.S.)—Guidebooks.   2. West (U.S.)—Guidebooks.   I. Rabkin, Anna.   II. Title.
Z732.W48R33    1993
027.4'025'78—dc20                                                                93-34680
                                                                                  CIP

Printed in the United States of America
0  9  8  7  6  5  4  3  2  1

North American Press
a division of Fulcrum Publishing
350 Indiana Street, Suite 350
Golden, Colorado 80401-5093

*This book is dedicated to Heinz Wellman,
who stretched our minds and horizons.*

# — CONTENTS —

| | |
|---|---|
| Foreword | ix |
| Preface | xiii |
| Acknowledgments | xv |
| Introduction | xvii |
| Alaska | 1 |
| Arizona | 7 |
| California | 25 |
| Colorado | 107 |
| Hawaii | 131 |
| Idaho | 145 |
| Montana | 155 |
| Nevada | 169 |
| New Mexico | 183 |
| Oregon | 201 |
| Texas | 223 |
| Utah | 267 |
| Washington | 283 |
| Wyoming | 311 |
| Index | 323 |
| List of Architects | 331 |

# — FOREWORD —

Anna and Marty Rabkin have developed an eclectic, personal and somewhat idiosyncratic guide to libraries in the 14 Western states. They visited hundreds of libraries in large cities, places near well-known tourist attractions and some that are not on the main tourist paths. The emphasis of the book is on public libraries, with a few museum or special libraries included that are open to the public.

What has resulted is a guidebook that you can take along with you as you travel, dip into as you plan your trip or take side trips as the spirit moves you. The book is arranged by state, then alphabetically by city. The perspective of the narrative is that of an interested library user who spots positive, interesting or perhaps unusual services or facts about the libraries that are described.

Look around you as you travel. Notice how the public spaces in public libraries are used. Often you will find that a community's public library is one of the few places where everyone can go. They are places where the generations mix without much conflict. Public libraries are also places where our diverse, multicultural communities can connect with ease. The information needs of our era require institutions like libraries that welcome everyone. Libraries can have comfortable enclaves or quiet spaces for contemplation. They can also be as busy as a department store during the after-Christmas sales. Anna and Marty Rabkin found that libraries have distinct personalities which often reflect the ambiance of the community. A large inner-city main library might be all business and somewhat impersonal while the branch or small city library can be more folksy and personal.

You may find a description of a service or activity that interests you, or a collection that has special or different approaches. The

Rabkins are interested in both the inside and the outside of libraries, and you will find much mention of architectural elements and details that lend themselves to better use or ease of operation by the public. They also describe how some older buildings, particularly Carnegie libraries, have been remodeled to serve modern needs without destroying the integrity of the original architecture and layout.

A good library is the heart of the community and will reflect that community's interests. As the Rabkins visited many public libraries in the West, they found that often local support of a library is directly related to the way that libraries complete their mission. This guide will help you look at libraries in other communities and see the kinds of services and events they offer to their community. Public libraries are one of the few publicly supported services that you visit just because you want to, without making an appointment and without knowing ahead of time what you want. You just walk in and you are welcome. Your public library will help you answer questions, and it will help your children complete their school assignments. It is also the place for you to find items to help you recreate, from a juicy novel to a video tape, to a compact disc, to a story hour for your children.

This book describes many different services provided by the public libraries. Many of these are the traditional ones that we all expect, books, books and more books. As our society has become more technological, public libraries also have made databases available, specialized reference services, magazine articles on-line, specialized business resources and the like. You can also find your community's records, the decisions of your city council, important documents related to development, Environmental Impact Reports and other public documents that will help keep you an informed citizen. In addition to all that technology, you will also find libraries that loan out toys, libraries that have little nooks for children so they can get away and pretend as they read, some that have "discovery" rooms to stimulate creativity and adventure for kids. Many libraries now recognize the importance of literacy and provide a venue for adult learners and their tutors. You will also find mention of art galleries, historical collections and other kinds of services. Take a look at these descriptions and you will be amazed at what libraries throughout the Western states are doing.

Most of all, your public libraries belong to you. You pay for them with your taxes. Your library is only as strong and responsive as your community wishes it to be. You can make a difference. As you visit these libraries, large or small, take the time to notice what they do and how they serve their communities. If an idea has merit to you, take it home and share it with your local library. Get active. Speak up. Tell your librarians and your public officials what you want from your library. If you are persistent, you have a good chance of getting what you want. An excellent library is one that knows how to give the community what it wants, when it wants it. You are a part of your community. You can make your library excellent by making sure that your library gets the resources it needs.

Regina Minudri<br>
Director, Berkeley Public Library<br>
Past President, American Library Association

# — PREFACE —

My love of libraries dates back to my discovery of bays of books in a room on the top floor of my small-town high school.

The room was open for student use only Mondays, Wednesdays and Fridays during lunch hour. On those days, I rushed to the top floor to comb the shelves for my favorite authors. Then I would ensconce myself in one of the window seats with my latest "windows on the world." In no time at all the daily anxieties of high school life receded. I often felt these were the most educational hours of my school week.

I have since lived in London, Paris, New York, San Francisco and, most recently, in Berkeley, California. I have had the pleasure of visiting some of the world's largest and best known libraries. Yet in none of these grand institutions was I able to recapture the excitement of those three hours a week or the tranquility of my first library experience. Perhaps the whimsical yet enduring hope that some day I might find the library of my dreams has been one of the motivating forces behind my life-long treasure hunt among the libraries of the world.

My husband and I have travelled extensively throughout North and Central America, Europe and Asia. When we were raising our two children, travel was one of the central features of our family life. And visiting libraries became a family tradition. Our children spent many happy hours in the children's rooms of libraries all across the United States. Sometimes they managed to finish entire books by reading a chapter in each town library we stopped in.

Searching for and visiting libraries greatly enriched our numerous road trips. Our quest for libraries took us off the usual tourist routes and into genuine neighborhoods. As we wound our way past schools and city parks, through residential streets and retail districts, we were exposed to the authentic culture, architecture and cuisine of the region. We often stumbled upon interesting local events, services or celebrations. Once we reached a library we could learn about special places or occasions from the bulletin boards, newspapers in the periodical section or library staff and patrons we met. Reference librarians appeared to welcome even our most obscure questions.

This project was conceived at the White House Conference on Libraries and Information Services in the summer of 1991. As a delegate to the conference I listened to President and Mrs. Bush, Members of Congress, the Librarian of Congress, educators and academicians all extol the virtues of libraries. They reminded us about the importance of libraries in a democratic society, the role they play in citizenship, literacy and productivity.

They preached to the choir. The choir was pleased to be appreciated. They wanted more than appreciation, however, they wanted help. I left Washington convinced that public libraries are in dire need and that we as citizens must increase our support for this culturally, historically and economically important institution.

In discussing the conference with my husband the idea for this book was born. No travel guide to significant U.S. libraries exists. There are travel guides to university campuses, museums, cemeteries, places of architectural interest, hot springs and churches ... to name just a few. By their existence they alert the public to the value of the particular subject they highlight. This book fills a void. We hope it will spur many visits to libraries. For frequent users of libraries these visits may be a reminder of libraries' importance in our local and national life. For less frequent library users we hope this will be a voyage of discovery and involvement.

Libraries are public assets funded mostly through local tax dollars. They compete for funding with police, fire and public works. Often they are underfunded, as local tax dollars are stretched to cover more and more needs, especially in urban communities. However, as we speed into the information-driven 21st century, government underfunding of libraries might be one of the worst investment decisions a democracy could make.

Libraries are at a critical point in their development. They can become museums or archives or they can continue as the public's information providers.

They can evolve and become even more.

# — ACKNOWLEDGMENTS —

Some books are individual efforts, some are collaborations and some the result of the work of a lot of people. This book could not have been completed without the help of hundreds of people. We want to express our gratitude to all of them, especially librarians. There seems to be something in the nature of people connected with libraries that makes them friendly and willing to help. We never ceased to be amazed and pleased at the assistance library staff gave us during our trips. They showed us around their libraries, told us about other libraries we should visit, told us about good restaurants and cheap motels ... they were always helpful.

We sent out over 1,500 questionnaires—to Anna's fellow delegates at the 1991 White House Conference on Libraries, to architects who had designed libraries and to librarians. Many of these busy people returned the questionnaires, which became major guideposts in our travels. One of our great regrets is that we did not have room to use more of the photographs so many librarians were kind enough to send us.

From the start we got key encouragement from some knowledgeable friends. Barbara Robinson, library consultant and "guru" was very helpful, as were Malcom Margolin, publisher of Heyday Books and Andy Ross, owner of Cody's Books, both in Berkeley. Two librarians who were especially helpful were Susan Nyfeler for the Central Texas Library System and Regina Minudri, director of the Berkeley Public Library and former president of the American Library Association.

A special group of friends encouraged us when the project grew in complexity and took much longer than expected. Tom Bates, Mal Burnstein, Loni Hancock, Karen Paget, Catherine Trimbur and Mal Warwick never failed to lift our sometimes flagging spirits.

Our daughter Michele provided tough and expert editing assistance. She and our son, Mark, were unwitting participants in this project, when as children, they sampled many of the libraries we are now revisiting.

Marty's office building colleagues never once let on how tired they must have been with one more interruption of their work with another library picture or tale. Elizabeth Cisse, Jodene Goldenring, John Heisch, Sandy Horwich, Ruth Ingram, Bruce Krumland and Ilsa Perse are Saints of Patience, at the very least.

Some people we met on the road really stand out. In the George Memorial library in Richmond, Texas, the front desk dispensed some freshly baked blueberry muffins to an obviously tired and hungry library researcher. In Albany, Oregon, Bill Bush, owner of the beautifully restored Marshall House, invited us to sit in the shade on his porch to rest our weary feet. Derik Ivens, a voyaging Britisher, shared a lot of miles, laughs and cockroaches with Marty in North Texas.

And if you're going to drive the vast distances of twelve states in the western continental United States (we drove 40,000 miles), the western edition of "Radio on Wheels," by Paul Rocheleau, published by Berkley Books, New York, is a life-saver. It categorizes radio stations and tells you where they are, on the map and on the dial. This book is a personal selection that just scratches the surface of the marvelous selection of libraries that abound in North America. For a complete index and guide, we used the detailed 2,400 page *American Library Directory,* published by R.R. Bowker, New Jersey.

Shirley Lambert of North American Press was always an enthusiastic, calm and patient center in the midst of a myriad of publishing detail.

Finally, we need to acknowledge that we didn't see all of the libraries in the fourteen states we cover in the book. And some we did see, we couldn't include in the book. But the choice of what to include was ours, and we feel that our choices, though eclectic, are representative.

Marty and Anna Rabkin<br>
Berkeley, California<br>
April 1993

# — INTRODUCTION —

This is not a "stand-alone" travel guide to Alaska, Arizona, California, Colorado, Hawaii, Idaho, Montana, Nevada, New Mexico, Oregon, Texas, Utah, Washington and Wyoming. It is a guide to new, interesting and useful destinations in these states not found in other travel books.

The guide describes libraries that we think you will enjoy and gives some additional local information. For quick reference we have included symbols that classify the libraries:

| Symbol | Meaning |
|---|---|
| A | An architecturally outstanding building |
| E | An exciting place worth a visit as a destination on its own |
| H | A building of some specific historic interest |
| T | A library near a popular tourist attraction |
| V | A library with a spectacular view |

You will find that library visits add new perspectives to your travels. They take you off the beaten tourist path into interesting neighborhoods and locations. They give you a window on both the diversity of populations served and the diversity of services provided. They will make you recognize the changing role libraries play in their communities. They will make you appreciate communities that insisted on architecturally sensitive buildings for their libraries or found creative ways to "recycle" old buildings.

Libraries are incredibly useful—in far more ways than in their classic functions of storing and disseminating information. Certainly they are the repository of the sum of humankind's knowledge, but they're also a lot more. Public libraries are also community centers, bulletin boards, places to relax, places to wash up, places to get out of the sun or the rain or the heat, places to find out what's going on in town and all around you. If kids traveling with you are starting to squabble over who gets to sit by which window, why not stop at a library for some quiet relaxation? And when you're traveling, where else can you go to sit and relax without having to buy something to put in your mouth?

Many of the libraries we have listed were originally "Carnegie" libraries. Over 1,400 American communities received over $55,000,000 from Andrew Carnegie and his nonprofit Carnegie Corporation for the construction of more than 1,600 library buildings. This huge building program started in the 1890s. Andrew Carnegie's primary requirement was that the local community agree to fund the operation of the library in the future. His magnificent act of philanthropy was key to the development of the entire American library system. Now most public libraries are supported by local tax dollars. The country has a huge investment in public libraries. As we enter the "information age" that investment should be protected and maintained.

We have listed mostly public, tax-supported libraries. Some membership libraries, some privately supported and some adjuncts to other institutions have been included, but our essential thrust is public, tax-supported libraries. Many academic and private libraries are splendid, both in architecture and in collections, but they are not easily accessible to or useable by the general public.

The arrangement of the book reflects this thrust. Entries are arranged by state and by city within state. The main public library for the city or town (if selected for inclusion) is the first entry, followed by any branches that we think are worthy of mention. Other kinds of libraries—research, museum, film, genealogical and so on—are arranged alphabetically after the public libraries under the heading "Also of Note."

Unless otherwise stated, all of the libraries we have described are wheelchair accessible. Since most libraries have local history and genealogy collections, we have only mentioned these collections when they are larger than usual. Hours and days of operation change rapidly, so we've supplied a telephone number for each library. If you're on a tight schedule, you might want to call before you arrive. Even though you are not a permanent resident in a place you are visiting, you can usually check out books. Check with the circulation desk—most libraries issue temporary cards (although in some places you may have to put down a deposit).

This book was written from the perspective of two library buffs ... and pretty idiosyncratic ones at that. We are not librarians, so we were not burdened by having to recommend that you visit only those libraries that work well for the staff. In fact, staff find some of our favorite libraries awkward to use; we hope they'll forgive us.

If a library isn't listed it may mean that we weren't able to visit it, or that there was a more attractive library within a few miles or that it just didn't stand out. We mailed 1,500 questionnaires to libraries and our travels were greatly influenced by the returns we got. If you want to see all the libraries we visited (including the ones we didn't list) prepare to drive 40,000 miles and visit about 550 public libraries (out of 3,500 in the 14-state area).

If we missed a public library that you think should have been included, please write us at The Library Guide Project, 930 Dwight Way, Berkeley, CA 94710. Also let us know about favorite libraries for inclusion in guides to other regions or in updates of this guide. As they say at your local library, "Check it out."

Look around any public library and you'll see a fascinating mix of people, young and old, white and nonwhite, English speaking and not—the true picture of the local society. More people of all ages are being trained in the use of computers in libraries than any place else; just take a look at the children's areas and you'll see young people looking up books (and playing educational games) on computers. Libraries are where millions of people are being introduced to the latest in technology on a day-to-day basis.

# · ALASKA ·

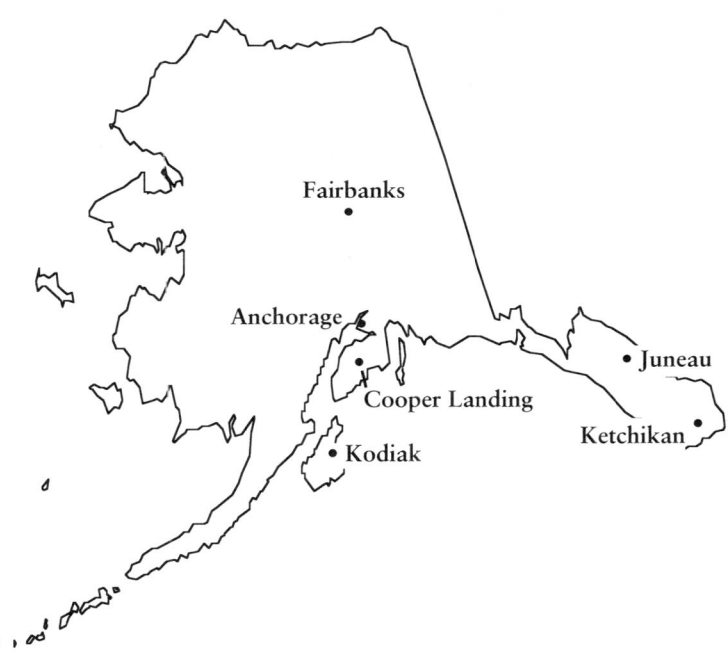

# ANCHORAGE

## Z. J. Loussac Public Library

| | |
|---|---|
| 3600 Denali | A, E |
| (907) 261-2975 | Open every day in fall and winter |
| | Call during summer |

Rather than build its new library in constricted space in the heart of downtown Anchorage, the city instead chose a location on 17 acres at 36th and Denali. An exciting, multi-purpose building, this modern four-story structure also houses the Anchorage Municipal Assembly Chambers as well as the 232-seat Wilda Marston Theater. On the first level is a bronze sculpture by Joan Bugbee Jackson; *Arctic Echoes*, a large fabric wall hanging by Janet Kummerlain, overlooks the circulation desk. While thoroughly modern, the building's huge columns and the dome over the Alaska collection recall older and more formal buildings. The library was designed by Environmental Concern, Inc. of Spokane, Washington, and opened in 1986.

A bridge from the third level of the library leads to a striking three-story circular wing housing an excellent Alaska collection. On the bridge you'll find an art gallery and the opulent Ann Stevens reading room. In the Alaska collection wing a mezzanine circles the main reading room, just as a mezzanine in the third-level reference area looks down to the main entrance.

The children's area, with a story theater and a section for young adults, is on the entrance level. You'll find interesting art and displays throughout the building and its parklike setting.

Anchorage, AK
Z.J. Loussac Public Library
Photo by Harry McBeth

*Also of Note:*

## Anchorage Museum Library

121 West Seventh Avenue
(907) 343-6189

Closed Saturdays, Sundays in summer
Closed Saturdays, Sundays, Mondays in winter

The Anchorage Museum of History and Art is the largest museum in the state. It has collections devoted to Alaska's history and native cultures as well as Alaskan art from many ages. There's a cafe on the premises; in summer the flower gardens are marvelous.

The Museum Library has a collection of over 200,000 images and photographs of Alaska and Alaskan art. It also has biographical files on Alaskan artists.

# —— COOPER LANDING ——

## Cooper Landing Community Library

Bean Creek Road
(907) 595-1241

Closed Sundays

The library in rural Cooper Landing is a log cabin, made from logs cut in this area. It was built by Tom Walker, a well-known photographer, author and log cabin builder. The library is warm and cozy, with an easy chair, wood stove and tea for the asking. A collection of Walker's photos hangs in the library.

The nearby Kenai River is famous for its salmon and bald eagle populations. The town has Athabaskan Indian, Russian and gold mining sites of historic interest.

Juneau, AK; Juneau Public Library
Photo courtesy Minch, Ritter, Voelckers Architects

## —— JUNEAU ——

### Juneau Public Library

| | |
|---|---|
| 292 Marine Way | A, V |
| (907) 586-5324 | Open every day |

If your tour ship ties up at a dock next to a four-story garage with a glassed-in structure on top, you're docked next to the Juneau Public Library. This unique solution to finding space in a crowded downtown area has produced a gem of a library, with some of the best views to be found. There had been a huge local outcry over the building of a four-story garage on the waterfront, but retrofitting an 18,000-square-foot library to the top floor has proven universally popular. An express elevator takes pedestrians straight up, while those who park in the garage can use the "local."

Bookshelves and circulation desks have been carefully placed to preserve as many views as possible. Most service facilities are in the center of the library. From some windows you can see the waterfalls on Mount Juneau and from others the marine and seaplane traffic on

Gastineau Channel. A high-walled foyer at one corner and peaked multi-use rooms at others provide more great views.

Architects Minch, Ritter, Voelckers of Juneau provided a splendid design for this unique library.

## —— KETCHIKAN ——

### Ketchikan Public Library

629 Dock  
(907) 225-3331   Open every day

Ketchikan, an island city of just over 8,000, is Alaska's southernmost city. It is also America's rainiest city, with annual rainfall of more than 150 inches. Its most famous tourist attraction is Creek Street, with art galleries, shops and a museum built on boardwalks over Ketchikan Creek.

The library is built right along Ketchikan Creek. Wall-to-wall windows overlook the creek from this 1967 building. In early spring you can watch fly fishermen fishing for steelhead. In July and August you can see salmon swimming upstream to spawn.

## —— KODIAK ——

### A. Holmes Johnson Memorial Library

319 Lower Mill Bay Road  
(907) 486-8680   Open every day

Though small, this is one of the busiest libraries in Alaska. Many of its patrons are employees at the nearby fish processing plants who live in tents or cannery dorms during the summer. The library specializes in the Russian settlement aspect of local history, with additional material on anthropology and archaeology.

Kodiak was founded by Russians in 1792, and the Russian Orthodox church and seminary are near the library. It's also only a short walk to the Baranov Museum, which is housed in the oldest building in Alaska.

# · ARIZONA ·

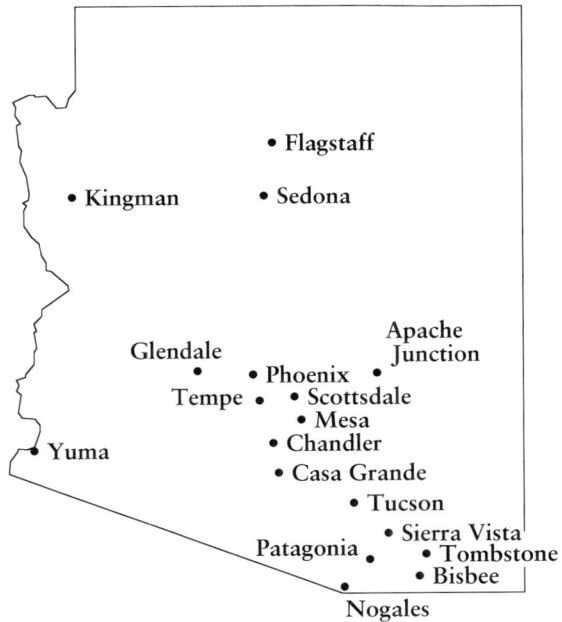

# —— APACHE JUNCTION ——

## Apache Junction Public Library

| | |
|---|---|
| 1177 North Idaho Road | V |
| (602) 982-0204 | Closed Sundays |

The view of the Superstition Mountains through the library's 20-foot-high windows is spectacular. You don't see out over a new real estate development or shopping center since the library is on the edge of the desert. You can walk right out into it if you're tired of the highway.

Stop and cool off inside. This pleasant community library shares a building with a senior center. One end of the tiled, 25-foot-wide hall between the library and senior center is all windows (in front of a tiled lounge area) looking out at the mountains.

Apache Junction is about 30 miles from Phoenix on the scenic Pinal Pioneer Parkway (State Highway 89) route to Tucson and Nogales.

Apache Junction, AZ
Apache Junction Public Library

# BISBEE

## Cochise County Library

Old Bisbee High School  T
(602) 423-9250  Closed Saturdays, Sundays

This historic old mining town is in the bottom of Mule Pass Gulch. The ravine is so steep that the library (in the Old Bisbee High School) is built on a hill with ground floor entrances on four different levels. Downtown Old Bisbee is alive with restored buildings and stores that sell crafts and Western art.

# CASA GRANDE

## Casa Grande Public Library

405 East Sixth Street  T
(602) 421-8690  Open every day

Casa Grande National Monument contains mysterious Hohocam Indian ruins (the main building is a three-story packed-mud creation) out in the desert near Casa Grande. The town was named after the ruins. This thinly developed country is about 50 miles southeast of Phoenix. The interpretive center and museum at the ruins raise as many questions about the disappearance of the Hohocams as they answer.

It gets really hot out at the monument even though the visitor center is air conditioned, and the library (about 5 miles away in a small park in the middle of town) is a good place to drop off anyone who doesn't want to explore the ruins.

## —— CHANDLER ——

### Chandler Public Library

| 25 South Arizona Place | A |
|---|---|
| (602) 786-2314 | Open every day in winter; closed Sundays in summer |

Chandler, southeast of Phoenix, is one of the early planned communities of this area. The library is on the street floor of a large commercial building in the heart of the city's downtown center, across the plaza from the upscale, historic San Marcos hotel and golf resort.

You can't miss the town's center because of the striking colorful colonnade and plaza that extend for several blocks. This is a good example of how to make an otherwise plain town center memorable.

## —— FLAGSTAFF ——

### Flagstaff City–Coconino County Public Library

| 300 West Aspen | A, E, T, V |
|---|---|
| (602) 774-4000 | Open every day |

Perhaps it's the unpainted wood, the local stone or the comfortable furniture, but in any case, an accurate observer has said, "One does not so much enter this building as put it on, like a favorite flannel shirt." And this is especially unusual in a very large library.

Flagstaff, AZ
Flagstaff City–Coconino County
Public Library

There simply aren't many other libraries that have four stone-faced fireplaces or upholstered wing-back chairs sitting in front of spectacular views. There's even a footbridge over a stream leading to one entrance. Throw in a fine selection of handwoven rugs, a good children's room and an interactive tourist information computer and you have a real winner.

When you think about Arizona, you normally don't think of mountains, but the altitude in Flagstaff is 7,000 feet. This alpine-style library would be at home in the Alps or the northern Rocky Mountains. The view of the San Francisco Peaks (the state's highest mountain range) makes the use of huge wood-laminate trusses and cathedral ceilings totally appropriate. The architects were Snowdon and Hopkins of Vail, Colorado, who also did the award-winning library in Vail.

Flagstaff is only 80 miles south of the Grand Canyon. The 30-mile drive south from here through Oak Creek Canyon to Sedona is spectacular, while 45 miles to the east of Flagstaff is the best preserved meteor crater on earth (570 feet deep).

## —— GLENDALE ——

### Glendale Public Library

5959 West Brown Avenue     E, A
(602) 435-4900     Open every day

Glendale's main library is large, bold and exciting. As you approach you see three tall, green, copper-covered towers. Up close, the glass-roofed main area seems open to the sky. An interlaced set of white metal trusses supports huge expanses of glass. There is a marvelous open feel to this library which backs up onto Sahuaro Ranch Park, where a ranch/orchard is in the process of being restored. Incredibly, the park has peacocks everywhere, on the grounds, the buildings and even in the trees. This is an exciting place to visit.

The interior of the library is as bold as the exterior. From burgundy bookshelves to its complete gift shop, this library seems to have it all. The children's room is large and full of kid-oriented exhibits.

# KINGMAN

## Mohave County Library

3269 North Burbank
(602) 692-2665                                                  Closed Sundays

Kingman is 200 miles east of Barstow and 140 miles west of Flagstaff, so its library makes a convenient stopping place (take the Stockton Hill exit off Highway 40). Surprisingly, it's a huge gray stone building with a striking blue metal roof.

Massive laminated beams crossing between stone columns and enormous bridge-style trusses support the high ceilings. The rough-cut stone blocks contrast well with the wooden beams and trusses. Clerestory windows spill light onto rather utilitarian furnishings. Comfortable chairs and tables are well lit by light reflected off the paneled ceilings.

# MESA

## Mesa Public Library

64 East First Street
(602) 644-2702          Closed Sundays in summer; open every day in winter

This library is on the ground floor of the building that houses Mesa's municipal offices. The building, with an interesting bas-relief sculpture in front, is near the city center of this neighbor of Phoenix and just down the street from the local historical museum. The library is large and open.

Truly exciting for almost any type of hobbyist or news hound are the racks and racks of periodicals—the library subscribes to 2,300.

*Arizona*

## Dobson Ranch Branch Library

2425 South Dobson Road
(602) 644-3443                                Closed Sundays, Mondays

This pleasant neighborhood branch shows how a library can be integrated into a community park. The library is almost hidden behind earthen knolls in a park with lots of playground equipment. Try this one if you have children who would like to play while you relax.

# —— NOGALES ——

## Nogales City–Santa Cruz County Public Library

518 North Grand Avenue                                              T
(602) 287-3343                                            Closed Sundays

If someone in your group doesn't feel like going across the border into Mexico at Nogales and being pushed into shops to buy rugs, ceramics and silver, you might drop them off for an hour or so in the Nogales Library, about a half mile from the border.

It's a pleasant building with a small park outside and a good place to spend some time even though the library itself isn't terribly exciting.

# —— PATAGONIA ——

## Patagonia Public Library
## Nogales City–Santa Cruz County Library

Duquesne Avenue
(602) 394-2010                                            Closed Sundays

This tiny, old-fashioned library on a back street in a small desert town surrounded by mountains is across the street from Lopez's Pool Hall. It will give you a good idea of what a hidden library can be like. One full-time librarian position is shared by two people plus one clerk. Try out this truly rural town and library.

Patagonia, on the outskirts of the Coronado National Forest, is on the route from Nogales to Tombstone. If you're a little overwhelmed with people from the crowded, crooked streets of Nogales, this is a nice route to get back to "country."

# —— PHOENIX ——

## Phoenix Public Library

12 East McDowell Road
(602) 262-4636     Open every day

This older facility next to the Phoenix Art Museum will be moved—probably after 1995. The plaza which the library shares with the museum is frequently used for sculpture exhibits. From the inside, mezzanines look down over large reading areas and out into the plaza through floor-to-ceiling windows.

Since there is a pleasant open atrium (with a small garden) in the center of the building, the reading rooms get a fair amount of daylight from all sides. So far there has been more investment in branch libraries and libraries in surrounding communities than in this location, even though the collection here is quite large.

## Cholla Branch Library

10050 Metro Parkway East (Metrocenter Mall)     E, A
(602) 534-3770     Closed Sundays in summer; open every day in winter

Located in a shopping mall, this iconoclastic library was designed by local architect William Bruder. It's a knockout. Its curious structure is like a three-story Quonset hut standing on end—concrete and metal walls with a semicircular concrete front.

On the outside of the building are shiny creations that look like television guns. These are part of a kinetic art sculpture that was recently added to the complex. They gather the ever-present Arizona sunshine and scatter its extracted colors across the interior surfaces of the library. Inside, neon signs direct you to the reading areas and there's a plastic "yellow brick road" leading up to the check-out desk. Modern

Phoenix, AZ
Cholla Branch Library

and almost kooky in appearance (it sure doesn't look like any other library you've ever seen), it's also quite comfortable. The use of industrial materials in the interior design sets up a warehouse-like effect that contrasts with nooks and corners furnished with comfortable chairs for resting and reading.

There's no forgetting that this library is in a shopping center. It's located between two movie complexes and a pizza parlor.

## Ironwood Branch Library

| | |
|---|---|
| 4333 East Chandler Boulevard | A |
| (602) 534-1900 | Open every day |

The black iron elements of the fence surrounding this small library are carried over in the interior design. Inside, the black trusses supporting the ceiling of the main reading room are exposed (on a smaller scale than the grand expanses of the Glendale Public Library) to produce a light and airy feeling.

This is a good place to stop if you want to get off the freeway and unwind before getting caught in Phoenix traffic. If you have some questions about Phoenix the friendly staff will probably be able to answer them for you. This new building is on the very southern end of Phoenix, about 1 mile east of Interstate 10, the main route from Tucson. It's in the heart of a rapidly expanding residential area—one housing development after another, some single family homes, some apartments and condominiums.

## Mesquite Branch Library

4525 Paradise Village Parkway North
(Paradise Mall)
(602) 262-7299

Closed Sundays in summer;
open every day in winter

On the edge of the Paradise Valley Mall, a huge, upscale shopping center, this library is very handy if you've been "malling" for a few hours. At least here you can sit down and rest your feet without having to buy anything.

*Also of Note:*

## Arizona Hall of Fame Museum and the Carnegie Library

1101 West Washington
(602) 255-2110

A, H
Closed Saturdays, Sundays

A classic example of an early Carnegie library, this solid brick pile is no longer used as a library. It now houses the Arizona Hall of Fame which focuses on the people and history of the state. First opened in 1908, it was designed by W. R. Norton in the Classic Eclectic style.

On the national register of historic landmarks, the library was built for $25,000. In 1984 it underwent a $1.3 million renovation after more than 20 years of nonlibrary use. It's surrounded by a pleasant park, but the neighborhood, between the county and state government sections of downtown Phoenix, is somewhat run-down.

## Arizona State Library

State Capitol, Room 200, 1700 West Washington
(602) 255-4035

T
Closed Saturdays, Sundays

This relaxing, wood-paneled room with nice light and comfortable leather chairs is on the third floor of the State Capitol building—a legislative research library and reading room that is open to the public. It's a pleasant place for relaxing if you have some business at the legislature and would like to unwind for a while.

In the basement of the same building is a genealogy library, called "The Root Cellar." It's not big in size, but it's packed with all sorts of genealogical research materials. Across the hall is a comprehensive map room. We saw some fascinating computer-generated county maps.

## Desert Botanical Garden, Richter Library

1201 North Galvin Parkway, Papago Park     T, V
(602) 941-1217     Closed Saturdays, Sundays

Not everything that thrives in the desert is a cactus. This library is in the beautiful desert botanical garden in Papagao Park. The park (which charges a small entrance fee) has a gift shop, snack bar and places for outdoor eating in addition to beautiful walks around the well-tended desert botanical displays. Trail guides are available and desert plants can be purchased at the nursery. The library staff will be glad to answer your questions about desert plants in general as well as about the plants you see in the garden. The staff will also help you with questions about plants that you have or are thinking of getting for your home.

The area surrounding the library and garden shows the desert in its natural state. It gives you an idea of what this area looked like before contemporary downtown Scottsdale and Phoenix came into being.

## Phoenix Art Museum Library

1625 North Central Avenue     T
(602) 257-1880     Closed Saturdays, Sundays

Currently located in one room in the basement of the Phoenix Art Museum, this library eventually will be moved across the courtyard to the quarters of the Phoenix Main Public Library. An interesting place to go if you get "museum feet" after having explored the museum for a while or if you need some more detailed information about the collection. Expect a lot of information about art; not much comfort.

Finding the library is difficult—down the end of a bunch of halls and a flight of stairs. The museum is well worth a visit.

## —— SCOTTSDALE ——

### Scottsdale Public Library

| | |
|---|---:|
| 3839 Civic Center Boulevard | A, T |
| (602) 994-2476 | Open every day |

This complex shows how successfully regional architecture can be realized. A pleasant blend of old and new in Spanish-style, adobe architecture, the solid white library is set in the sculpture and fountain garden of Scottsdale Civic Center. Between the library and the city hall is a peaceful swan pond surrounded by whimsical sculptures.

The library's multistory, open construction allows you to go up on the balcony to reading rooms that look down into central reading areas. They are divided into a number of sections, some quite small and intimate. Comfortable upholstered furniture invites you to sit and read for a while.

The library is currently planning an expansion which will more than double its size. The Western art room has a large collection of Kachina totems (although if you are really interested in these, visit the Heard Museum in Phoenix).

The modern, well-designed Civic Center complex in which the library rests is near Scottsdale Old Town, with its many art galleries, and about five blocks from Scottsdale's more glitzy Galleria shopping area.

### Mustang Library

| | |
|---|---:|
| 10101 North 90th Street | A, V, T |
| (602) 391-6061 | Open every day |

Mustang Library, while not huge, has architecture so striking it has been featured on the cover of *American Libraries* magazine. On the edge of town, its powerful architecture has the feeling of a ship sailing up out of the desert. A branching concrete tower echoes nearby saguaro cactus plants. The library boasts a 50-foot brick bas relief of its namesake on the Mustang Wall. This is a good looking and very useable modern library with pale mauve upholstered furniture and lots of windows.

The large children's section is separated from the rest of the library by glass walls so you can see what the kids are doing but their noise is contained. The children's story room features a small stage and puppet theater.

This branch is near Architect Paolo Solari's Cosanti foundation and school, as well as Taliesin West (Frank Lloyd Wright's Arizona headquarters, now an architectural firm and school).

Scottsdale, AZ
Mustang Library

## —— SEDONA ——

### Sedona Public Library

| | |
|---|---|
| 395 Jordan Road | E, T, A |
| (602) 282-7714 | Closed Sundays |

Natural red rock and weathered copper and glass in this brand new building reflect the glorious red rock scenery in Oak Creek Canyon (Highway 89A) that runs north from Sedona to Flagstaff. The library is supported by contributions, not taxes, so the operators have to watch operating costs even more carefully than most. The building's architects, Design Group, designed it with such care for natural resource conservation that during most days they won't have to turn on the lights.

Sedona is a marvelous art center with many shops and museums set in splendid red-rock country. The library underscores the town's artistic commitment with six display areas (indoors and out) to accommodate rotating displays of art.

There's a lot to do in Sedona, including hot air balloon rides, back country four-wheel-drive trips and gallery browsing. The brand new library is a good place for contemplating some of what you've seen.

## —— SIERRA VISTA ——

### Sierra Vista Public Library

| | |
|---|---|
| 2950 East Tacoma | V |
| (602) 458-4225 | Open every day |

On the edge of a mountain town this library sits in the midst of community athletic fields, all of which are lit so they can be used day and night. The views of the surrounding Huachuca Mountains (snow-capped in the winter) are terrific.

Sierra Vista is 22 miles north of the Coronado National Memorial. The main industries here are nearby Fort Huachuca and horse breeding, with horse shows most weekends.

Tempe, AZ
Tempe Public Library

## TEMPE

### Tempe Public Library

| | |
|---|---|
| 3500 South Rural Road | E, A |
| (602) 350-5555 | Open every day |

When you drive up to Tempe's new main library, in a complex with the Tempe historical museum and tourist center your first reaction will be, "This place is big." Once inside the library, your reaction will be, "This place is bigger than I thought it was." But even though the library is big and modern, it's comfortable and airy. There are lots of windows and it's decorated in a contemporary Southwestern style.

The large reading rooms are divided by shelves and tables so you have a sense of privacy. The upholstered furnishings are very comfortable. One room of study carrels has a wall of glass brick that lets in a lovely, warm light to add to the artificial lights. This is the type of place you wish your kids had access to for their studies.

In 1992 the staff believed there would be enough expansion room for the next ten years. It's rare to see a library with so much extra shelf space.

Massive numbers of computers are connected to the main catalog. One wall has 24 PAC (Public Access Catalog) terminals in a row. Part of the basement level looks like the library of the future. Dozens of computer terminals, CD readers and microfilm projectors sit side-by-side so you can do research on almost any electronic information system.

## —— TOMBSTONE ——

### Tombstone Reading Station

| | |
|---|---|
| Fourth and Toughnut Streets | T, H |
| (602) 457-3612 | Closed Saturdays, Sundays |

Even the home of the "Shoot-Out at the OK Corral" has a public library. This Old West town full of gift shops, souvenir stores and privately operated museums is fascinating for the devotee of western history. You can walk down wooden sidewalks to the library at Fourth and Toughnut streets.

In fact you can ride up and tie your horse to the hitching post in front of the library. Then you can visit the famous corral where the shoot-out actually took place. Touristy but fun.

## —— TUCSON ——

### Tucson Public Library

| | |
|---|---|
| 101 North Stone Avenue | E, A |
| (602) 791-4114 | Open every day |

A truly exciting library! Don't miss this large, distinguished four-story angular building on a plaza in the heart of downtown Tucson. It holds its own with the glittering high rises nearby. The sedate entry to

Tucson, AZ
Tucson Public Library

the building is highlighted by a huge, fire engine red metal sculpture that stands in contrast to the straight lines of the building.

Inside the decor creates a feeling of comfort. Some reading areas are glassed off from more active reference areas. There are many small conference rooms that groups can use for studying or meeting.

Most people would be happy to have these elegant and comfortable chairs and couches in their home. The light purple and mauve upholstery contrasts pleasantly with expanses of gray carpet. In the spacious children's room there is a special Southwest collection. There are separate areas for children and young adults.

## Bear Canyon Branch Library

8959 East Tanqueverde Road (Bear Canyon Shopping Center)
(602) 791-5021                                                                           Closed Sundays

In the eastern outskirts of Tucson, fully occupying one of the buildings in a large shopping center, this modern branch is not a bad place to stop while you replenish your supplies. As in most of Tucson, there is a nice view of the mountains.

## River Center Branch Library

5605 East River Road (River Center Shopping Center)                                     V
(602) 791-4979                                                                           Closed Sundays

A branch library in a shopping center but with a different feel—the library is *in* the shopping center, not on one edge of it. Its entrance is near upscale restaurants and cafes, a Southwestern craft gift shop and a cafe with outdoor tables. The library has neon signs to compete with the glitz of the stores in the center.

If you feel like a beer or a cocktail while your kids take a break with a book, this is a good place. The outdoor tables of the cafe are within a few feet of the library entrance, so it's a fabulous place to sip a margarita while those too young for that kind of refreshment spend some time in the library.

There are marvelous views of the mountains from the shopping center.

# YUMA

## Yuma County Public Library

| | |
|---|---|
| 350 Third Avenue | T |
| (602) 782-1871 | Closed Sundays |

After driving across the desert from San Diego or Los Angeles on the west or Casa Grande on the east, it's refreshing to find the oasis of green lawn surrounding the Yuma County Public Library.

Pleasant but somewhat old-fashioned, this library is located in the cultural/historic district of Yuma. It is only a few blocks from the Colorado River which marks the boundary between Arizona and California. A curious bit of history near Yuma is the remnants of the old Plank Road, which was a wooden road built through the sand dunes, in service from 1915 to 1926.

# · CALIFORNIA ·

## ——— ANAHEIM ———

### Anaheim Public Library

500 West Broadway     T
(714) 999-1880     Closed Sundays

While it seems heresy to suggest it, some members of families have had enough visits to Disneyland. The Anaheim Public Library is only five minutes away, and makes a good drop-off place while other family members spend the day with Mickey, Minnie, and friends.

The library was built in 1963. The recently recarpeted main room has been repainted in calm blues and grays. The library is brilliantly lit by what seems like a whole ceiling of light panels. This is very much an urban library with lots of tables and chairs for study.

There's a very large children's room although most travelling children will prefer Disneyland. The library does have one of three Disney Research collections in existence, the other two being at the Burbank, California studio and in Florida.

## ——— ARCATA ———

### Arcata Branch Library, Humboldt County Library

500 Seventh Street
(707) 822-5954     Closed Sundays, Mondays

It may be the influence of a branch of the California State University or left-over "vibes" from former resident author Bret Harte, but Arcata is a remarkably eclectic community. This is, after all, the starting point of the annual May "World Championship Great Arcata to Ferndale Kinetic Sculpture Race" as well as home to a host of good restaurants and community activities.

The library is light chocolate brown in color, all wood, with a small barrel dome skylight near the entrance. The small picnic area just outside invites you to sit and relax with a book (although this area is frequently foggy). There's a children's section to the left as you enter— find a cassette player so your kids can sit and listen to music or stories.

One unique touch is a large, clear aerial photograph of the city under glass on a tabletop. It really gives you a good idea of your surroundings.

## ——— ATASCADERO ———

### Atascadero Public Library

| | |
|---|---|
| 6850 Morro Road | A |
| (805) 466-0142 | Closed Fridays, Sundays |

Stocky columns supporting a heavy canopy the length of the building give this new library a unique appearance. The overhang is mauve, the recessed wall in back of the columns is white. The library is located only about a block from Highway 101.

The ceiling rises to a 30-foot peak above the entrance, and reflected light bounces down from white panels. One end of this elegant room opens onto a patio.

At the back of the library reading areas face fenced-in gardens. One end of the library is the children's area, well signed and very pleasant. It has comfortable reading chairs for both adults and children, and adjoining it is another enclosed outdoor reading area, this one with garden furniture. The library was designed by Ken McIntyre of San Luis Obispo.

## ——— BAKERSFIELD ———

### Beale Memorial Library, Kern County Library

| | |
|---|---|
| 701 Truxtun Avenue | A |
| (805) 861-2135 | Closed Sundays |

Bakersfield has a smaller population than either Fresno or Stockton, two other major cities in California's great San Joaquin Valley, but its library situation is immeasurably better.

The Beale Memorial Library, Bakersfield's main library, is only a block or so from the glitzy new Kern County administrative building.

The library is a large ocher building (over 120,000 square feet) that looks big from the outside, and even bigger inside. The overall feeling you get as you wander around this multi-story building is of generous space. Even the check-out and reference desks seem larger than expected.

A grand staircase with oak banisters leads upstairs from the main floor. Large expanses of gray-green carpet and teal upholstered furniture complement the interior design. From the second floor, smaller staircases lead to mezzanine stacks. This level also has lots of reading spaces and comfortable furniture, as well as enclosed special collection rooms for collections on Local History and Geology, Mining and Petroleum. These spacious and well furnished rooms have outside windows, and their inner windows let the light flow through into the main reading library.

Parsons, Brinckerhoff of San Francisco designed the building, which was completed in 1987. It is centered around an atrium that provides a pleasant reading area on days when the valley temperature is not overwhelming. The large children's room is on the main floor.

Bakersfield, CA
Southwest Branch Library, Kern County

## Southwest Branch Library, Kern County Library

| | |
|---|---|
| 8301 Ming Avenue | A |
| (805) 664-7716 | Closed Sundays, Fridays |

The library is in a rapidly developing new section of Bakersfield and only a few blocks from the Ming exit of Highway 99. A modern and striking building, it is radically different from the more traditional Beale Memorial library in downtown Bakersfield. A high black canopy mounted on four white two-story columns dominates the entrance. High-tech black glass panels contrast with stone walls. This could be the headquarters of a Silicon Valley computer firm.

Inside, huge heating and air conditioning ducts sweep across the ceiling. Exposed structural beams and fluorescent light fixtures hang down past them on 20 foot rods. The ceiling is at least 30 feet high, with a mezzanine above the main floor. Upstairs you can relax in a comfortable and well lit reading area.

The soundproofed glass walls let lots of light into this cool library. Most of the chairs are oak, some are upholstered, set on a dark gray carpet. The outer wall is stepped back at one corner to provide lots of light for the children's section. There's something almost nautical about the stairway to the mezzanine, perhaps it's the light gray paint, perhaps the blue-gray carpet or the iron railings. David Malazzo from Bakersfield was the architect of this six-year-old building.

# —— BERKELEY ——

## Berkeley Public Library

| | |
|---|---|
| 2090 Kittredge Street | E, T, V |
| (510) 644-6100 | Open every day |

This four-story, ocher, Art Nouveau building (with a startling green frieze of Egyptian images) is a beehive of activity. In downtown Berkeley, one block from the entrance to BART (the Bay Area Rapid Transit system), it's one of the busiest libraries on a per capita basis in the nation.

Berkeley, CA
Berkeley Public Library

Whether you want to know how many aardvarks there are in Australia or the number of zoos in Zanzibar, the famous reference staff will unfailingly get you your answer. Of course they can also answer almost any question about Berkeley and the Bay Area.

Check the piles of free newspapers and flyers and the bulletin boards to find out what's going on in this city of unusual interests. Take a look in the high-ceilinged main reading room, furnished with dark oak tables and chairs, and you'll see a cross-section of the area's population. There's a marvelously painted ceiling, 40 feet above. The library has large art, music, reference and local history collections

The large children's room on the top floor is busy, pleasant and a little old-fashioned. It has a large, crowded collection. Cushioned window seats also have fabulous views of San Francisco Bay. The Berkeley Library is the epitome of community libraries—the activities, the enthusiastic staff, the community support, and good (if old-fashioned) architecture. James Plachek was the architect of this 1930 building.

The library is a just short walk from the campus of the University of California, and the critically acclaimed Berkeley Repertory Theater is just around the corner. You might time your trip to be near mealtime as the library is surrounded by restaurants for all tastes and budgets.

## North Berkeley Branch Library

| | |
|---|---:|
| 1170 The Alameda | A |
| (510) 644-6850 | Closed Sundays |

This 1936 library was a WPA project designed by James Plachek, the same architect who designed Berkeley Main. In a quiet neighborhood, it sits just below the upscale residential area. The entrance to this Spanish-Romanesque style building is through a squat hexagonal central tower. A gem of a building, it has light orange walls with dark brown trim, except for the windows, which are trimmed in blue. It is set in a beautifully landscaped corner plot.

Two wings angle off from the entrance, with stucco arches above each entrance and a wide rainbow painted on the children's wing. Both wings have marvelously carved and painted wooden trusses supporting wooden ceilings. The library had 8,000 books when it opened and now has 50,000, so there isn't as much room as there once was. Still, this is a delightful and calm neighborhood library.

## Tool Lending Library

1901 Russell Street
(510) 644-6101                                     Closed Sundays, Mondays

This is one of only four tool lending libraries in the country. Its 2,500 tools are not available to nonresidents, but you might want to go by and see what innovative services libraries can offer. It has most of the popular equipment available in tool rental shops.

The library is located just in back of the South Berkeley Branch Library, across the street from a set of public tennis courts.

# ——— BEVERLY HILLS ———

## Beverly Hills Public Library

444 North Rexford Drive                                              A, E, T
(310) 288-2200                                                 Open every day

The Beverly Hills Civic Center is just what you would expect in the headquarters of Hollywood glitz. Byzantine towers, a dome with blue and gold tiles, tall narrow arches, manicured grass and tall palm trees are all at home here.

As one librarian describes, "The library is Spanish Renaissance, verging on Baroque, with Art Deco elements in the custom lighting fixtures and Moorish influence in the archways and elaborate tilework."

# Public Libraries: Travel Treasures of the West

Beverly Hills, CA
Beverly Hills Public Library
Photo courtesy City of Beverly Hills

This fascinating three-story building has a mezzanine above a main floor, and large arches in back of the mezzanine. The insides of the 2-foot-thick arches are tiled in shiny blue. The prevailing color in the library is cream, with green highlights. There are lots of plush upholstered chairs set on beautiful carpets. Much of the furniture is dark mahogany. The countertops are polished green marble from Thailand, lit by light fixtures of polished brass and frosted glass. You'll find sculpture, interesting archways and angled columns wherever you look.

The vaulted reference room at one end of the library's main floor has its own very quiet reading and study area. The ceiling is made of ash from North Carolina. Deep green carpets are surrounded by marble tile.

Upstairs you can enjoy a huge fine arts section with lots of room to sit and study. The desks and carrels are dark Philippine mahogany. The collection is particularly strong in 19th and 20th century art, and interior design. The library even has a circulating collection of 21,500 art slides.

*California*

# ——— BURBANK ———

## Burbank Public Library

110 North Glenoaks Boulevard
(818) 953-9737                                                             Closed Sundays

An enjoyable place with a pleasant garden outside, this medium-sized library has recently been remodeled.

You can browse through a sizeable art collection—some in open shelves, some locked. There is also an interesting collection of rare and older books and a recently acquired significant collection of Californiana. The more valuable books are secured in wooden glass-fronted cases, a fine contrast to the more modern furniture of the newly remodeled library.

Upstairs is a good-sized, comfortable children's room with a big story corner for kids. There is also a collection of pet rats!

## Warner Research Library

Entrance at rear of Burbank Central Library
(818) 953-9743                                                     Open by appointment

Although operated by the Burbank City Library, this separate facility is not really open to the public; it's essentially a fee-for-service library, and you must call for an appointment. The collection (the former research collection of Warner Brothers Studios) has almost 40,000 volumes and over 2 million clippings and photographs in its files.

This is the place where people in the creative arts come to authenticate their work. The material ranges from diet around the world to costume to etiquette in strange places. It's not just a collection of pictures of national costumes, but a place where someone recently inquired about what types of signs he might expect to see inside a Middle Eastern jail. The library documents the fabric of societies all over the world, from hospital interiors in Asia to dating practices in Africa. The collection is accessible by subject and by geographical location.

This is a not a place for browsing. If you're interested, call and they'll tell you what their research fees are (modest, especially for students) and they'll have the material ready for you to review when you arrive.

## ———— CAMBRIA ————

### Cambria Branch Library, San Luis Obispo City–County Library

| | |
|---|---|
| 900 Main Street | A |
| (805) 927-4336 | Closed Sundays, Mondays |

Located on Main Street in this busy, artsy town that is only 8 miles south of San Simeon and the Hearst Castle, the Cambria Library is a small building with what looks like a cross between a shingled air vent and a lighthouse on top. Actually, it's quite attractive.

Inside, the light wooden ceiling is composed of unfinished planks that are neither sanded nor varnished. And the wooden beams angling up to the central skylight are even more rough-cut. Fluorescent fixtures hanging from the ceiling are bright orange, contrasting pleasantly with the light wood and complementing dark orange carpet and orange upholstered furniture.

The library is next to an old one-room schoolhouse that was built in 1881 and is now an art gallery. A block down Main Street is the Soldier Factory, an outstanding gift shop for people interested in toy soldiers. For a snack, try Chase's Olive Barrel for smoked, spiced, or garlic olives.

## ———— CARMEL ————

### Harrison Memorial Library

| | |
|---|---|
| Ocean Avenue at Lincoln Street | A, V, T |
| (408) 624-4629 | Closed Sundays |

This library was designed by the noted California architect Bernard Maybeck. Stone-lined brick paths curve through a small garden to the tile-roofed building. Impressive pine trees frame large arched windows that look in from the main promenade and shopping street. The blue painted window frames of this stucco building highlight their classic shape. This comfortable building wears its age well.

Maybeck was a master in the Arts and Crafts school of architecture, and the library and its furnishings reflect his era. The gently

Carmel, CA
Harrison Memorial Library

peaked wood panel ceiling of the two-story main reading room is a perfect setting for the massive stone fireplace, which is surrounded by comfortable wood and leather chairs. The bookcases throughout the library are wooden. The walls of the library are replete with historic paintings by local artists and artists who have painted here. Architects Flesher + Foster of nearby Pacific Grove designed a sensitive modernization for the library, retaining its handcrafted character.

There are lots of windows in the library, which is just above street level. It's a great place from which to watch the downtown shoppers stroll. There is no children's section here. Children have their own library three blocks away at Mission and Sixth streets (see below). It's a nice walk. In fact, there may be more art galleries, boutiques, restaurants, and stores between these two branches than between any other two library branches in the world.

## Park Branch Library

Sixth Avenue at Mission Street
(408) 624-4664  Closed Sundays
Local History closed Saturdays, Sundays, Mondays

You would probably never guess that this shake-shingled, stone-fronted building surrounded by pine trees is a former bank. Now it houses a colorful children's library and a fascinating local history collection.

The children's room is divided into a number of comfortable areas. There are window and bean bags seats, lots of small pieces of furniture, fuzzy toys, cushioned couches and a good story corner.

The local history and writers rooms are also inviting, but in a very different way. The Henry Meade Williams local history room is paneled, with books in glass-fronted cabinets that allow you to see what's available. There are two rooms of books, formal, pleasant, quiet and well lit. This is both the archive for the city and a literary history museum. The library has a nice collection of Edward Weston photographs. The rooms are well worth a visit if you're interested in local history They are staffed Tuesday through Friday afternoons.

## —— CHICO ——

### Chico Branch Library, Butte County Library

| | |
|---|---|
| 1108 Sherman Avenue | |
| (916) 891-2762 | Closed Sundays, Mondays |

Chico is not in one of California's better known population areas; it only has about 40,000 residents. It is, however, a lively, outgoing place. Historic Bidwell Mansion is fun to visit, as is the Sierra Nevada Brewing Company and the Upper Crust Bakery-Restaurant.

The library is surprisingly large for a city this size. A large, modern, low-slung brick building on its own grassy block, surrounded by bushes and trees, it's in a quiet residential area near a school.

On the walls in the large children's room is a colorful mural. For each letter of the alphabet there's a cheerful picture of a character from a children's tale; A for Alice, B for Babar, C for the Cat in the Hat, etc. Bring your children and see how many of Scott Teeple's delightful paintings they can identify.

## —— CHULA VISTA ——

### Chula Vista Public Library

| | |
|---|---|
| 365 F Street | A |
| (619) 691-5164 | Open every day |

With a population of over 140,000, Chula Vista is no longer merely a bedroom community for San Diego. Its very attractive library is only a short distance from the freeway. An expansive red tile roof dominates the exterior of the building in a pleasant park across the street from the civic center.

Bold burgundy, orange and blue furniture and carpets enliven the interior. Ceiling heights vary all over the library, and brilliant colored banners hang throughout the building. Some are just for decoration, others are signs that give directions. Large circular windows look out into the surrounding park.

This library is devoted to finding and filling community needs. It even has a darkroom and a soundproofed piano practice room with an electric keyboard. The children's room is bright, large and comfortable. Some of the reading rooms have fireplaces. Much of the staff is bilingual to serve a large Spanish-speaking population.

Designed in 1976 by Richard George Wheeler and Associates, this bright building still looks modern and new in 1993.

## ——— CORONA DEL MAR ———

### Sherman Research Library and Gardens

2647 East Pacific Coast Highway  
(714) 673-2261  

T  
Closed Saturdays, Sundays;  
Garden open every day

Perhaps the most surprising thing about the Sherman Library is that it is not a library about botany, plants or flowers even though it shares a block with the Sherman Gardens, an absolute delight of manicured displays of plant life from around the world. The library concentrates on the history of the Pacific Southwest during the last 100 years. Both a research library and an archive, its books do not circulate, but they do provide an amazing amount of information on recent regional history.

The library buildings, which resemble a pueblo, grow out of a home that a newly married couple built with their own amateur hands in 1940. When you find their cottage, you see a truly homemade adobe type structure. As additions were built for offices and then the library, their original style was carefully followed.

The library has a comfortable reading room and main storage area, a small collection of California impressionist paintings, and a significant closed archive collection. While there's a nominal fee for entrance to the garden, the library is open for research at no charge.

## —— CORONADO ——

### Coronado Public Library

640 Orange Avenue  
(619) 522-7390       Open every day

Besides its wide and white beaches the most famous attraction in exclusive Coronado is the Del Mar Hotel, a magnificent concoction of towers, cupolas, turrets, and Victorian style gingerbread. It was built in 1888 (the hotel is so big it offers tape-guided tours) but now offers the latest in modern conveniences.

Coronado's library is much like the "Hotel Del"—it combines both old and new with style and grace. In the 1970s a major modern addition was grafted onto the back of this library built in 1909 in the fashion of a Grecian temple. The library is located in a parklike setting and fronted by a rose garden.

If you tire of tennis, swimming or fine dining while you are visiting Coronado, the library is a pleasant 1-mile stroll from the Hotel Del on Orange Avenue.

## —— COSTA MESA ——

### Costa Mesa Branch Library, Orange County Public Library

1855 Park Avenue  
(714) 646-8845       Closed Sundays

This is one of those buildings with a totally circular theme—a circular fountain out front, a circular trellis at the entrance, and a huge circular skylight above the reading room. The roof is a striking bronze tint.

The library is only a few minutes drive from the marinas at Newport Beach. The Costa Mesa Historical Society has an interesting archive next door. It is formally open only on Thursdays, but occasionally someone is there who might let you in on another day.

Costa Mesa, CA
Costa Mesa Library

## —— DANVILLE ——

### Danville Branch Library, Contra Costa Public Library

555 South Hartz
(510) 837-4889                                                          Closed Sundays

    Danville and, hence, its library are at the foot of Mount Diablo, which rises almost 4,000 feet above the valley here. This is also the home of the new Behring Museum and its collection of classic cars, as well as the Blackhawk development, Northern California's most concentrated collection of ostentatious architecture. The museum has its own noncirculating research library that has, among other parts of its collection, 40,000 sales brochures.
    The smallish triangular public library is not as elegant as you might expect here, but its high windows have a nice view of the mountain through the trees growing just outside. The drive to the observation

tower at the top of the mountain is about 45 minutes, and the road is pretty curvy, so anyone with a tendency toward car sickness might want to meet the more adventurous drivers here. The library is only a block from Danville's upscale main shopping street and near the well known and elegant Bridges Restaurant.

## ─── FAIRFAX ───

### Fairfax Branch Library, Marin County Library System

| | |
|---|---:|
| 2097 Sir Francis Drake Boulevard | A, V |
| (415) 453-8092 | Closed Sundays, Mondays |

This lovely wood-shingled building is near the end of the heavily populated areas of Marin County northwest of San Francisco. While the library is in the well-populated green hills, above it you see Mount Tamalpais and its foothills. Magnificent black oaks grow in front of the building.

The library has small collections in an amazing number of languages: Spanish, German, Czech, Finnish, Dutch, Russian, Swedish and Italian. This may be for the convenience of the *au pairs* hired from abroad by the wealthy residents of this area. The bright children's room is separated by glass walls from the main part of the library. Off the children's room is a sunroomlike extension from which you get a magnificent view of the mountain. There's also a small foreign language children's collection.

The library is predominantly wood inside as well as outside. Light wood bridge trusses support a wood-paneled ceiling. Black light fixtures hang down into a semicircular library of angled sections. In back of the main reading room a lovely deck looks up at the mountains and watershed, but at the time of our visit the library district was so underfunded that it could not afford to make needed repairs, and the deck was closed. The library was designed by Bull, Field, Volkmann, Stockwell in 1976.

## —— FAIRFIELD ——

### Fairfield–Suisun Community Branch Library, Solano County Library

1150 Kentucky Street
(707) 429-4636     Open every day

    Fairfield, about halfway between San Francisco and Sacramento, the State Capitol, is home to Travis Air Force Base and a huge Anheuser-Busch brewery (which has guided tours). It's also home to a pleasant, low-slung brick library.
    A vine-covered wooden trellis in front of the library shades an outdoor reading area. One whole end of the building is set aside for children, with comfortable lounging furniture, a good story area and a huge fairy tale mural on the wall.
    This is an interesting, long library, with cylindrical yellow light fixtures hanging down past exposed yellow air conditioning ducts. At the back of the building a quiet reading area looks out over a pond with ducks and geese.

## —— FERNDALE ——

### Ferndale Public Library

807 Main Street     T
(707) 786-9559     Closed Sundays, Mondays

    Ferndale, with its population of 1,430 people, is just 15 miles south of Eureka, and one of the most completely preserved (and still functioning) turn-of-the-century villages in California. The village is a state historical landmark and lots of fun to visit, especially the Gingerbread Mansion on Berding Street. You can get good walking tour guides at the Chamber of Commerce.

The public library in Ferndale fits right in. A Carnegie library, it was built in 1910. It's a square, solid, yellow stucco building with red steps. From the library you can see a few blocks to the ornamental facades of the downtown area. The inside walls of the library have been papered with light-colored grass cloth, so it's very pleasant and light. In 1977 a children's section was added to the back—so well done that you can hardly tell there's been an expansion. The new section has a brightly colored free-standing fireplace and bean-bag furniture for children.

As a reminder that this is earthquake country, look at the bookcases and you'll see iron braces anchoring them firmly to the floor. A major earthquake a few years ago knocked most of the books to the floor but didn't do too much other damage (to the library, at least). Old Andrew Carnegie's picture still hangs on the wall.

## —— FORT BRAGG ——

### Fort Bragg Branch Library, Mendocino County Library

499 Laurel Street
(707) 964-2020                                    Closed Sundays, Mondays

This neat, low-slung, gray wooden library is at one end of Laurel Street. Four blocks west is the terminal of the Skunk Railway that travels through redwood groves and above the Noyo River (it gives you a good look at what clear cutting will do). Both full-day and half-day trips are available.

Built in 1989 to replace a facility that was destroyed by arson after being in service for 77 years, you'd never guess that this pleasant, bright, and well-furnished library is in a building that used to be a mortuary. There's a working fireplace, and in one corner is a small children's room and a young people's area next to that. The paperback exchange has lots of material for trading.

This is a good place for relaxation, and a lot of residents do that here. The park across the street has an extensive play yard for kids with imaginative slides and swings all mounted in sand.

# —— FOUNTAIN VALLEY ——

## Fountain Valley Branch Library, Orange County Library

17635 Los Alamos  
(714) 962-1324                                             Closed Sundays

    The way to describe this library depends on how it's approached. At the front a curved and polished stone element over the entryway is reminiscent of a beached whale; from the side, sets of saw-toothed roof elements that provide clerestory windows make the building look like a railroad repair yard, and a reflecting pool at one end completes the confusion.

    The clerestory windows let in lots of light, and cool gray carpets and upholstery combine for a calm feeling inside. The library has a well lit gallery wall for rotating art exhibits. The light fixtures inside and outside the library are similar.

    The building is in Fountain Valley's Civic Center, next to a restored fire company, real estate company, etc., the city's "Heritage Park." A nice place to take the kids.

# —— FREMONT ——

## Fremont Main Branch Library, Alameda County Library

2400 Stevenson Boulevard                                         A, E, V  
(510) 745-1400                                              Open every day

    The Fremont Main Library is a long, large building with clean lines and half-circle sections extending from both the front and rear. The exterior is tiled with two shades of gray and one shade of blue.

    The entrance to the building is through a bright rotunda with plain blue columns under a circular skylight two floors above. Gray carpet and ivory walls lend the feeling of peace. Remarkably large square white and round blue columns give a solid feeling to the library (and a sense of security to anyone who knows how close they are to a major earthquake fault). Hanging above two stairways to the second floor is a remarkable sculpture, *Dream Voyage*, by Larry Kirkland. A plaque near the sculpture reads, "Opening a book is an invitation to take a wonderful and private journey; to explore our singular place in the universe."

To the rear of the library, leather-covered lounging chairs in a large glassed-in reading room make you feel like you're reading in a park. There is a young adult magazine area and a large, colorful children's area that includes a very good parenting collection.

The reference, business and nonfiction sections are upstairs in an area that is almost 300 feet long, with a unique view of Sunol Ridge from the east end. The business collection is extensive—until 1993 it was a separate Business Library in Oakland (about 25 miles north of Fremont). Clear gray and white signs hang from the ceiling and stand out in this cream and blue library. The building was completed in 1989. It was designed by Simon Martin-Vegue Winkelstein Moris of San Francisco.

# —— FULLERTON ——

## Fullerton Public Library

353 West Commonwealth Avenue
(714) 738-6380                                              Closed Sundays

Located next to the Fullerton City Hall, the library is a brown cut-stone building. It has several levels, and feels almost like a shopping mall as you look down into the main reading room from the mezzanine. The combination of lots of wood trim, columns partially faced in stone and pastel rugs make this multilevel library inviting.

The Mary Laura Campbell Children's Book Collection is a real find. A noncirculating reference collection, it has over 350 rare and 1st editions of children's books, some dating back to the 17th century. The library has published a fascinating pamphlet, *Cobwebs to Catch Flies or a Sampler of Books from the Mary Laura Campbell Collection*. If you are interested in either early children's books or the history of printing, don't miss this collection, some of which is always on exhibit.

The children's room is warm and inviting, an example of a children's room with no windows that works well. The walls are almost totally covered with bright posters and paintings, and there are also a number of doll houses.

The local history room has a wonderful picture of the orange groves that were eliminated to make way for this highly urban city. You can find early street plans and other old archival material as well as clippings and oral histories.

## —— GLENDALE ——

### Glendale Public Library

| | |
|---|---|
| 222 East Harvard Street | A |
| (818) 548-2020 | Closed Sundays |

This very large library was recently remodeled and enlarged (adding 16,000 square feet of public space); it continues to be a fine-looking building. The large main reading room is surrounded by a mezzanine on three sides, and the fourth side is a high wall of windows that adds to the expansiveness of the room. Lots of chairs provide for comfortable lounging.

The recently expanded children's room gives you the impression that kids come first. There are unique bay windows for children in floor to ceiling windows at one side of the room. Rather than window seats there are slightly sunken carpeted pits, large enough for a few small people to read or play in while they look down to the street below. It's a fascinating way of creating contained safe spaces in a large room.

Glendale has one of the three largest cat collections in the world. The other two are at Yale University and in Switzerland. While in large part this world-famous noncirculating collection is aimed at serious cat breeders (stud books dated back to the early 1900s, feline medical books, etc.) there's also material on cats in fiction, in magic, in music, in art and in religion, books on how to photograph cats, zodiac signs for cats—and on and on.

If you drive north on Brand toward the Brand Library and Art Center (see below) you'll see some fantastic houses sitting up in the foothills of the Sierra Madre. You'll also see how mudslides can start rocks rolling down that might end up in the middle of Glendale.

## Also of Note:

## Brand Library and Art Center

| | |
|---|---|
| 1601 West Mountain Street | T |
| (818) 548-2051 | Closed Sundays, Mondays |

The official description given by the library is: "The architecture is considered Saracenic, with crenelated arches, bulbous domes and minars combining characteristics of Spanish, Moorish and Indian styles." It looks like an exotic white Indian temple, on its site in front of the Verdrugo Mountains. It was built in 1904, patterned after the East Indian Pavilion at the 1893 World Exposition held in Chicago.

This is the art and music section of the Glendale Public Library. The collection of over 40,000 volumes sprawls through all the rooms of what was once a palatial private residence. The music collection is enormous. It includes piano rolls, records, sheet music and over 8,000 compact disks. The library claims to have one of the largest circulating collections of music west of the Mississippi River. There's a large and unique collection of videos tape on artists. Most of the library is

Glendale, CA
Brand Library and Art Center

circulating and in open shelves, but the more valuable and rare books are kept under lock and key.

A gallery added since the building became a library has constantly changing exhibits that focus on Southern California artists. There's also a small recital hall that seats 150.

As you explore the library, you'll find some original woodwork and Tiffany glass, although much of it was hidden during an unfortunate "restoration" in the 1950s. One room still has silk damask wallpaper with a gold-on-gold pattern. Times change—a wood trimmed fireplace in back of the circulation desk is now filled with shelves of videotape cassettes.

## —— GLENDORA ——

### Glendora Public Library

140 South Glendora Avenue
(818) 914-8291                                      Closed Sundays

Glendora's appearance is somewhat odd. Catalina cherry trees the length of its main street have been manicured so that they look like inverted ice cream cones. Blocks of these trees lead up toward the San Gabriel Mountains.

For a lower floor library with practically no exterior windows (except in the children's area) this is a remarkably bright and open place. An interesting change is that the Friends of the Library Gift and Book Shop is in the center of the main library reading room, not pushed off to a corner or a basement as so many are.

The direction signs in this library are outstanding—a good lesson on how to make a library user-friendly. White-on-brown colored signs hang from the ceiling wherever you look, pointing the way to Sports, Literature, True Crime, etc. In the children's room, similar signs indicate Fairy Tales, Mythology, Animals and so on.

## —— HALF MOON BAY ——

### Half Moon Bay Branch Library, San Mateo County Library

620 Correas Street
(415) 726-2316

Closed Sundays

The medium-sized Half Moon Bay Library might be a good place to take a break on a half-day excursion from San Francisco. A 25-mile drive down Highway 1 brings you here along the Pacific, and you can then return on a circular route going east on Highway 92 toward San Francisco Bay.

The library has some lovely shade trees out front, and a well-gardened patio in back. It can get windy around here, and this is a good place to get out of the gusts for a while.

Half Moon Bay (with a population of under 10,000) is one of those throwback cities that haven't been "discovered" yet. The library is only a block or so from City Hall, the elementary school, the church and the center of town. And if you decide you like it here, there are lots of bed and breakfasts.

## —— HEALDSBURG ——

### Healdsburg Branch Library and Sonoma County Wine Library, Sonoma County Library

139 Piper Street
(707) 433-3772

A, T
Closed Sundays

This well-designed library would be worth a mention even if it didn't have a premier wine library. Below a dark orange tile roof, square concrete columns support a vine covered wooden trellis. A small fountain and garden highlight the corner on which the library sits. The Sonoma County Wine Library is in a large suite of rooms at the back of the general library.

This is much more than a tourist's guide to wineries. Over 3,000 books range from rare and historic books on the history of wine to the latest material from technical symposia. There are even oral histories from people who have made the Sonoma County wine industry famous. The library is near more than 50 wineries, many of which are open for tours and tasting.

While the wine library is industry supported, it is housed in this branch of the county library and open whenever the regular library is open. Much of the time the director of the wine library is here; if he's not, the general librarians are very knowledgeable about the collection.

If you're travelling with children, you'll find a very pleasant children's section near the circulation desk. This might be a good place to rest for a while if you think you've tasted at one winery too many.

## —— HOOPA ——

### Kim Yerton Memorial Library

| | |
|---|---|
| Loop Road (behind the schools) | A |
| (707) 625-4447 | Closed Sundays, Mondays, Wednesdays, Fridays |

This is both the Hoopa library and the Hoopa tribal archives. It was a joint effort, with the Hoopa Tribe putting up half the money and the county putting up the balance. This is one of very few county libraries in the country on an Reservation. It opened in 1992.

Hoopa, CA
Kim Yerton Memorial Library

The small building dramatically adapts traditional local construction motifs to contemporary use. Three sides are unfinished vertical cedar planks, with earth berms rising against the building. It's a small, clean-cut, one-room library finished in contemporary decor. Small skylights help with the lighting. At one end a series of three rectangular clerestory windows sit next to a circular window which looks out at the mountains. The design is by Phil Holcomb of Holcomb and Lusso in Redding.

The forested country near here gives you a feeling of an older Northern California, and the library has an extensive collection on both contemporary and historical Native American life. Hoopa is 11 miles north of Willow Creek, off State Highway 299, which is a rarely used but fascinating drive from Eureka on the coast toward Redding and Mt. Shasta.

# HUNTINGTON BEACH

## Huntington Beach Library

| | |
|---|---|
| 7111 Talbert Avenue | A, E |
| (714) 842-4481 | Closed Sundays |

Huntington Beach, with a population of almost 200,000, tends to disappear in the Los Angeles metroplex, but it's by no means a sleepy little beach resort. Architects Anthony & Langford recently completed a major expansion of this exciting multilevel library (originally designed by Richard Neutra) that saw it grow from 74,000 square feet to over 110,000. It has an intriguing design with lots of different spaces and places in which to sit.

This library is unique. There's a whole set of terraces inside the library that you can see from other levels. Some raised balconies contain stacks, others are reading areas. From each level you see fountains below and outside. Some good-sized trees grow next to fountains on the ground floor, so that wherever you look you see lots of greenery. There are five levels of operation and from many places you can see all the levels between the various bridges and terraces in this amazingly high library. Huge glass wall windows open onto the city's Central Park.

The main entrance is on an upper level, in the new section, as is the children's area. The Orange County Genealogical Society has its collection here as well.

*California* 51

Huntington Beach, CA
Huntington Beach Library

## IRVINE

### University Park Branch Library

4512 Sandburg Way
(714) 786-4000                                                                                      Closed Sundays

Irvine is a planned community of 110,000 and home to one of the campuses of the University of California. It's generally upscale and neat, as is the University Park Branch library. This angular building is set on a carefully gardened corner near University Community Park.

Inside, huge wooden trusses radiate from the center of an almost circular library. The pervasive use of wood gives the library an alpine feel. The center of the building is a large circular office complex. A circular concrete circulation desk contrasts with the full carpets, wood ceiling and paneled walls. This is a warm and comfortable building.

There's a pleasantly green enclosed outdoor reading area, and you can take a book out there to read without having to check it out. This branch is just down the street from an elementary school so it's not uncommon to find lots of kids studying here.

## LA JOLLA

### Athenaeum Music and Arts Library, Library Association of La Jolla

1008 Wall Street
(619) 454-5872                                                                 Closed Sundays, Mondays

La Jolla's Prospect Street has so many upscale shops, galleries and restaurants that it can get a little tiring. A good rest stop is this classically formal Music and Arts Library just a block away. It's a private library (books circulate to members only), but the general public is welcome to come in, browse and relax.

Dark wooden ceiling beams, oriental rugs on highly polished wood floors, solid wood bookcases, a grand piano in the music room and a significant fine arts collection make this two-room building a beautiful stop. The collection includes historic and contemporary material in

La Jolla, CA
Athenaeum Music and
Arts Library

dance, theater, visual arts and architecture. There are frequent art exhibits and concerts in the library. At one time this small, lovely old building was the La Jolla Public Library.

## —— LAKEPORT ——

### Lake County Library

1425 North High Street
(707) 263-8816                                   Closed Sundays, Mondays

Lakeport is on the shore of Clear Lake, the largest fresh-water lake in California (Lake Tahoe is partially in Nevada). There's nothing fancy or upscale about this area, and for that reason it's one of Northern California's more reasonable tourist spots. Lakeport is primarily a resort town, and Main Street is only a block from the lake with beautiful views of the water and the mountains.

The library is in a plain, contemporary building built in 1986. There are very few windows but even on a dull rainy day there's plenty of light. The large children's room is totally glassed off from the main library—handy to separate you from either other people's kids or your own.

## —— LARKSPUR ——

### Larkspur Public Library

| 400 Magnolia Avenue | A |
| --- | --- |
| (415) 927-5005 | Closed Sundays |

Larkspur is a small, wealthy community in the Marin County hills less than 10 miles north of the Golden Gate Bridge. Like the city, the library is plush and cozy. It's nestled in the back of a Mission Revival city hall; you enter through a multicolored door in leaded glass studded with glass balls.

This elegant little library is a cross between Craftsman Style and Art Deco design, with Victorian lampshades and moldings. Stained glass windows (installed to cover up dreadful views) add to the period nature of the design. Even the stack areas are carpeted. From the stacks, a circular window looks into the children's room. The lovely 1982 Swanson and Associates design of this small space almost hides the fact that the library holds over 60,000 volumes.

## —— LONG BEACH ——

### Long Beach Public Library

| 101 Pacific Avenue | A |
| --- | --- |
| (310) 437-2949 | Open every day |

The Long Beach Public Library is just across the street from the southern end of Los Angeles' new light rail system and near the Marina and convention center. Its main library is a suitable size for California's fifth largest city.

This low-lying beauty is mostly underground—the roof is part of a park surrounding City Hall. Even so, the building has a spacious and airy feeling. Sitting in comfortable chairs you look out through huge windows to gardens, city hall and waterfront activity.

This large, modern library serves such a diverse population that the "information" sign over the main desk is in eight languages. The large children's area has a 100-seat auditorium.

Don't miss the Loraine and Earl Miller special collection rooms (downstairs). If you like formal libraries you'll love this glorious, fully paneled set of rooms with walnut bookcases, pegged oak floors and lighted niches for artwork. The furniture, Queen Anne, Chippendale and Windsor reproductions, matches the formal design. The rooms house a fine arts collection emphasizing Asian art, rare texts and the archives of opera singer Marilyn Horne.

## —— LOS ANGELES ——

### Los Angeles Public Library

| | |
|---|---|
| 630 West Fifth Street | A, E |
| (213) 612-3200 | Call for days open |

After two disastrous fires kept this facility closed for over seven years, the Los Angeles Public Library's historic facility reopened in late 1993. Truly a sight to see, the original 210,000-square-foot, 1926 building has been magnificently restored, and a huge addition of 340,000 square feet has created adequate space for the nation's third largest public library collection.

The building, designed by Bertram Goodhue, has regained its original splendor. There are restored murals, sculptures and decorative stencils throughout. The rotunda features 1932 murals by Dean

Los Angeles, CA
Central Library, Los Angeles Public Library
Model of new building
Photo courtesy Los Angeles Public Library

Cornwall and a 2,000-pound bronze chandelier representing the solar system. Stucco and glazed tiles combine to create what has been called a "Spanish/Egyptian/Deco" architectural style. The historic building houses the Popular Library, Children's Literature, Music and Rare Books, as well as administrative offices. As befitting its size, the library has a number of Special Collections, including more than 2,000,000 photographs, 500,000 of which are historic images of Southern California. The library also has one of the nation's largest fiction collections.

The new Tom Bradley East Wing has eight stories, four of which are below street level. Natural light flows through a grand atrium to the lower levels, illuminating escalators leading to the subject departments housed in the wing. Significant art projects are located in the atrium, including 13-foot pole lanterns by Ann Preston at the escalator landings and three glass chandeliers by Therman Staton. Don't miss the elevators, decorated by David Bunn with catalog cards, with windows showing more catalog cards on the elevator shaft walls.

The new building, designed by Hardy, Holzman, Pfeiffer Associates of New York, includes the 235-seat Mark Taper auditorium and the Klos children's story theater. The library is near the Museum of Contemporary Art and the Los Angeles Music Center. The complex includes underground parking, a 1 1/2-acre public garden, cafe and restaurant.

## Frances Howard Goldwyn Hollywood Branch Library

| 1623 Ivar Avenue | A |
| --- | --- |
| (213) 467-1821 | Closed Sundays |

This aggressively modern building was designed by well-known California architect Frank Gehry. It's a tall white and glass structure with huge structural beams. From the outside the building looks completely closed in, but once inside you discover a four-story high atrium. The entrance is on the ground floor, the main library on the second and then two more levels of windows, all under a fourth-floor skylight.

About 60 percent of the library's collection is in the performing arts. There's a good collection on the history of the motion picture industry as well as a lot of how-to books. The special collections room has many movie and television scripts, preserved by special lighting and air conditioning. The room is open to the public, but you need to obtain permission to use it.

Around the library are marvelous blow-ups of some of the most celebrated movie posters and also some framed originals. This is mecca for film buffs. The reference desk staff specializes in film esoterica and answers questions about films and film history from all over the world.

## ── LOS GATOS ──

### Los Gatos Memorial Library

110 East Main Street
(403) 354-6891                                                       Open every day

This contemporary library shares a brick plaza with Los Gatos' municipal offices. The plaza is only a short walk from the main shopping area on University Avenue. Los Gatos, at the base of two small mountain ranges, is home to a good number of people who made their fortunes in nearby Silicon Valley.

You'll enter this small library upstairs and instantly be struck by a parklike feeling—on two sides large windows open to trees surrounding the building. The columns supporting the coffered concrete ceiling are brick, and there's plenty of fluorescent light. With its own entrance, the children's room is almost totally separate from the main library.

Downstairs is a good-sized reference room and a series of photographs and drawings of early California, going back to houses built in the 1840s.

## ——— MANHATTAN BEACH ———

### Manhattan Beach Branch Library, Los Angeles County Library

| 1320 Highland Avenue | T |
|---|---|
| (310) 545-8595 | Closed Sundays |

It's sometimes easy to forget that Los Angeles is really a beach community, and that there are lots of little beach-resort and boutique areas like Manhattan Beach. The beach here is fabulous—broad and white with a lovely surf and a paved path along its edge.

This busy, medium-sized, solid brick building is just a block above the beach. Inside, the walls are all brick, but there are so many books you can hardly see them. There's a bright mural in the children's section that is also jammed with books.

There's a "peek" view of the ocean if you dodge your head to one side and look around an apartment house across the street. This isn't a great library, but it's a good place to come and get out of the sun or the rain if there's too much of either on the beach.

## ——— MARYSVILLE ———

### Yuba County Library

| 303 Second Street | A |
|---|---|
| (916) 741-6241 | Closed Fridays, Saturdays, Sundays |

Marysville, an agricultural town of about 12,000, is in the Sacramento Valley 40 miles north of the capital. It is surprising to find such an impressive building in such a small community. On the other hand, Marysville was one of the first cities west of the Mississippi to have a public library.

A well lit ceiling stretches out across the two-story reading room from the entryway to a mezzanine of stacks on the far side. There's an indoor garden under a skylight in the main reading room. You could sit there on a sunny day and imagine yourself to be in a pleasant garden at home. The California history room is one of the best in Northern California. It's a separate, glassed-off room with lots of material. There are fascinating directories from the 1870s and a handwritten index to local newspapers from the 1850s through the 1940s.

Comfortable orange and red furniture contrasts with the carpets and large expanses of brick wall. The tall columns supporting the roof are brick. Combined with the indoor garden/patio, this extensive use of brick gives the library a very warm feel.

## —— MENDOCINO ——

### Mendocino Community Library

| 45141 Williams Street | T, V |
|---|---|
| (707) 937-5773 | Closed Sundays |

Mendocino, the premier tourist site on California's north coast, has just about everything—glorious coastal roads and scenery, beautiful state parks, trails, bed and breakfasts, galleries, performing arts, shops, good restaurants.

It also has a unique library, one run totally by volunteers and supported wholly through membership fees, fines and fund raising. While not truly a "public" library, it is open to the public for browsing and reading. Books only circulate to members (who pay ridiculously low fees to join). Especially good for travelers are the ongoing used paperback sales and the free magazine exchange section. You can donate your old magazines and pick up someone else's.

The library is on the corner of Williams and Little Lake streets, across the street from a busy center of cultural activity, the Mendocino Art Center. This library has been in existence at various locations for 85 years.

It is now in a pleasant old house, and the odd-looking pillars on the north porch may seem strangely familiar. The porch was used for scenes outside a house of prostitution in the famous film, *East of Eden*. There's a picture book room for small kids (just inside the porch, in fact) and a newly added children's room.

You can see the ocean from a window in back of the service desk and the library is near a good spot for whale-watching in the Mendocino Headlands State Park.

## —— MERCED ——

### Merced County Library

| | |
|---|---|
| 2100 O Street | |
| (209) 385-7643 | Closed Sundays |

Merced, in the heart of the agricultural San Joaquin Valley, is the western gateway to Yosemite National Park. The Merced County Library is a two-story concrete building near the Merced Courthouse Museum.

As you enter the library you can look over a wooden sculpture and a fountain to trees outside a wall of windows at the back of the building. The fountain and sculpture are surrounded by upholstered chairs. This well-designed building was built in 1976. The large main reading room is surrounded by a mezzanine around the second floor, and a skylight adds to illumination from hanging globe light fixtures. A California history room is on the mezzanine floor.

The library has a collection of books in Hmong, Lao and Japanese for the rapidly growing Asian immigrant population in this area.

## —— MILL VALLEY ——

### Mill Valley Public Library

| | |
|---|---|
| 375 Throckmorton Avenue | A, E, V |
| (415) 388-4245 | Closed Sundays |

There is an enduring quality to good design. The authors discovered this library in the early 1960s, and it is as welcoming now as it was then.

Not only are there redwoods in back of this library, there are redwoods growing right next to its front entrance. The stucco building nestles into the trees of a park behind and below it. It was designed by Wurster, Bernardi and Emmons and landscaped by Lawrence Halpirin and Associates.

Inside, white walls contrast with a high-beamed wooden ceiling. At each end of the library tall bay windows rise to the peak of the ceiling and let in gentle light, filtered by redwoods. Four unique dormer windows (with glass on three sides) project from the street side of the long roof of the building and let in even more light.

The window at the west end of the library (in the children's room) looks up at Mount Tamalpais. The children's room is just what you would hope for—stuffed toys, comfortable cushions and lots of redwood.

Leather and wood lounge chairs specially designed for the library by Art Carpenter sit around a fireplace (which is used on dark and dreary days). Outside the fireplace wall a deck runs the length of the library. Several large redwood trees actually grow up through the deck. Downstairs is a gallery as well as good local and Marin County history collections maintained by the Mill Valley Historical Society.

Mill Valley, CA
Mill Valley Public Library

## —— MODESTO ——

### Stanislaus County Free Library

1500 I Street
(209) 558-7824                                  Closed Sundays, Fridays

Two-story rectangular white columns hold up an enormous overhang the length of this large white building. Fittingly, since this is very much a large agricultural community, there's a farmers' market right next to the library every Saturday.

This is a large utilitarian library. To the left as you enter is the pleasant children's room with large murals and paintings up on the wall. This room has more outside windows than any other place in the library. It's a pleasant place for children to sit and read or play quietly. They also have a good collection of song books.

For those interested in San Joaquin Valley history, the McHenry Mansion is across the street and the McHenry Museum is up the block.

## —— MONTEREY ——

### Monterey Public Library

625 Pacific Street                                              A, T
(408) 646-3930                                          Open every day

Monterey is the central tourist attraction of the Monterey Peninsula area, and there's so much to see here that a good library is a good place to rest tired feet. The library, one of California's first, established in 1849, is near many of the historic adobe houses in Monterey. It's also near the Monterey Peninsula Museum of Art and the Allen Knight Maritime Museum.

Designed by William Wurster, the library has dull orange balcony railings and steel "I" beams that contrast strikingly with knotty wood paneled walls. A curving wall of windows at the front of the library lets in lots of light. In addition, large circular light fixtures supply bright light, even on foggy days. Large expanses of blue and orange carpet add to the open feeling of the library.

The main reading room has lovely vistas through a curving front window wall, and there's an outside patio for reading in good weather. You'll find a good children's section, with a separate section for picture books.

The library displays a significant collection of original paintings by well-known California and Monterey Peninsula artists. It has a good California and local history collection, as well as some special architectural collections. If you want to find out what's going on in town other than what you find in the guidebooks, check the large bulletin boards here.

## MOUNT SHASTA CITY

### Mount Shasta Branch Library, Siskiyou County Public Library

515 East Alma Street
(916) 926-2031

T
Closed Sundays

Mount Shasta, as well as being one of California's most beautiful mountains, is home to lots of hiking, skiing, consciousness raising, and just plain relaxing. The plain, small library was built in 1969. It's right at the foot of Mount Shasta, as is, of course, the entire town of Mount Shasta City.

For a small library, it's quite spacious inside. This is a good place to pick up some extra information on the area's mountains and trails.

## OAKLAND

### Oakland Public Library

125 14th Street
(510) 238-3134

Closed Sundays

This imposing granite building was designed in the 1940s and opened in 1951. Its formal stone construction and three-story windows seem to shout "public library" as you drive up. Near the county courthouse and administration buildings, the library is only a block or so from Lake Merritt and is also only one block from the large but semihidden Oakland Art Museum.

The old-fashioned reading rooms in this library seem to go on and on forever. In fact, they go completely around the periphery of the building, with elevators and service space in the center. The library has a big collection of sheet music and a large magazine and periodical section on the second floor.

The Oakland History Room (closed Sundays and Mondays) has a significant collection, with photographs dating back to 1850 and voting records dating back to the 1870s. Its large study room is not fancy and upscale—it has a musty, archival feeling, but it's fun to explore. Author Jack London spent a significant part of his life in Oakland and there's a large London collection here that holds many early editions (some autographed), a big file of photographs of the author at all stages of his life, some partial manuscripts and other memorabilia.

## Golden Gate Branch Library

5606 San Pablo Avenue
(510) 652-3584                                         Closed Sundays, Mondays

This white-trimmed brick building is not only a small community library, it's also home to the Northern California Center for Afro-American History and Life. The library has a general collection as well as a fairly large African-American section, but the center is a treasure trove of an archive, concentrating on the history of black Americans in California. It has over 500 original manuscripts and letters, 2,000 titles dealing with African-American life in the United States, letters, and nearly 10,000 photographs telling the story and lives of early and present day black Californians. The small museum also displays historical artifacts and manuscripts and publishes a quarterly newsletter.

It's on a busy commercial street in a predominantly African-American neighborhood.

*Also of Note:*

## Kaiser Permanente Health Education Center

Kaiser Hospital, 482 West MacArthur
(510) 596-6204                            Closed Saturdays, Sundays

    Kaiser Hospitals are the largest health maintenance organization (HMO) in the country. Most of the hospitals have health education centers, and the one in Oakland is one of the largest.
    The goals of the centers are to promote both health education and health maintenance. Health education involves educational services that help patients and their families cope with acute or chronic medical conditions and diseases by emphasizing the patient's role as an active partner in health care. Health maintenance involves educational services that encourage members and staff to make changes in their behavior and environments to reduce health risks and enhance quality of life.
    The center operates like a membership library. Only members of the Kaiser HMO can take out books, videotapes and audiotapes, but anyone can drop in to browse. There are comfortable viewing areas (equipped with headphones) so that up to five people can sit and watch tapes without disturbing each other. There are also books for children on various health matters.
    The comfortable one-room library has lots of books on nutrition, diet, parenting, children, etc. There is more on health maintenance and recovery than on medicine and sickness—this is not a medical library. There is a lot of material on health for the general public. The center is also a bookstore, selling books on health and health maintenance at cost. A resource file lists community-based health support groups.

# —— OCEANSIDE ——

## Oceanside Public Library

330 North Hill Street                                        A
(619) 966-4690                                          Closed Sundays

    In front of this white building trimmed with blue tile is a reflecting pool, with palm trees growing out of square islands in the pool. The

Oceanside, CA
Oceanside Public Library

building is even more surprising inside, with high, narrow columns and arches in white and blue. There's a Moorish feeling to the design, suggested by the tall arches trimmed in patterns of blue around a central courtyard below. Private reading desks (under more tile-trimmed arches) look down from the mezzanine into the center of the library.

The building, designed by Charles Moore, opened in 1990. There's a view of the ocean from the second floor stacks; Oceanside has 3 1/2 miles of marvelous beaches. The Civic Center carries on the theme of the building (or vice versa) with colored tiles highlighting the white buildings.

## —— OXNARD ——

### Oxnard Public Library

| | |
|---|---:|
| 251 South A Street | A, V |
| (805) 385-7500 | Closed Fridays, Sundays |

Oxnard grows strawberries year round and has a busy harbor, an upscale waterfront area, miles of beaches and an intriguing new library. Both at the front and the back of this two-story brick building stocky columns on the second level support huge brick arches around large, clear windows. Through the imposing arches and windows you see an impressive, white, coffered, barrel-vaulted ceiling.

The short columns, so prominent outside, are repeated throughout the library. They're about 2 1/2 feet wide and about 5 feet high, mostly painted a deep burgundy. The carpets are a lighter burgundy, with green paths along them. While the entrance to the library feels monumental, the reading areas are of quite human scale and very comfortable.

The lobby floor is gray slate tile and a beautiful green tiled staircase leads to the second floor. The large windows at front and back of the building provide lovely clear light. The back wall faces west, affording views of the magnificent sunsets.

Reading and stack sections lead off to both sides from the top of the stairway. The second floor is almost totally ringed with outside patios that have comfortable deck furniture for outdoor reading. Throughout the library are framed quotations and poems from well-known authors, philosophers and poets, in Spanish and English.

The children's area is quite large with a generous story area. It is one of the largest children's rooms we visited.

## —— PACIFIC GROVE ——

### Pacific Grove Public Library

550 Central Avenue
(408) 648-3160                                        Closed Sundays

Originally a Carnegie library, building was begun at this site in 1907. It was enlarged in 1926, 1938, 1950 and 1970. A lovely Mission style colonnade along the front of the library supports the overhang of a sweeping roof.

The library has a collection of histories and accounts of voyages in the South Seas, including a number of rare books. You'll need to ask to see it. There's also a significant collection of older bound periodicals in a separate formal reading and conference room. The children's room is large, high, quiet, well lit and nicely closed off from the main library by glass walls.

The library is directly across the street from the Pacific Grove Museum of Natural History and only one block from Ocean View

Boulevard, a lovely street along the ocean. It's only about a mile's walk from here along the ocean to the fabulous Monterey Bay Aquarium. A lot of people come to Pacific Grove for conferences at the state-run Asilomar conference grounds. This would be a lovely place to spend some time if someone you're with is in a conference at Asilomar.

## —— PALM SPRINGS ——

### Palm Springs Public Library

| | |
|---|---|
| 300 South Sunrise Way | A, E |
| (619) 322-READ | Closed Sundays |

Palm Springs is a busy, elegant resort, and its matching library is one of the busiest about. The building hunkers down into the park, with bluff slanted walls all around, but once you enter it's a different story. A large skylight over a fish pond in a central atrium highlights its center. The pond is surrounded by tile, which in turn is framed by the library's mauve carpets. Around the sides of the building are enclosed gardened patios with tables and chairs for outdoor study or relaxation.

This is no quiet repository for dusty books. The library has so many exhibits, displays and special collections it's hard to know how to describe them. "Prickly Pears" is a collection of videotaped interviews that are portraits of historical Palm Springs. A charming "Palm Springs Golden Anniversary Quilt" commemorates local activities—you can even buy notecards with a color reproduction of it. One month there may be a display on the police department, the next month a display on the Agua Caliente Cahuilla Indians, another month a display on Railroads.

Young people are celebrated here. A flyer called the "Kid's Calendar" announces children's events ranging from a "Teddy Bear Tea" to "Mother's Day Ice Cream Social." There's even a "Dial-A-Story" phone number supported by the library; kids can call the number and hear a story. And of course the library has books, lots of them, and comfortable chairs on which to sit and read.

## —— PALO ALTO ——

### Palo Alto City Library

| | |
|---|---|
| 1213 Newell Road | A |
| (415) 329-2436 | Open every day |

The main library in Palo Alto is a long building surrounded by a brick screen that keeps sun out and lets light in. Almost all you can see from the outside is the brick screen, a sweeping roof, trees and a chimney. At each end the screen encloses a reading patio. Flowering trees, pines and shrubs surround the building.

The interior of this large building is lovely. Over the service area wood-trimmed light fixtures reflect the same pattern as the brick screen outside. In the peaked central section, chandeliers hang over comfortable chairs. Floor to ceiling windows look out to the brick screen and greenery. There are peaked clerestory windows at the ends of the main reading room. A huge fireplace brightens rainy days. There are lots of upholstered couches and chairs—some wicker furniture. Very comfortable.

A gallery wall near the circulation desk displays art. There's also a media section where you can relax on upholstered furniture and listen to some of the library's compact discs over headphones. The original building, designed by Edward D. Stone, opened in 1958 and was remodeled in 1984 with a design by Spenser Associates. There is no children's section here, but just three blocks away the city has an entire library devoted to children.

### Palo Alto Children's Library

| | |
|---|---|
| 1276 Harriet Street | |
| (415) 329-2134 | Closed Sundays |

Built in 1940, this tile-roofed Spanish style building was the only library in the country built for the express purpose of serving children. A fireplace with hand-painted tiles from nursery tales, a scene from *The Secret Garden* and the library's own secret garden based on the book are only a few of the attractions. (Even the fireplace grate has scenes from children's tales.)

It's not just that the library has a large collection for children—this place is totally for children. A pelican model hangs from the ceiling among other cut-outs and a large ship's model graces the top of one of the bookcases. There's even a carousel horse. The "Secret Garden" in the back of the library is subdivided into child-sized sections. With hedges for borders instead of fences it's a lovely imaginative place for kids.

The library has wonderful folk and fairy tale collections, a teacher's shelf, a parent's shelf and grandparent's kits.

The library is part of the Lucie Stern Community Center Complex, which includes the Community Theater and the Children's Theater. It is near the Junior Museum and Rinconada Park. Palo Alto is most famous for being the home of Stanford University, but your children might be more interested in knowing that it's also home to the Barbie Doll Museum and Hall of Fame. The librarians can tell you about all sorts of children's activities in the area.

## —— PASADENA ——

### City of Pasadena
### Department of Information Services Library

| | |
|---|---:|
| 285 East Walnut Street | A, E |
| (818) 405-4041 | Open every day |

If you like your libraries formal and grand, this is the place to come. The Pasadena Central Library is a yellow stucco Spanish Renaissance building. Designed by Myron Hunt (who also designed the Rose Bowl, Huntington Library and Occidental College), the library opened in 1927. Recent extensive restorations have returned the library to its original beauty, while unobtrusively providing for contemporary electronic services. For example, there are many computers, but most are hidden in specially designed wooden carrels.

This library is worth a visit just to see the huge main reading room. The original oak reading tables (now glass topped with individual table top lamps) sit on a cork floor under a carved wood ceiling 40 feet above. Bronze and copper pendant light fixtures hang above between high clerestory windows.

Even the children's room has high wooden ceilings and formal carpets, although a great deal of thought went into making the room child-friendly. Chairs and benches for various sizes of small folks were carefully selected, and special "read-to-me" leather and wood chairs were designed to fit a parent and a child.

The Pasadena Centennial Room is one of the most elegant local history sites around. Here, while the primary feeling is of elegance, form hides function. What's hidden are special controls for light, humidity and security to preserve a very special collection. Throughout this library elegant carpets, dark wood bookcases and formal display cases remind you of earlier days of elegance.

## —— POMONA ——

### Pomona Public Library

| 625 South Garey Avenue | A |
|---|---|
| (909) 620-2033 | Closed Sundays, Fridays |

This striking building in the Pomona Civic Center is a two-level library set into a tiled plaza surrounded by trees. The main floor encloses inner patios with overhead wood screens that make for pleasant indoor reading areas and also let a lot of light into the library. The architects of this 1965 building, which has endured very well, were Welton Becket & Associates.

The quiet and private special collections room on the lower level is fascinating. Besides a larger than usual genealogical collection it has over 4,000 citrus labels, 10,000 wine labels and a splendid archival collection of over 40,000 photographic images by Burton Frasher. His work covers western America from the early 1900s through the 1940s.

The large and colorful children's room has a comfortable deep red carpet. In the middle is a large circular reading table with a padded bench all around that displays a large model of a California mission. There's a permanent Laura Ingalls Wilder exhibit (author of the *Little House on the Prairie* series). It covers her life, her books (in several languages), the characters in her books and her personal correspondence. There are books about her and books about pioneer and frontier life. An alcove contains other Wilder memorabilia.

## —— REDDING ——

### Shasta County Library

| | |
|---|---|
| 1855 Shasta Street | |
| (916) 225-5756 | Closed Fridays, Saturdays, Sundays |

Redding is a major crossroad in northern California and a good place to stop if you're on Interstate 5 north or south or have just come across from the Pacific coast on Highway 299. Redding, like most of northern California, is not terribly prosperous, and there is a distinct lack of library funding.

In spite of this, this large library has a recently remodeled children's room and some interesting special collections. The children's room is bright and cheery. The rest of the library is somewhat drab, mostly due to poor lighting—but it's pleasant, spacious and well worn. On a clear day you can see Mount Shasta from the windows on the north side of the library.

In the large local history section a collection details the building of Shasta Dam, which is an important part of this area in California. If you're camping at Lake Shasta and want some information on the local dams, this is a good place to look.

## —— REDLANDS ——

### A. K. Smiley Public Library

| | |
|---|---|
| 125 West Vine Street | A, E, H, T |
| (714) 798-7565 | Closed Sundays |

This library and the Lincoln Memorial Shrine just behind it are worth the 60-mile trip to Redlands from downtown Los Angeles. The original Moorish/Mission style building was donated to the city in 1898. It's been carefully expanded five times since then. The additions in 1926 and 1930 were designed by Myron Hunt, the architect who designed the library in Pasadena. A 1990 addition, designed by Cathleen Malmstrom of Architectural Resources in San Francisco, is outstanding.

*California* 73

Redlands, CA
A.K. Smiley Public Library
And this is one of
the *new* rooms!
Photo courtesy A.K. Smiley
Public Library

An ornately carved stone entrance under a square, Moorish tower leads from a beautifully tiled entryway past bas-relief sculptures to a main hall with a brilliantly polished oak floor. The main reading room to the left is spacious and has carved, oak beams crossing a coved ceiling that gently angles up at the sides. A beautiful round stained glass window dominates the far wall. Along the side walls are rows of small, high, arched windows, with leaded diamond-shaped panes. Light flows through them and reflects from white walls and ceilings to create an almost ethereal feeling in this light building. The wood in the structure is golden oak—light, cheery and almost glowing.

In one of the original 1898 rooms a carved wooden staircase displays a beautifully carved wooden relief below its complexly curving banister. Even on a dull day the sets of small clerestory windows let in lots of light.

The stack area is floored with travertine marble while some floors in the newest section are of Shanghai slate. Anyone interested in turn-of-the-century American furniture will enjoy this library—all of the original furniture is still here, recently refinished by a local craftsman. The seamless 1990 expansion added a conservatory that looks out through a formal courtyard to the Lincoln Shrine.

A children's garden outside features topiary figures (hedges grown to look like animals) and in a hall outside the children's room is a series of signed Norman Rockwell prints. This is one of those must-see surprises.

## —— REDWOOD CITY ——

### Redwood City Public Library

1044 Middlefield Road
(415) 780-7020                                        Closed Sundays

    The entrance to the library is the facade of Redwood City's old Fire Station No. 1. It is an interesting preservation effort. Even though they essentially put up a new building, architects Ripley Associates of San Francisco preserved some of the city's past by using the facade and small available space of the old station. Library doors now fill the arches through which fire trucks used to drive. The old facade is beige brick, and the new addition is matching stucco. The trim around the arches is painted an attractive blue.
    When you first enter, the library seems surprisingly small because all you see is a large information desk. As you go further in you discover that this is now a 47,000-square-foot library, nicely spread out, with soft leather furniture.
    Even though this is a busy library, many of its areas are quiet and comfortable.

## —— RICHMOND ——

### Richmond Public Library

325 Civic Center Plaza
(415) 620-6561                                         Open every day

    This library serves a truly mixed community, including a small artists' community at Point Richmond near San Francisco Bay, a poor inner city area and new developments around the large Hilltop Mall. It is a bustling, big library. Both its collection and friendly staff reflect the multicultural nature of its clientele. It has more books per square foot than most libraries. The shelves are really high, with top shelves up about eight feet.
    The library, built in 1949, is a large red brick building with aluminum trim. It's a center for African-American studies collections,

and the library is developing a core African-American videotape collection so it can act as both a regional and national resource for other libraries.

There is a Richmond history collection with lots of information on the development of Richmond during World War II, but you need to ask at the reference desk as it's not part of the regular collection. The children's library is like the main library—utilitarian, crowded, plain and useable.

## —— SACRAMENTO ——

### Sacramento Public Library

| | |
|---|---|
| 828 I Street | A, E, T |
| (916) 440-7800 | Closed Sundays, Mondays |

Just a short walk from the state capitol building, this striking new building takes another approach to preservation. Rather than restoring or expanding the 1918 Carnegie library that stood on this corner, an impressive new building was wrapped around the old one, with terrific results.

The main entrance to the library is through a five-story glass-fronted atrium galleria. Three large glass sculptures hang high in the air over 5,700 square feet of travertine floor inlaid with bronze symbols. Balconies and catwalks go around the space on three sides, and, in the back, reading rooms overlook the space. The galleria is used for cultural or educational events, and it can be rented for private events.

Sacramento, CA
Sacramento Public Library
Atrium Galleria

The I Street entrance shows the joining of the new building to the old. Here, in another high interior space, four floors of curving white and glass walls meet the terra cotta walls of the old library under the fifth floor skylight. Once again, reading rooms look down into open space.

The interior is equally well designed. As a convenience, just inside the entrance is Central Express, a browsing library where patrons find the latest in best sellers, videotapes, audiocassettes and compact discs. On upper floors, comfortable lounge chairs sit next to windows looking down into the entryway on one side and the galleria on the other. The Sacramento Room, comprising the second floor of the original Carnegie library, reflects the original architectural finishes of that period. It houses a significant collection of local history and rare books.

The Kids' Place, the children's and young adults' area is on the lower level. Light flows in from the first-floor windows, past a 100-foot mural sculpture, to a brightly colored room. A multicolored wood-paneled circulation desk highlights this long, well-furnished area.

A significant number of artworks were commissioned for the library as part of Sacramento's Art in Public Places program that mandates a percentage of public construction spending for art. Architects Kaplan, McLaughlin and Diaz joined with designers Simon, Martin-Vegue Winkelstein who did the interiors to produce a splendid library.

It is sad that due to California's financial crisis this magnificent new building that opened in 1992 is only open 35 hours a week, Tuesday through Saturday, 11:00 A.M. to 6:00 P.M.

*Also of Note:*

## California State Library

| | |
|---|---|
| 914 Capitol Mall | A, H, T |
| (916) 654-0183 | Closed Saturdays, Sundays |

Just before the Capitol is a stately granite building with huge granite columns holding up a massive pediment. That's the library. Directly in front of it is a fountain surrounded by carefully tended flowers. Many lovers of formal architecture consider the lobby of this building, the

Neo-Classical Library and Courts Building, to be the most beautiful in Sacramento. A World War I memorial, the lobby is embellished with inscriptions, black Italian marble columns, an ornamental ceiling and 12 paneled murals illustrating the history of warfare by Frank Van Sloane. Urnlike lamps hang 20 feet above a brilliantly polished tile floor. Throughout the building are intricately carved and painted ceilings.

The circulation and reference rooms on the third floor have marvelous bas-relief sculptures by Edward Sanford and murals by Maynard Dixon.

The reference collection is probably one of the best state history collections in the United States. It includes rare books dating from the 16th century, works on the California missions, letters pertaining to the Gold Rush and over 100,000 cataloged photographs.

Even if you don't get to the library, don't leave Sacramento without visiting the exquisitely rehabilitated state capitol building. It's lots of fun, and tours are given on a regular basis.

## California State Railroad Museum Library

113 I Street  T, H
(916) 323-8073  Closed Sundays, Mondays

---

Located in historic Old Sacramento, next door to the railroad buff's dream attraction, the California State Railroad Museum, this may well be the nation's largest center for the study of railroad history. The modern 100,000-square-foot museum houses perfectly restored locomotives, sleepers, private cars, dioramas, videotapes—the whole works.

The library is home to a huge collection of railroad history. This is not a circulating library, but the plain 19th-century-style reading room is staffed by friendly archivists. If you'd like to research a specific topic, call in advance so the librarians are prepared to help you.

Collections include over 5,000 books, over 1 million photographs, 4,100 glass plate and film negatives from the Pullman Company from 1880–1940, 25,000 rolling stock drawings from the Atchison, Topeka and the Santa Fe, and on and on. They also have financial and land records of the Central Pacific and Southern Pacific railroads (and their predecessors) going back to the early 1860s, route maps and dining car menus. This is truly a national collection, with information on over 4,000 railroads.

Old Sacramento, with its raised wooden sidewalks, boutiques, restaurants and antiquarian book shops is great fun. Also in the area is the Delta King paddle wheel steamer, now a deluxe hotel.

# —— SAINT HELENA ——

## George and Elsie Wood Public Library, Napa Valley Wine Library

| 1492 Library Lane | T, V |
| (707) 963-5244 | Open every day |

Just as the Lahaina Library in Hawaii opens on the beach, the Apache Junction Library in Arizona is right in the desert and the Bonney Lake Library in Washington is right in the trees, this library is surrounded by vineyards, with grape vines within twenty yards of three sides.

This interesting building—stucco with a slate tiled roof—has very few windows on the front, as the windows all peer out at the vineyards. Circular skylights and light panels make for a very bright library and carry out the circular theme.

About a third of the library is a children's room. There's a separate room for California history, local archives and rare books. It may be the proximity to wine country and the area's obsession with food and wine, but this library does seem to have a larger than usual cookbook collection (check area 641 in the shelves). One of the Napa Valley's finest restaurants, Tra Vigne, is only a half mile from here.

The Napa Valley Wine Library collection, started in 1961, has over 2,000 titles. The library, constantly involved in wine education, sponsors annual wine tasting events and publishes periodic reports.

In front of the library is the Silverado Museum, a collection devoted to the works of Robert Louis Stevenson. The red-carpeted museum has over 8,000 items including original letters, manuscripts and other memorabilia. A delightful place to visit, it's closed on Mondays.

## ──── SALINAS ────

### John Steinbeck Library

350 Lincoln Avenue  
(408) 758-7311   Closed Sundays

Native son and Pulitzer Prize winner John Steinbeck wrote *The Grapes of Wrath*, *Cannery Row*, *Of Mice and Men* and a number of other works not terribly complimentary to the West of his day. He is remembered and acclaimed far more kindly in Salinas today then he was at the peak of his career. Today the Salinas public library is named after him and houses a collection of 30,000 items relating to him. A lifesize statue of Steinbeck graces the front of the library.

The Steinbeck Archives were started in 1964 and include manuscripts, first editions, correspondence, etc. A detailed description of the holdings has been published and is available from the library. The Steinbeck room displays material from the archives and the Steinbeck Boutique sells books by and about the author. To finish off your trip you can visit the John Steinbeck House and even eat lunch in its restaurant.

## ──── SAN BERNARDINO ────

### Norman F. Feldheym Central Library

555 West Sixth Street   A, E  
(909) 381-8201   Closed Sundays

Plan to spend a lot of time here. Set amidst tall palm trees in a downtown park, this sprawling, 64,000-square-foot, two-story library is a comfortable beehive of activity.

To the right of the red-tiled entrance is an auditorium that seats 200, a two-story art gallery, and meeting rooms. The main reading room is large and spread out, with shelves arranged so that you can see out to the large windows around the sides of the library. There are lots of comfortable reading areas, some study carrels, lounging chairs and private alcoves. Overhead an angular skylight casts gentle light into the main reading area.

San Bernardino, CA
Norman F. Feldheym Central Library
Computer room over reading room

An upstairs microcomputer room projects like the prow of a ship over the main reading room. A joint school/library project, the computers are set up for desktop publishing and other computer tasks. The staff is helpful, and the library gives frequent free classes.

Across the hall from the computer room is a large literacy training section which offers tutoring and training for people of all ages. And just around the corner is the California Room, with good genealogical, local history and photo archive collections.

The children's room, with its own entrance, has a story corner that will seat up to 75 kids. There's also a set of three tropical fish aquariums (donated by McDonald's) arranged in a triangle around a post. The architects were Gregory Villanueva and Oscar Arnoni.

California                                                                  81

# —— SAN DIEGO ——

## San Diego Public Library

820 E Street
(619) 236-5800                                                    Open every day

    This three-story central city library has become pretty tired in its declining years. The city is currently in the planning process for a new facility and using its resources to open branch libraries (see below).
    On the other hand there is a huge collection in the central library, including the Wangenheim Room with its collection of materials on the history of the book and the history of printing. The California Room has a wide array of resources on southern California and San Diego history and large general collections.

## Linda Vista Branch Library

2160 Ulric Street                                                              A
(619) 573-1399                                                    Open every day

    Here is a library that shows how cities adapt to changing population patterns and how innovative architecture can be used to create a community center. While plans for a new main library for San Diego are on hold, neighborhood libraries like Linda Vista have shown innovative new planning and design.
    Striking solid bluff walls on two sides are pierced by arched entrances under a curving roof. On another side a beamed metal triangle

San Diego, CA
Linda Vista Branch Library
San Diego Public Library

rises above a wall of windows. Inside, a spiderweb of wooden columns and struts supports a high roof in a bright and airy main room. In places it looks like an upside-down umbrella. Rob Wellington Quigley's design is delightful and so light that very little artificial light is needed.

Linda Vista is a neighborhood that has developed a significant Asian population (to add to its older Spanish-speaking population) in recent years. Library signs are in Korean and Thai as well as Spanish and Chinese. Inside, patrons can find books in their own language. This is also a neighborhood that doesn't have much of a center, and this innovative library at a 1960s shopping mall creates an anchor for the community.

## Otay Mesa Branch Library

3003 Coronado Avenue
(619) 690-8374    Open every day

This library is probably one of the very few from which you can see into another country. It's high on a hill, a few miles from Tijuana, Mexico. On clear days patrons can see Tijuana's bull rings from an outside terrace.

Inside, clerestory windows let in lots of natural light that reflects off white walls, furniture and furnishings. This isn't a huge library, but it is modern and useable. A lot of thought went into making it user-friendly. For instance, the checkout, information and return counters are low enough so that children won't be intimidated by them.

It's not the closest library to Tijuana, that one is in San Ysidro, which is between Otay Mesa and the border, and is a much smaller library. For now, this is a good waiting place for people who don't want to visit Mexico, while the rest of the family visits Tijuana for a few hours.

*California*

## —— SAN FRANCISCO ——

### San Francisco Public Library

Civic Center, Larkin Street  T
(415) 557-4400  Closed Sundays

This grand old building is across a reflecting fountain and mall from San Francisco's classic domed city hall (the dome is higher than the U.S. Capitol's) and only a block from the Symphony Hall and Opera House. There's a lot of new construction going on in this area, but the large number of homeless people who congregate nearby can make the area somewhat sad.

Built in 1917 in Italian Renaissance style, the white granite building has imposing columns and huge arched windows all around. It's great fun to explore even though it's quite overcrowded. The library reached its projected capacity in 1944 and has been squeezing things in ever since.

On the other hand, walking up the marble stairway to the main reading rooms is a marvelous exposure to early 20th century grandiose public architecture. Three-story-high carved and vaulted ceilings loom above marble stairs. Colonnaded mezzanines around the landings have huge murals on their walls. The main reading room in the "circulating library" is 200 feet long with painted wood beamed ceilings high overhead and tall arched windows the length of the enormous room.

The San Francisco Room on the third floor, which also houses the Museum of the Book, is much less crowded. It's worth coming to the library just to see this room and its collection. There's a lot of early San Francisco history here, including a lovely stained glass depiction of the waterfront and stereoscopic pictures of the earthquake of 1906. There are special collections on the History of the Printed Book, Calligraphy, Early Children's Books, Humor, Robert Frost, Sherlock Holmes and the Panama Canal.

This library is so big and has so many interesting features that on the third Wednesday of each month they give walking tours. Ground has been broken for a new library one block down Larkin Street from here. This new facility, with 375,000 square feet, will open early in 1996.

## Chinatown Branch Library

1135 Powell Street
(415) 274-0275                                    Closed Sundays, Mondays

    Another sign of the diverse population in the San Francisco area, this is the second largest branch of the San Francisco Public Library. If you'd like to get a little further into Chinatown than the crowded shopping streets, souvenir stores and produce markets, take a look in here. You won't see many tourists, but you will see a lot of people. Besides a large collection in various Asian languages, the library has a multilingual staff, speaking English, Cantonese, Mandarin and Vietnamese.

    The building, an old Carnegie library erected in 1915, will be undergoing rehabilitation and expansion in early 1994.

## Eureka Valley–Harvey Milk Memorial Branch Library

3555 16th Avenue
(415) 554-9445                                    Closed Saturdays, Sundays

    This small, brightly lit neighborhood library with its enclosed brick courtyard was built in 1961. It's named after one of the country's first openly homosexual elected officials. The library is near the Castro District of San Francisco, home to beautifully restored Victorian homes and a large and politically active gay community. To serve its local readers, the library has both fiction and nonfiction Gay and Lesbian collections.

    In front of an ivy-covered stone block wall in the entryway is a lovely polished gray marble sculpture, *Torso*, by the late Beniamino Bufano, a noted San Francisco sculptor.

## Mission Branch Library–Biblioteca de la Mission

3359 24th Street
(415) 695-5090                                    Closed Sundays, Mondays

    Around the large arched windows of this solid, square, stone 1915 building are carved stone books and flowers and wreaths, painted to show off the stonework. Inside, arched windows are set off by more grandiose carvings of books, scrolls, leaves and shields, topped by an old carved ceiling. The building is a throwback to a different era.

Catering to a neighborhood that has more roots in Central and South America than in North America, the library has over 13,000 Spanish language books and a large Latino interest collection in English. There is always a bilingual staff in attendance.

Besides the fun Mexican/Central American ambience of this neighborhood, there are lots of nearby places of interest. The Mission Cultural Center, the Galería de la Raza, Mission Dolores and the Women's Building are all located nearby. There are so many bookshops, cafes, galleries and other good places to visit in the neighborhood that the library produces a "Book-Lover's Guide to the Mission."

## Richmond Branch Library

351 Ninth Avenue
(415) 666-7165                                   Closed Sundays, Mondays

This library is in an area sometimes called "the Richmond" and frequently referred to by natives as "the Avenues." Not far from Golden Gate Park, it's between Geary and Clement streets, two of San Francisco's most international streets. Exploring this neighborhood is fun, not just because of the older houses you'll see, but the restaurants and shops cater to Russian, Greek, Chinese, Polish, Italian and Indian residents (and a lot more, besides).

Built of square granite blocks in 1913, this medium-sized library has several tall palm trees growing out front. A carved serpentine pattern goes up the sides of the arched front doors. The trim on the arched windows of the library is painted robin's egg blue. This is a bright, high, one-room library. Downstairs, a large children's room opens onto a mini-park with a kiddy playground in a sand box.

*Also of Note:*

## California Academy of Sciences Library/Biodiversity Resource Center

Golden Gate Park                                                         T
(415) 750-7102                          Library closed Saturdays, Sundays
                                 Center closed Sundays, Mondays, Tuesdays

The huge California Academy of Sciences is directly across the band shell and Music Concourse from the M. H. DeYoung Memorial

Museum and the Asian Art Museum. The Academy includes the Steinhart Aquarium, the Natural History Museum and the Planetarium.

The research library is on the second floor, and there is no admission if you're just going to the library. But the museum and aquarium are so outstanding that they are well worth an admission fee. The kids will love the dinosaur exhibit and its sound effects.

The library's collection emphasizes natural history and the natural sciences, but there is also a large collection of maps, including all of the U.S.G.S. topographic maps of the western United States and the archives of the Academy. Everything is cataloged, and the staff will be glad to help if you'd like to follow up on anything you couldn't get answered by the museum staff or the staff of the Biodiversity Center on the main floor.

The library's Biodiversity Center is in one of the main exhibit halls of the museum. It provides access to an immense variety of resources that describe the diversity of species on the earth, threats to it and human efforts to preserve it. Both the information and the center are more accessible than the more formal research library upstairs. The center has a large collection of pamphlets and of environmental and conservation newsletters and magazines such as *Sierra, Hawaii's Forest and Wildlife, Oaks and Folks, Colorado Wildlife*, etc. There are usually several videotapes running on the conservation of various species.

## Helen Crocker Russell Library of Horticulture

| Strybing Arboretum, 9th Avenue at Lincoln Way | T, V |
|---|---|
| (415) 661-1514 | Open every day |

According to the dictionary, an arboretum is "a place for the scientific study and public exhibition of many species of trees and shrubs." That's what's here as well as a fine botanical garden. The 70-acre arboretum and garden are beautiful, and it's hard to believe that they are in the middle of a big city. The fascinating collection is arranged geographically, with collections ranging from Chile to Southwestern Australia.

The friendly and comfortable library contains more than 12,000 volumes, including a number of rare books, and also receives over 200 periodicals. It's at the main entrance to the arboretum. There is even a small children's section, a convenient arrangement so kids will have something to do while parents do a little garden research.

After exploring the library, the garden and the nearby gift and book shop, you're just a short walk from the Japanese Tea Garden next to the De Young Museum.

## J. Porter Shaw Library at the National Maritime Museum

| | |
|---|---|
| Building E, Fort Mason Center, Bay and Laguna Streets | T, V |
| (415) 556-9870 | Closed Sundays, Mondays |

For anyone interested in maritime history, this library is an absolute must. This is one of the largest collections of maritime history in the country, and most likely the most accessible. With over 14,000 volumes, back issues of 500 periodicals, oral histories and over 100 sea chantey recordings the collection is simply enormous. There's a library of ship's plans from 1878 to 1966, and copies of Lloyd's registers from 1764 to the 1980s. It's tucked away on the third floor of a yellow concrete building in the Fort Mason Center, a conglomeration of over 50 nonprofit organizations in former army buildings (this area is well worth a half-day visit by itself).

The library recently secured the Barbara Johnson collection of 3,600 books, 5,000 pamphlets and thousands of other items on whaling. This is the largest single collection of library material on whaling in existence.

The comfortable library, with a general reading area, private study rooms and its more formal Lyman Reading Room is a pleasant place. It's also quite modern; archival and rare material (including films and over 250,000 photographs) is carefully stored in climate-controlled vaults.

This library may have one of the best views going. The back window looks out across San Francisco Bay to Sausalito; there's even a brass telescope to help you look at the boats on the bay. There's also a lovely stained glass window of an early steamship.

# SAN JOSE

## San Jose Dr. Martin Luther King, Jr. Main Library

180 West San Carlos  
(408) 277-4846

T  
Open every day

Located centrally in one of California's fastest growing cities, the library is near the Children's Discovery Museum, the Center for the Performing Arts, TheTech Museum of Innovation, the McEnery Convention Center and the Hilton Hotel. The Convention Center stop of the Light Rail Vehicle system is right in front of the library.

There are three library floors in this five-story yellow concrete building. Escalators moving people up three flights toward skylights make the library look like an upscale department store. The building is open from top to bottom. The ground floor is particularly bright, with light from wide arched windows complementing the central light from the fourth floor skylight.

The large children's room has a friendly feel—rocking chairs, lots of stuffed toys.

An extensive African-American collection is located in the Martin Luther King, Jr. area on the second floor.

## Biblioteca Latino Americana

690 Locust Avenue  
(408) 294-1237

Closed Sundays

Just a few blocks from San Jose's main library, this library is in a different world. In a plain building with a large colorful mural outside, the Biblioteca Latino Americana caters to the 30 percent of the population in Santa Clara County that speaks Spanish. Most of the libraries near here have some Spanish language books; here the majority of the books are in Spanish.

It's unfortunate that funding for this branch seems limited. The building is crowded and old, although the enthusiastic bilingual staff works hard to make up for the lack of financial support. This is where good intentions get crossed with inadequate funding.

## —— SAN JUAN CAPISTRANO ——

### San Juan Capistrano Branch Library, Orange County Public Library

| | |
|---|---|
| 31495 El Camino Real | A, E, T |
| (714) 493-1752 | Closed Sundays |

Designed in 1983 by world-famous architect Michael Graves, this superb building is one of the most comfortable and attractive small libraries you are likely to find.

Starkly modern outside, the inside of the library does a remarkable job of both replicating the shape of the nearby mission and providing comfortable, quiet spaces for reading.

An inner courtyard is surrounded by covered walkways and is reminiscent of central courtyards in the California missions. There are reading rooms off some of the walkways and enclosed outdoor reading areas off others.

San Juan Capistrano, CA
San Juan Capistrano Branch, Orange County Public Library

The small reading rooms—some with room for only six to eight people—are exquisitely furnished and provide more comfortable reading and lounging space than most of us have in our homes. The small rooms and built-in bookcases in this showpiece make it much more popular with visitors than with librarians.

Even children are provided with private space. There's a main children's reading area with four tables for five kids per table, and there are also four distinct storytelling areas so kids can be read to in small groups, as opposed to one large group with one storyteller.

Throughout the library there's careful attention to detail. Table lamp shades are inverted pyramids that complement the squareness of the individual rooms and their pyramidal skylights. Sconces on the wall have flat angles that match the angles of the ceiling and square hanging lamps cap it all.

The library is just a block from the grounds of the Mission at San Juan Capistrano that encompasses three different churches, including one in use for over 200 years. The Amtrak Station in San Juan Capistrano has been in use as a train station since 1895.

## —— SAN LUIS OBISPO ——

### San Luis Obispo City–County Library

995 Palm Street
(805) 781-5991                                                Closed Sundays

If you're taking either Highway 1 or Highway 101 up and down California, San Luis Obispo makes a convenient and interesting stop. Home to the world's first motel (1925) and also home to a fantastic fantasy motel (the Madonna Inn), this agricultural and tourist center of 42,000 has lots to offer.

The contemporary Mediterranean-style brick library was designed by Bruce Fraser and opened in 1989. Right in the center of town, its brick tower and entrance contrast with yellow/orange concrete walls. A brightly lit building with comfortable lounging furniture, the library has lots of attractive art on its walls and a generous children's room.

The library is not only in the center of town, it's just a few blocks from the Mission San Luis Obispo. From the Mission there's a self-guided walking tour of historic places. There's also a large farmers' market every Thursday and concerts during the summer. Interesting shopping is available on the tree-lined streets of San Luis Obispo.

## —— SAN MARINO ——

### Huntington Library, Art Collections and Botanical Gardens

| | |
|---|---|
| 1151 Oxford Road | T, E |
| (818) 405-2100 | Closed Mondays |

For those interested in art, literature or growing things, the Huntington Library may be the highlight of a visit to southern California. A research library that includes 3 million manuscripts, 357,000 rare books and 321,000 reference books, three separate buildings for exquisite art collections and 120 acres of botanical gardens displaying over 14,000 carefully labeled plants is not to be missed.

The library concentrates in British and American history from the 11th century to the present. While the actual library is open only to qualified researchers, the Library Exhibition Hall is open to the public and displays outstanding parts of the collection.

The library building is as formal as the U.S. Supreme Court. The exhibition hall is long, dark and formal. Exhibits fill the room, and above are rare books in cases on a mezzanine. One of the more popular exhibits is a 500-year-old vellum (parchment) choir book that you can

San Marino, CA
Huntington Library,
Art Collections
and Botanical Gardens

actually touch. There's also a Gutenberg bible, an early Chaucer, letters of George Washington and Benjamin Franklin, manuscripts by Wordsworth, Shelly, Mark Twain and many others. One of the original copies of *Audubon's Birds of America*, in its huge double elephant folio size is usually on display. Exhibits change periodically.

On one side of the library you see through a bank vault door into the rare book stacks. A sign says "On three levels are shelved three fourths of more than 340,000 rare books in the library. Adjacent to these floors are the manuscript stacks, housing three-fifths of the more than 2.2 million manuscripts in the Huntington." This is the epitome of literary history in a dark formal room that just begs you to come back with credentials and study in the library.

# ——— SAN RAFAEL ———

## Marin County Free Library

| | |
|---|---|
| Marin County Civic Center, | |
| North San Pedro Exit, U.S. 101 | A |
| (415) 499-6056 | Closed Saturdays, Sundays |

The Marin County Civic Center is the only government building designed by Frank Lloyd Wright that was ever built. The library is under a blue dome in the center of the structure. It's between one wing that houses the county's Administration Building and another that houses the Hall of Justice. The elaborately detailed building is pale orange stucco, with a sky-blue roof.

You don't have to be an architecture buff to have fun exploring these buildings. Skylights run the length of the multistory wings, over plantings on the ground floor. Balconies galore run throughout this unique structure. It is easy to get lost, though, trying to find the fourth floor and library. If the elevator you get in doesn't go that high, find another one. The elevator to the library is near the central breezeway.

The ceiling of the main reading room in the library is a shallow low dome with lights all around. Shelves radiate from the sides out toward the wall. Originally all the shelves were much more in tune with the room, but overcrowding has forced some significant changes. The furniture in the library was designed by Wright's associates. The Anne

Kent Historical Room has a good California collection and also a great deal of material on Wright and the Civic Center.

## —— SAN RAMON ——

### San Ramon Valley Branch Library, Contra Costa County Library System

100 Montgomery Street                                            A
(510) 866-8467                                            Open every day

San Ramon is only 35 miles from San Francisco and not terribly well known. However, the development of the huge Bishop Ranch Office Park and a significant number of similar facilities has moved much of the contemporary office scene here from San Francisco. Its library is in an area that has shopping, residences and offices within a few blocks of each other.

The contemporary building is on the corner of the Marketplace Shopping Center. At first glance it looks more like the anchor store of the shopping center than a library. An eye-catching building with an imposing barrel vault overhead, it's surrounded by green shrubbery. Just outside the library entrance is a pay phone in a bright red British telephone booth.

While the vault runs the full length of the library, reading and reference rooms lead off at interesting angles inside. A large children's area (almost a third of the space) is uniquely identified by horizontally hanging bright yellow scalloped banners. They shade the fluorescent lights, retain noise within the area and give the area a real sense of identity.

The library looks much larger than it actually is, thanks in large part to the way sections are separated from each other. Comfortable and modern, it opened in 1987 and was designed by Clifford Moles Associates of San Francisco.

# SANTA BARBARA

## Santa Barbara Public Library

| 40 East Anapamu Street | A, T |
|---|---|
| (805) 962-7653 | Open every day |

The city of Santa Barbara is rich, well put together and elegant, and so is its main library. (In fact, so are all of its libraries—they're all over the place here.) The public library is right in the heart of the downtown area, one block from State Street, the main downtown avenue and directly across the street from the county courthouse. You can get a good view of the library, the city's acres of tile roofs and the mountains to its east from the observation tower of the sprawling Spanish/Moorish courthouse.

The block-long library is light brown with tall, arched and recessed windows on three sides and surrounded by trees. The original wooden entrance door (carved, gilded and painted) is no longer used, but it is fun to find its carvings of the shields of four famous European libraries. The modern main entrance is adorned with a fountain and lots of places to sit.

Although the library is formal, it's not intimidating. Perhaps it's the simple elegance of the tall arched windows, perhaps the plethora of upholstered reading and lounging chairs, perhaps the huge fireplace and carved ceiling—but the overall combination makes this library very inviting. Light pours through a skylight over stairs leading to the second floor mezzanine. The views of Santa Barbara's street life from the comfortable chairs in the mezzanine are entrancing.

There are several art galleries in the library as well as some remarkable murals.

Santa Barbara, CA
Santa Barbara Public Library

*Also of Note:*

## Blaksley Library, Santa Barbara Botanic Garden Library

| | |
|---|---|
| 1212 Mission Canyon Road | T |
| (805) 682-4726 | Closed Saturdays, Sundays |

This charming small library has a collection of almost 9,000 volumes and 2,500 bound volumes of periodicals on the flora of California and the West in general, plus a wide variety of reference materials on flora of other areas. It has hundreds of current journal and newsletter subscriptions. The library is open by appointment only because it is frequently used for meetings and classes.

The building, designed by Lutta Riggs in 1941, was carefully placed to look out at the gardens and up to La Cumbre Peak. Plain wood floors, French doors and an open wood beam ceiling give this room a natural feel. The large windows in the north wall of the library frame the mountain peaks beautifully.

The Botanical Garden has signs with both the Latin and common names of plants. There are also trails of varying length, so you can get as much or as little exercise as you want.

## The Karpeles Manuscript Library

| | |
|---|---|
| 21 West Anapamu Street | T |
| (805) 962-5322 | Open every day |

For anyone interested in original manuscripts or original writings, this library is a great find. This is a museum of the original written word, hardly a library, but well worth visiting. It is one of several sites of a private institution operated by David Karpeles, whom we were privileged to meet in this building. His institution is "Dedicated to the Preservation of the Original writings of the Great Authors, Scientists, Philosophers, Statesmen, Sovereigns and Leaders from All Periods of World History" and is a remarkable example of private philanthropy for the public good.

One item on display is a response from the future President James Buchanan to a job seeker in San Francisco in which Buchanan as Secretary of State, replies that " ... no such appointment could be made at this time as California is not part of the United States, but when the proper time arrives, a new application would be considered." There are original writings of Cotton Mather; John II, King of Aragonne and Count of Barcelona; Martin Luther's handwriting; letters signed by Harry Truman; and the original manuscript of A. A. Milne's *Winnie the Pooh.*

Manuscripts are beautifully displayed in oak and glass cases. Pages from some are framed and beautifully hung. The main archive, where scholars study more of the work, is in Montecito, just south of Santa Barbara, but it is only open to the public occasionally.

## Santa Barbara Museum of Natural History Library

| | |
|---|---|
| 2559 Puesta del Sol Road | T |
| (805) 682-4711 | Closed Saturdays, Sundays |

This is a triple hit: an extension of the incredible amount of information available in a good museum, an historic replica of an early 20th century Trophy Room and a splendid collection of rare and unusual books. The museum itself is only a few blocks from the Mission Santa Barbara.

In the library you'll find friendly people working in a formal, tall room. It has a timbered and carved ceiling, lots of game trophies on the walls and a stone fireplace at one end framed by a pair of 6-foot-long elephant tusks. The tusks came from an elephant shot by Major Max Fleischmann (of Fleischmann's yeast) in 1910. Fleischmann was the major benefactor of the museum as well as the library. While it seems odd to find hunting trophies in a museum now so totally dedicated to conservation, it is also illuminating to see how standards have changed.

This noncirculating research library has extensive collections on malacology, natural history and the anthropology of the Channel Islands, Santa Barbara, the Chumash Indians and the western United States. The rare book room includes many old voyage records and an extensive collection of early Western history. There is also an extensive collection of antique natural history prints.

Formal wooden bookshelves stretch 10 or 11 feet high all around the room, and above them whitewashed walls reach the dark timbered ceiling. If you want to see an old-style but beautiful and useable research library, just take a look here—and if you want to do research, you'll rarely find friendlier people.

The museum is a wonderful place for both children and adults. Well-designed and vibrant displays bring natural history and conservation alive. Children particularly like the 70-foot skeleton of a blue whale mounted in a garden outside the library.

## —— SANTA MONICA ——

### Santa Monica Public Library

| 1343 Sixth Street | A |
| (310) 458-8600 | Open every day |

This large, heavily used public library in the heart of a busy urban center was built in 1965, but it has been maintained well. It does not have the tired feeling of some other libraries in similar settings. It shows

Santa Monica, CA
Santa Monica Public Library
Photo by Cynni Murphy

that good architecture with good maintenance can successfully survive heavy urban use.

Santa Monica, on the ocean edge of Los Angeles, is an intellectually stimulating community. One look at the library's huge bulletin board shows an incredible variety of activities.

Over the two-story main reading room is a marvelous sculptured ceiling of white triangular elements, fluorescent lights and skylights. Huge colored banners fly beneath this airy structure. Light from the ceiling combines with that coming in from a striking concrete screen wall at one end of the reading room. From comfortable reading areas in second floor balconies you can look down into the main reading room below. There's also a large, well-furnished children's room on the second floor. The library has quite a foreign language collection including books in Spanish, French, German, Chinese, Korean, Vietnamese, Russian and Japanese.

# —— SANTA ROSA ——

## Sonoma County Library

| | |
|---|---|
| Third and E Streets | A, T |
| (707) 545-0831 | Open every day |

This library, in the hometown of famous botanist Luther Burbank, is like most of Santa Rosa—the more you look, the more you find. Santa Rosa is home to a restored 1920s shopping district, the Burbank Home and Memorial Gardens and the Church of One Tree, a Gothic church (now the Robert L. Ripley Museum) built entirely from the wood of one redwood tree.

Two of the library's walls use a complex redwood screen for shade. The screens also make the block-long building seem somewhat unassuming. It comes as quite a surprise to see how large it really is once you get inside. And the patterned light that filters in through the redwood screen is quite pleasant. Apparently pigeons dislike the redwood, making it a more successful material than metal.

One corner of the library is a circular meeting room. From the main reading room, windows look into an enclosed patio (next to the main entrance) where you can sit and read in fine weather. Tinted ground-level windows look out onto city streets from a large children's room.

The library maintains a thorough and up-to-date list of the clubs and community organizations in the county on its computer, and it also has a small collection on wine. This spacious two-story library was built in 1966 to a design by Francis Joseph McCarthy.

## —— SAUSALITO ——

### Sausalito Public Library

| | |
|---|---:|
| 420 Litho Street | A, T, V |
| (415) 289-4120 | Closed Sundays |

Sausalito, an ex-artists' colony, is still a charming and busy tourist attraction. From the deck outside its combined civic center and library you can see down to Bridgeway, the main tourist avenue, and you can also see the masts of boats rising from marinas. Across Richardson's Bay is a lovely view of the mansions on prestigious Tiburon and Belvedere. Just below is a well-equipped children's playground.

The library is small inside, but a series of 20-foot-high arched windows face the bay. The colors in the room are delightful umber and orange and purple, with a brown rug. An intriguing staircase goes up to stacks on a mezzanine—it's interesting because it narrows as it rises.

There's a special collection on sailing and navigation that makes sense for a library so close to a big pleasure sailing center. It's only two blocks from the big marinas and six blocks north of the Village Fair, the heart of downtown Sausalito, a two-minute drive or ten-minute walk. It's also only a half mile from the working scale model of San Francisco Bay built by the U.S. Army Corp of Engineers.

## —— SIERRA MADRE ——

### Sierra Madre Public Library

| | |
|---|---:|
| 440 West Sierra Madre Boulevard | |
| (818) 355-7186 | Closed Sundays |

Most people think of Los Angeles in terms of its beaches, glitzy downtown high rises or wealthy neighborhoods. Sierra Madre is none of the above. It is a town of 12,000 on the northeast side of Los Angeles, nestling up against the base of the San Gabriel Mountains.

The library itself sits in the midst of ivy and trees on the side of a wide street in this middle-class residential community. Things seem oddly "normal" here after visiting Glendale, Pasadena and San Marino. Part of the collection includes a small number of oral histories, and it typifies the nature of the community since many of the interviews are with people who have lived here for most of their lives. That's rare not just for Southern California, but for most of the state.

This is a pleasant, small library with an angled ceiling of patterned stucco. There's a piano for programs in the main reading room and separate California and children's rooms. The latter is solidly stocked with lots of books and a happy mural of the sun smiling over clouds. The design of this pleasant library makes it more interesting than many libraries of its size. It's somewhat worn but very warm.

## —— SIMI VALLEY ——

### Simi Valley Branch Library, Ventura County Library System

2969 Tapo Canyon Road
(805) 526-1735                                                     Open every day

Northwest of Los Angeles, Simi Valley is surrounded by the Santa Susana Mountains. A lot of Western films and television thrillers have been shot here, where the Chumash Indians used to live. The library, in the civic center of this spread-out bedroom community of over 100,000, is deceptive. From the outside it looks plain, almost drab, but inside it's high-ceilinged, modern and airy.

In the children's room and other places huge photo murals depict local sites, including Chumash Indians, mission and rancho days and mountain scenery. Some of the murals are as much as 20 feet high and 30 feet wide. The children's room also has a life-size replica of a tree house.

The main reading room is so large you can step back and get beautiful views of the clouds through its high clerestory windows. Just outside the periodical section is an enclosed patio for lounging and reading. There's a comfortably furnished business reference section, again with some lounging chairs as well as study chairs and tables. There are quite a few upholstered couches—you can really sit back and relax in this library. There's even a rose garden in the public patio.

## *Also of Note:*

## Ronald Reagan Presidential Library

| | |
|---|---:|
| 40 Presidential Drive | T, V |
| (805) 522-8444 | Museum open every day |
| | Library closed Saturdays, Sundays |

It seems somewhat symbolic that the first street you cross when you get off Highway 118 at Madera Street and turn toward the Reagan Library is Easy Street (honestly!). The library's magnificent location looks out over the mountains, and on a clear day you can see across the ocean to Santa Cruz Island 50 miles away. Housing developments are beginning to encroach on the open space, but for now there still is a lot of wild country around here.

A large courtyard and fountain grace the center of these contemporary Spanish Colonial buildings. The complex is light orange stucco with huge expanses of red tile roof. A huge red-tiled peaked canopy looms over the entrance to the library in the main courtyard.

This is really an archive rather than a browsing library. Appointments are recommended. One of the 15 archivists will assist patrons by bringing requested materials from storage. This is the home of what ultimately will be a collection of over 50 million source documents. The staff is very service-oriented, so if you would like to hunt up some information about something you see in the museum, try the library.

The walls of the formal beige-walled reading room are lined with shelves of general reference materials, and on the back wall is the large presidential seal. There's a lovely view out the windows that helps with the good overall lighting of the room. A very comfortable lounge/conference room is located in this part of the complex.

Then there's the museum, a nicely exhibited, comprehensive history of Ronald Reagan's public life that includes narrative text, display cabinets of memorabilia, videos and interactive exhibits. There's a full-size replica of the Oval Office as it was when Reagan was president. It's interesting to see the seat of real power in human size—

the desk, the chairs, the fireplace, the items that the president uses on a day-to-day basis.

You might even meet Nancy Reagan here signing copies of her biography or other books in the gift shop—there are many books by and about her and the former President and all sorts of videotapes and other gifts (ranging from date books to jelly beans).

## —— SUNNYVALE ——

### Sunnyvale Public Library

665 West Olive Avenue
(408) 730-7315                                          Open every day

Much bigger than it looks from the outside, the Sunnyvale Public Library is a one-story brick building with an attractively gardened entrance. It's almost always busy. The city's Public Art Program has provided a number of outstanding creations, the sculpture *Out to Lunch* at the entrance, a large abstract tapestry over the information desk and a major stained glass window for the library's east wing.

In a typical example of how libraries follow the needs of their community, Sunnyvale has a microfilm copy of the General Military Specification, of great use to people who manufacture for the government, but far too costly for many small businesses to buy. This is in Silicon Valley, so there is (or was) a lot of defense department work around here.

This is a very open building with a large and comfortable children's room off to one side, separated from the rest of the library.

## —— UKIAH ——

### Mendocino County Library

105 North Main Street
(707) 463-4491                     Closed Sundays, Mondays, Tuesdays

Ukiah was recently rated as the sixth best small town in the country. It has a pleasant older library, a one-story building with some exterior walls of random sized stone. Other walls are light beige with redwood trim.

This library and others in Mendocino County are a tribute to the staying power of people who like libraries. Most of the staff here are volunteers. Although severe budget cutbacks once forced the library down to two days a week of operation, it's now back up to four, and they're even talking about five days a week. This library has only one professional librarian even though it is the headquarters of the County Library System.

Children's art from school and library projects is on display in the children's room. It changes every month. Soft sculptures hang there permanently. The room is nicely carpeted and has lots of stuffed toys for kids to play with as well as a small tropical fish aquarium.

## —— VALLEJO ——

### Vallejo Naval and Historical Museum Library

734 Marin Street  
(707) 643-0067                             Closed Sundays, Mondays

This is really an off-beat place. The building that houses both the museum and the library is a rather unattractive Spanish Renaissance Revival structure that was built in 1927 as the city hall. Since 1979 it has been a museum. Inside it still looks much like an old city hall, but it is surprisingly elegant. The prow of a sailing ship, bowsprit and all, looms up out of the wall and hovers over the stairs. On the second floor there's a periscope from a submarine that actually fought in World War II. It's mounted through the ceiling. You can look through it at the city and Mare Island Naval Shipyard outside. There are rotating historical exhibits as well as maritime shows.

The small library specializes in naval history, which comprises about 60 percent of the collection. Much of it is local history, but the unique part of the collection deals with naval history of the Pacific Northwest. They have a photo collection of about 7,000 images dealing with the nearby shipyard and Vallejo. General maritime history is covered more thoroughly at the J. Porter Shaw Maritime Library in nearby San Francisco, but for navy buffs, this is the place to come. The library is always open on Tuesdays and Wednesdays, or by appointment, or if some of the staff happens to be around and has the time to help you.

## —— WEAVERVILLE ——

### Trinity County Free Library

| 229 Main Street | A |
| --- | --- |
| (916) 623-1373 | Closed Saturdays, Sundays |

If you're driving east from the Pacific coast on Highway 299 or south from Yreka on Highway 3, you're liable to need a good rest stop, and the library in Weaverville is a nice one. Weaverville itself, at the foot of the Trinity Alps, is a surprise and worth a look. While the city has a population of only 3,000 it has California's oldest drugstore, a Chinese temple that has been functioning since the 1850s, a good museum and a fine new library.

The building has a gently angling roof and is built of bricks of different shades of orange, which give it an interesting texture. There are no street-level windows, so the height and lightness of the interior comes as quite a surprise. A peaked, white, corrugated metal ceiling, supported by white painted steel beams, reflects bright light all around. Clerestory windows at the sides and at the back of the room look out at the surrounding trees. This is an example of good design making up for the lack of windows. The architect was Bill Peckham of Redding.

## —— WILLITS ——

### Willits Branch Library, Mendocino County Library

| 390 Commercial Street | |
| --- | --- |
| (707) 459-5908 | Closed Fridays, Sundays, Mondays |

This attractive brick library opened in 1989. You can see into a park across the street from its generous front windows. It's located near the rodeo grounds and the County Museum and just a few blocks from the active and attractive railroad station. Upholstered oak chairs and warm carpets add to the comfort of this pleasant one-room library.

Even the children's section has upholstered furniture. (It also has a small aquarium.)

Willits is the terminus for the Skunk Trains to Fort Bragg (run by the California Western Railroad) and the Northcoast Daylight trains to Eureka (run by the Redwood Coast Railroad Company), and the library is a convenient and attractive place to wait for trains or passengers. If someone doesn't like railroad travel through pristine forests (hard to imagine, but there are people like that), he or she could wait in the library while traveling companions take the three-hour, half-day roundtrip to Northspur. Other railroad excursions are all-day or overnight.

## —— YORBA LINDA ——

### Yorba Linda Public Library

18181 Imperial Highway
(714) 777-2873                                              Closed Sundays

Just a few blocks from the Nixon Birthplace and Library, this major remodel shows a very interesting treatment of limited space. In front, a striking concrete frame sets off the face of the building. It encloses a staircase of pink tile with turquoise trim.

The library is well lit and nicely carpeted. Art Deco light fixtures add to fluorescent lights to set off peach and pastel walls. There's a very private feeling in the various sections of the library. Near the front there are small reading rooms or alcoves that make you feel you're in a train compartment. They're windowed on three sides with comfortably upholstered window seats and individual reading lights so even at night you can sit within the library and be in a very private space. There's a very good children's library on the second floor with computers at low desks, circular tables with padded seats and some upholstered furniture for adults. The library was designed by Architectural Alliance, Inc.

A large (1,100 square feet) Friends of the Library bookstore in the basement sells used books—a good alternative to the Nixon Center for those not interested in political life (or for Democrats).

*Also of Note:*

## Richard Nixon Library and Birthplace

| | |
|---|---|
| 18001 Yorba Linda Boulevard | T |
| (714) 993-5075 | Open every day |

The Nixon Library and Birthplace is more of a museum than a library. A concrete building with a red tile roof, the museum is set across a reflecting pool from the small wooden house in which Richard Nixon was born. At the other end of the historic and technical spectrum, the museum even has an interactive theater in which visitors can select any of 400 questions to ask the president and have prerecorded answers played back on a video screen.

The modern and comfortably furnished John M. Olin Reading Room in this center will concentrate on Nixon's pre- and post-presidential papers. It will be strictly a research, non-browsing library, with a tremendous amount of material about the politics of Nixon's time. There will be a major emphasis on political campaigns. This will not be the archive of the Nixon presidential papers. If you want to do research here, call for an appointment.

The museum covers a long period of time—not only Nixon's activities while he was working his way through the political landscape to the presidency, but also his considerable elder statesman achievements since then. Exhibits on The Road to the Presidency, The House, The Senate and more present an incredible array of displays. Countless gifts and honors received by the former president are also exhibited. You can see and hear the debates with Kennedy, listen to the critical Watergate Tapes and in general, get a full picture of Nixon's political history.

A gift shop sells all sorts of Nixon memorabilia.

# ·COLORADO·

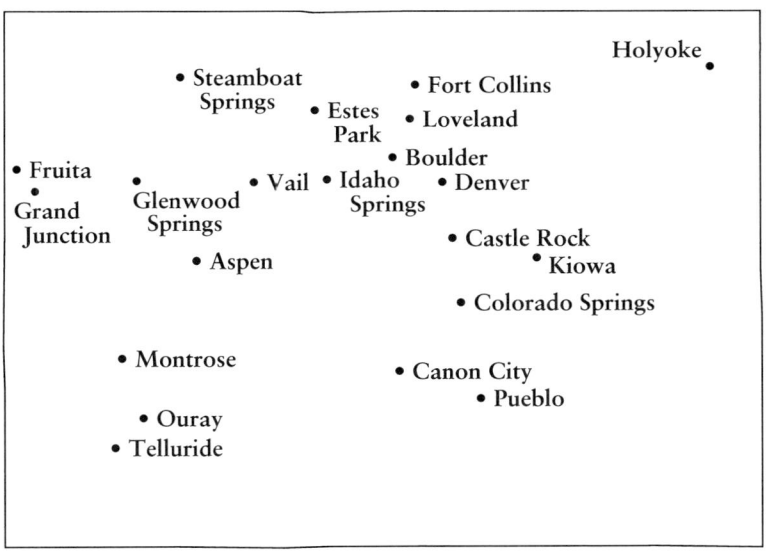

# —— ASPEN ——

## Pitkin County Library

| | |
|---|---|
| 120 North Mill Street | A, T, E |
| (303) 925-7124 | Open every day |

This beautiful library opened in the fall of 1991. It's a brick building with a large clock tower, loads of gables and wood-trimmed windows finished in dusty green. It was designed by John Wheeler.

Large white columns in the main reading room rise to lofty skylights whose rectangular panes allow a lovely, soft light to filter in. High sconce lights on the columns below the skylights reflect more light off the white ceiling. The open space is punctuated by lights hanging down from the ceiling over the reference and checkout desks. The result is a truly elegant space.

Built with later expansion in mind, it is sparsely furnished. This is a building with room for the future.

The downstairs music room holds the archives of the Aspen Music Festival (over 5,000 tapes), a huge record collection and lots of equipment for listening. The music collection is not always open so you need to check if you want to use it. There is also a large skiing collection in this winter sports oriented town.

Aspen is much more human in scale than some of the other Colorado ski resorts. Buildings over three stories are pretty well hidden. Many streets are reserved for walkers only. For drivers with good nerves who like mountain driving, Highway 82 South (which is closed in the winter) is one of the most beautiful drives around. It's a slow drive and vehicles over 35 feet are not permitted, but this mountain road goes over Independence Pass at 12,000 feet, and after you get off the road you can relax at the library.

Colorado

# —— AURORA ——

## Aurora Public Library

| | |
|---|---|
| 14949 East Alameda Drive | A |
| (303) 340-2290 | Open every day |

    This impressive building is the closest major library to Denver's new airport. It's next to Aurora's History Museum and Municipal Justice Center. The 12-year-old design, by Warner/Burns/Toan/Lunde of New York with Denver architect Brooks Waldman, is testimony to the staying power of good architecture. The beige brick structure has a striking angled glass and metal entrance set off by an abstract metal sculpture.
    The library is built into a hill and the entrance is on a mezzanine floor. Through the bright entryway, you see an art gallery, a courtesy desk, comfortable purple couches and an expanse of tall windows reaching down to the lower level of the building.
    Downstairs, one end of the library is a 30-foot-high glass wall, with a reading area just inside. The glass roof overhead makes it a huge sunroom. Although bookshelves are almost 8 feet high, the space isn't oppressive due to the room's height. Reading tables and plants line the glass walls.
    The library has easily accessible microfilms of magazines, lots of newspapers and a well organized selection of compact discs and videotapes. There are video cassette players in the adult and children's sections and a paperback exchange program. The library even has a public lunchroom, complete with vending machines.

# —— BASALT ——

## Basalt Regional Library

| | |
|---|---|
| 99 Midland Avenue | |
| (303) 927-4311 | Closed Sundays |

    Basalt is about halfway between Aspen's high peaks and Glenwood's hot springs. You can't miss the small Basalt Public Library—as you come into town it's the building with a bright red roof; just in front of it is a caboose used as a tourist information center. The library was recently enlarged, not so much to enlarge the collection but to increase energy efficiency and to allow more sitting and reading space.

The population of Basalt has doubled since 1985, as workers and their families at Aspen and other expensive resort areas have moved in this direction. Visitors to the hot springs at Glenwood Springs come for the hunting and fishing. There's a lot of sailing and other water activity at Ruedi Reservoir 11 miles east of here. Railroad buffs come here to visit Hagerman Pass and view remains of old trestle tracks and train wrecks. The library has a good collection of railroad history.

# —— BOULDER ——

## Boulder Public Library

| | |
|---|---:|
| 1000 Canyon Boulevard | E, A, T |
| (303) 441-3100 | Open every day |

Boulder is home to the University of Colorado, the National Center for Atmospheric Research, The National Oceanic and Atmospheric Administration, more good restaurants than one should reasonably find in a town of 100,000 and an exciting new addition to a large, busy library.

Geometrically, the entrance to the Boulder Public Library is a "truncated, skewed, coneoid." Less technically, it's a unique structure of flat rock, aluminum and glass. The newest in a series of three connected library buildings, this is the pinnacle of a quarter-mile-long complex. A passageway from this building to its predecessor goes over Boulder Creek and serves as a cafe, complete with a cappuccino vendor.

The entrance and design of this library reflect architect Vern Seieroe's philosophy that government buildings should be open and inviting. The openness of the building serves two purposes: (1) most of the lighting is from daylight, even on an overcast day, and (2) as you pass by you can see activity inside.

In the striking rotunda of the new addition there are very few columns, but radial trusses hold up concentric circles of ceilings, with clerestory windows allowing a remarkable amount of light into the library.

## Colorado

Boulder, CO
Boulder Public Library

This library is a model of energy conservation. The overall design saves a lot of energy by using natural light—55 to 60 percent of the energy used in most libraries goes to lighting, and more to removing the heat generated by the lighting. Much of the cooling in this building is done using fresh air, with automatically opening and closing windows and shades. There are even light switches on individual bookshelves with timers that turn the lights off after you leave. The heating system is a large swamp cooler that uses no chlorofluorocarbons.

Reading areas line the balconies of this user-friendly library. From above you see down into both inside and outside children's areas (the fenced-in outside area has its own pond). While some noise rises from the children's area, one of the major criteria in the building's design was an emphasis on children.

Rather than a check-out desk at the front of the library here you find a computerized information service (The Answer Place) with paraprofessionals who can help patrons with the equipment.

A lot of thought went into the design of this library, from the dusty pink bookshelves to carpet patterns that show where staff is located.

## ——  CANON CITY ——

### Canon City Public Library

516 Macon Street
(719) 269-9020                                                              Closed Sundays

    One of the advantages of looking for libraries is that it often gets you off commercial streets. Highway 50 through Canon City is pretty commercial and dull, but once you get off the main street (Royal Gorge Boulevard) and go back two blocks to the library, you find a pleasant old Western town.

    The small, plain Carnegie library was built in 1902 of big, solid granite blocks and was cleverly expanded in 1983. From the outside it's not immediately obvious that a large expansion took place. Inside, where the expansion enlarged the library, the old granite walls were left exposed as inner walls. In the older section the chairs, tables and bookshelves installed in 1902 are still in use. The bookcases have steel rods going from one case to the next, wooden shelving and cast-iron end pieces locking in heavy bronze supports. Fascinating stuff that still works quite well 90 years later.

    Tourists come to Canon City to visit the Royal Gorge 8 miles from here, where the world's highest (1,053 feet) suspension bridge crosses the Arkansas River. There's an incline railway to the bottom, a tramway across and a miniature railroad on the rim. The other main industry here is a number of regional and state prisons hosted by Canon City and nearby Florence. A history section is located in the basement. Children can check out toys in the very active children's section on the second floor.

## —— CASTLE ROCK ——

### Philip S. Miller Library

961 South Plum Creek Boulevard
(303) 688-5157                                                          Open every day

    The library search can always surprise you. Castle Rock is a town of about 5,000 just off the interstate south of Denver. Plum Creek

Boulevard leads to a striking library below a fountain and waterfall in the center of a divided road.

The library has a colonnaded walkway and the striking peaked roof is supported by white "I" beams. Inside, the high wooden ceiling is supported by laminated wood trusses.

The windows in the children's room are low, so a small child can see the library's parklike setting. The back end of this surprising library has large windows with a good view of the mountains to the south.

## —— COLORADO SPRINGS ——

### East Library and Information Center, Pikes Peak Library District

| | |
|---|---:|
| 5550 North Union Avenue | A, V, E |
| (719) 531-6333 | Open every day |

An entry hall with a ceiling of arched windows leads to the main reading room of this great contemporary library. Pots of ivy flourish on the entryway's walls under floods of natural light. The reading room has a 150-foot-long semicircular stretch of windows that look out at Pikes Peak and surrounding mountains. There is a marvelous seating area inside the windows, and outside, behind a glass screen, is another area available during fine weather.

The library is modern, white and bright throughout. Although bookshelves in the stacks are high, your ability to see through the picture windows at the end reduces the crowded feeling. Prominent signage helps you find the section you want; you are rarely out of sight of large directional signs for Reference, Periodicals, Children, etc.

This bustling place has a gift shop, a used bookstore and a whole raft of meeting rooms—it's almost a small convention complex. Walls in this area are moveable to open small rooms into bigger ones. This is truly an information center, with a major emphasis on electronic information, not just a library with a computerized catalog. The computerized Maggie's Place system accesses the library's catalog, and also gives you information ranging from child care providers to the city council agendas. You can access it from your home computer (with a modem)—call the main library number for information.

## Old Colorado City Branch Library

| | |
|---|---|
| 2418 West Pikes Peak Boulevard | H |
| (719) 634-1698 | Closed Sundays |

This classic yellow brick library with Ionic columns framing its door is behind Bancroft Park, only a few blocks from the center of the Old Colorado Historical District. Driving here from downtown on the tree-lined blocks of West Pikes Peak Boulevard, you'll pass a number of attractive older homes.

While the library is not very exciting, it is a good place for people to relax and browse after exploring either the Historic District or the red sandstone formations in the nearby Garden of the Gods park.

## Rockrimmon Branch Library

| | |
|---|---|
| 832 Village Center Drive | |
| (719) 593-8000 | Closed Sundays, Mondays |

This convenient library on the north side of Colorado Springs is only a short drive from the Pro Rodeo Hall of Fame and American Cowboy Museum. Located in the small Village Shopping Center, the library has a large enough parking lot for easy maneuvering of an RV. Take either exit 147 or 149 off Interstate 25. Decorated in bright colors, the library is surprisingly large, taking up two store spaces. Almost 40 percent of the space is devoted to the children's and young adult collections.

If you are leaving Colorado Springs and would like to stock up before you go, this is a useful stop. You could let younger passengers use the library while you shop in the small shopping center—it has a grocery store, liquor store, travel agency, Chinese restaurant, etc.

### *Also of Note:*

## Air Force Academy Library, U.S.A.F. Academy

| | |
|---|---|
| Exit 156B, Interstate 25 | A, T |
| (719) 472-2590 | Closed Saturdays, Sundays when classes are not in session |

When visiting the Air Force Academy, this showplace designed by Skidmore, Owings and Merill in 1958 and enlarged in 1982 should be part of your itinerary. An open design and spiral staircase add to its interest.

The library has an internationally known collection of Aeronautical History that covers the period before powered flight, and hundreds of personal papers dealing with the growth and development of military aeronautics and air power.

## American Numismatic Association Library

818 North Cascade Avenue
(719) 632-2646     Closed Sundays

This is the headquarters, museum and library of the American Numismatic Association. It's also mecca for those interested in the physical manifestation of money. The exhibits of all sorts of coins and bills are well lit, well displayed and well designed.

The basement library has almost 50,000 specialized items. Nonmembers can use the library, but only members can take out books. For members of the ANA admission to the museum is free; for nonmembers admission is $1.

## Fine Arts Center Library

30 West Dale Street
(719) 634-5581     Closed Mondays

Next to Colorado College and just a few blocks from the American Numismatic Association library, the Fine Arts Center Library has an extensive general collection on art history. The Art Deco building is in the National Register of Historic Buildings. While the library specializes, as does the museum, in the art, ethnology and anthropology of the American Southwest, there are books in the 25,000 volume collection on the art of Japanese, Jewish, Pacific Island and other cultures.

Entrance to the museum and library is $2.50 for nonmembers, but all visitors can use the library. This is one of the few museum libraries that actually circulates books to members. The three-room library is partly housed in the paneled space that was the office of Alice Taylor, the center's founder.

## —— DENVER ——

### Denver Public Library

| | |
|---|---:|
| 1357 Broadway | A |
| (303) 640-8800 | Open every day |

Denver is in the midst of a marvelous and thorough remodeling and expansion program for all of its public libraries. Construction of branches and the huge addition to the Central library will be completed in 1994. The renovation of the existing Burnham Hoyt wing of the new building will be completed in 1995.

The seven-story addition was designed by Michael Graves and Klipp Colussy Jenks DuBois Architects, P.C. The design bursts with an exciting variety of shapes and textures—a tower with a pyramid-shaped cap, another with an overhanging flat roof, a corniced drum and a huge number of windows. Special attention has been paid to the Children's Room on the first floor.

Combined with the existing central library, which will become a wing of the new structure, the building will have over 500,000 square feet of space. It is scheduled to open in mid–1995.

Denver, CO
Denver Public Library
Model of new Denver Public Library

# Ross–Cherry Creek Branch Library

305 Milwaukee Street
(303) 331-4016                                                    Closed Sundays

Not all of Denver's prodigious spending on library construction is going into the new central library—nearly $20 million in bond funds has been earmarked for improvements to 21 branch libraries. Denver's largest branch library, the 1962 Ross-Cherry Creek Branch had gotten a little old and small, so a major expansion and renovation was done in 1993.

An addition on the east side was specifically designed to connect visually with the vibrant and upscale Cherry Creek North shopping and business district. The new entryway is highlighted by large, colorful geometric forms in concrete and steel. Michael Brendle Architects' bright redesign includes a new children's area just inside the main entrance.

Technology for the twenty-first century combines well with the exciting and whimsical architectural touches. The electronic Kid's Catalog is a multi-media computer system that helps children find what they are looking for. Children with limited computer skills can avoid typing altogether by using a computer mouse to click through a verbal/visual wonderland of topics. More sophisticated children are guided along with text as they type their entries.

## *Also of Note:*

# Helen Fowler Library at the Denver Botanic Garden

909 York Street                                                              T
(303) 370-8014                                                    Open every day

While this library has only 2,000 square feet, it's packed with over 20,000 volumes and 500 periodical titles on botany, horticulture, xeriscapes, children's gardening books and anything else the avid gardener or landscape enthusiast might want to see.

It's on the ground floor of the education building at this beautiful eighteen acre expanse of gardens. Exhibits in the Gardens range from the award-winning Boettcher Conservatory structure to the Xeriscape Demonstration Garden which concentrates on plants that will survive arid climates.

## ——— ESTES PARK ———

### Estes Park Public Library

| | |
|---|---|
| 335 East Elkhorn Drive | A, T |
| (303) 586-8116 | Open every day |

Estes Park is the entrance to Rocky Mountain National Park, and the architecture of its library, which is located on the main street, reflects its mountainous setting. Roger Thorp, the architect, used brown rock with redwood paneling on the exterior. The roof is green shingles, and the entrance is solid rock and wood.

Lots of comfortable reading areas are scattered within its 13,000 square feet. Seating is mostly near the windows with a particularly attractive seating area near the front, where you can sit next to a fireplace and look out at the main street and rocky peaks.

Children can check out toys from a "toy-brary" for three weeks (and tourists can get a temporary card). This is a fine place to recover from mountain driving, shopping or rough weather.

## ——— FORT COLLINS ———

### Fort Collins Public Library

| | |
|---|---|
| 201 Peterson Street | |
| (303) 221-6740 | Open every day |

Fort Collins, one of the larger cities in Colorado (population 88,000), is home to Colorado State University and the Anheuser-Busch Brewery. The library shares Lincoln Park with the interesting Fort Collins Museum. Tall trees dot the rolling lawns of the park. The corners of the upper level of the library stretch out over the grass and provide shady sitting areas.

The children's area and media collection take up the first floor; the balance of the library is upstairs. History buffs will be interested in the library's local photography collection.

Bright, bright colors are everywhere: red, blue, yellow and green. The colors have even been used on exposed air conditioning and heating ducts.

Entire sections have their own color, such as yellow for children, green for adult fiction, etc. Bright banners are used for direction and information signs throughout. Even the banisters of the stairways are painted in bright colors. A cheerful space on even the dullest day.

## ——  FRISCO ——

### Summit County Library

43 Mount Royal Drive
(303) 668-5555                                                                Open every day

Since Frisco is at an altitude of 9,100 feet, Mount Royal, which is right above it, doesn't look so high, even at 10,300 feet. The library is only a block from one of Summit County's 47 miles of paved bike trails, and both half- and full-day raft trips on the Colorado River start here.

Although small, this is a warm wood and stone building. Large wood laminated beams support the ceiling. A stone-faced fireplace, skylights and upholstered chairs invite you to come in and relax either after strenuous vacationing, or while someone else is being adventurous.

This is one of the libraries that proves that you should always look for the library, even in a town of 1,600. You might be pleasantly surprised.

## —— FRUITA ——

### Fruita Branch Library, Mesa County Public Library

432 East Aspen
(303) 858-7703                                                      Closed Saturdays, Sundays

The Fruita Public Library is cute as a bug. Originally built as a WPA museum, this stone building with a red roof looks just like a witch's cottage. You almost expect to see Hansel and Gretel coming out the front door.

Built in 1938, the library stands on a lawn under a huge spreading tree, across the street from three churches. This is one corner of the Dinosaur Triangle, and there are fossil dinosaur tracks and bones in the stones of the two fireplaces in the library. There are also pieces of petrified wood, shells and semiprecious stones in the rocks making up one of the walls. This place is almost totally rock—even the floor is made of slate.

## —— GLENWOOD SPRINGS ——

### Glenwood Springs Branch Library, Garfield County Public Library

| | |
|---|---:|
| 413 Ninth Street | T |
| (303) 945-5958 | Closed Sundays |

A recent expansion of the library gave it a mildly Art Deco entrance, but what's most notable about this fairly plain library is its location. It's only two blocks from a bridge (both foot and car) over the river to one of the world's largest hot-spring pools.

The footbridge across the river is fun. The library is on Ninth Street, the Amtrak station is on Seventh Street, and next is the bridge. If your train is a few hours late and your skin is too wrinkled from the pool, wait at the library (or go off and visit Doc Holliday's grave).

## —— GRAND JUNCTION ——

### Mesa County Public Library

| | |
|---|---:|
| 530 Grand Avenue | A, T |
| (303) 243-4442 | Open every day |

As you walk around this library you might wonder why it looks the way it does, but the odds are you'd never guess it started off as a supermarket. Two stairways lead to a lower level, with large boxed desert garden areas below skylights.

This is a library that really cares about young people. The children's section is 12,000 square feet, and there's also a lot of young adult space in the main section of the library. It's fun to see bookshelves graded by height for different age children. Shag carpets, lots of loose pillows and carpet end pieces for kids to sit on fill the space. There's even a rocking chair for storytellers.

Signs in this section as well as in the rest of the building are large and obvious, which is a help to adults herding children as well as to the children.

Grand Junction is only a few miles from the awe-inspiring rock formations of the Colorado National Monument, and the area is replete with dinosaur remains and museums. It's also the first big town east of US 50 (which appropriately has lots of signs calling it "The Loneliest Highway in America").

The library is a good place for both adults and children to unwind and find out about this great vacation area.

## —— HOLYOKE ——

### Heginbotham Library

539 South Baxter  
(303) 854-2597

H  
Closed Sundays

There's not much exciting around rural Holyoke, especially to the east in the plains of Nebraska, but its library is a near-perfect example of Craftsman Style Bungalow architecture. This jewel-like building with English half timbering and its surrounding gardens is on the National Register of Historic Buildings.

The library was built in 1917 as the home of W. E. Heginbotham, a reclusive, tight-fisted banker who surprised the entire community on his death in 1968 by leaving a huge trust fund (as well as his house) for the benefit of the community. Thirty miles south of Interstate 80, Holyoke is a good rest stop.

## —— IDAHO SPRINGS ——

### Idaho Springs Public Library

219 14th Avenue
(303) 567-2020                                                    Closed Sundays

The Idaho Springs Public Library is a solid brick edifice. It's old-fashioned, inside and out, but conveniently located near the center of town. Idaho Springs is a good place to stop either before starting up over the highway westward, or before making the last push into Denver. You can either explore a gold mill or relax in a local hot spring or have a brew in the Buffalo Bar.

Just off Highway 70, Idaho Springs, an old mining town, isn't newly built up like the big ski resorts. There are enough of the old buildings left so that they are the fabric of the town and there is a large number of inviting saloons and restaurants. Many of the residences have also been treated with loving care.

## —— KIOWA ——

### Elbert County Library

331 Comanche Street
(303) 621-2041                                    Closed Sundays, Mondays, Wednesdays

Kiowa, CO
Elbert County Library

When you see the Catholic Church on the north side of Kiowa's main street, you'll really be looking at the local library. Built in 1903 as St. Ann's Catholic Church, it became the Elbert County Library in 1970. It still has the granite cross and rose window of a classic church (and, of course, once inside you'll find a cathedral ceiling). The librarians here are some of the most friendly around.

Kiowa, with a population of 206, is on the edge of the rolling high plain. Interstate 70 to Denver through Kansas can get pretty dull. You can turn west on State Highway 86 just above Limon toward Kiowa. There is a good chance you'll see commercial buffalo herds along this route.

## —— LITTLETON ——

### Koelbel Public Library, Arapahoe Library District

| | |
|---|---|
| 5955 South Holly | T |
| (303) 220-7704 | Closed Sundays in summer |

Suburban Littleton runs along the south side of Denver. Its Koelbel Library is a monumental new red brick building which fits the imposing residences in The Preserve at Greenwood Village across the street. The library is only about five minutes from the Denver Tech Center, a major business and technical center, so it's a good place for research by visiting business people.

The library occupies a corner lot, with its parking and main entrance on the inside of the corner. A huge two-story bay window structure on the north side of the building dominates the view from the street. On the entry side a copper-topped cupola highlights a broad set of entrance steps. The building was designed by Barker/Rinky/Seacat of Denver.

The great size of the library disappears when you enter. The rotunda over the entrance lobby is brightly painted with falcons, the library's emblem, and there are art galleries both to the left and right. The imaginative Wizard's Entrance to the large children's room is decorated with fairy tale paintings. An elegant curving stairway leads to the lower level. It's lined with narrow, ceiling-high clerestory windows separated by painted panels repeating the falcon logo.

124  *Public Libraries: Travel Treasures of the West*

The best place for relaxing is the upstairs reading area in the bay window section, which looks out over the new housing development. It's like sitting in the bow of a cruise ship. Comfortable upholstered chairs in an area screened from library activities by bookshelves and magazine racks make this a secluded area.

## Columbine Branch Library, Jefferson County Public Library

| 7706 West Bowles Avenue | V, A |
|---|---|
| (303) 932-2690 | Open every day |

The Columbine Library, a branch of the Jefferson County Public Library designed by Anderson, Mason, Dale of Denver, has a striking series of vaulted roof sections and a curved picture window wall. It's situated in Robert F. Clement Park, a vast park with picnic areas, soccer and football fields and tennis courts.

As you enter you face a curving wall of floor-to-ceiling windows. Shades and screens lower automatically when the sun gets too bright. The panoramic view stretches across a field of flowers and the park to the Front Range mountains. Southern Jefferson County is growing, but the library will never be totally surrounded by buildings because of its park location.

The library has an interesting combination of good reference books for the young professionals who live in the area and a large children's section for their offspring.

Littleton, CO
Columbine Library
Janet Stevens Mural,
Children's Area

## —— LOVELAND ——

### Loveland Public Library

| | |
|---|---|
| 300 North Adams Avenue | A |
| (303) 962-2665 | Closed Sundays in summer; open daily in winter |

It's hard to believe that the same architects, Barker/Rinker/Seacat of Denver designed this unassuming, low-lying building and the monumental Koelbel Library in Littleton. When you drive up to the civic center at the corner of Adams and East 4th Street in Loveland, you first see windows sticking up out of a grassy knoll. Then you realize you are looking at a delightful public library.

The red brick library seems to grow out of the ground. The green bordered windows all around the building make you want to go inside this lovely space. Bushes and plants go right up to the walls of the building, carrying out the lush feeling of its surrounding lawns. From inside, you see bushes, trees and grass wherever you look out.

The interior is dusty pink and light green. This is one of the few libraries we've seen with wicker furniture in reading areas. The children's and young adults' section takes up almost half the library, and the children's program room is particularly well designed for small people.

In the park there's a well-equipped playground with slides, mock railroads and lots of play equipment. You can sit in the library and see kids at play outside. The park also has a public pool, lots of tall trees, a lagoon and a number of amusing library-related bronze sculptures.

## —— MONTROSE ——

### Montrose Public Library

| | |
|---|---|
| South First Street and Uncompahgre Street | |
| (303) 249-9656 | Closed Sundays |

If someone you're with has had enough of exploring Colorado's great outdoors, you might leave them here while you drive 14 miles to the Black Canyon of the Gunnison, one of Colorado's more famous sights.

The brightly painted murals near the ceiling are the most interesting part of the library. At first they seem abstract, but if you look a little closer, you see that they are actual representations of the numbers and subject matter of the Dewey Decimal System. There was a recent controversy about the murals. When the library was repainted there was a move to paint over them because they had been done in 1972 and were considered "old." A user vote was taken, and the preservationists won.

# —— OURAY ——

## Ouray Public Library

| | |
|---|---|
| City Hall, 320 6th Avenue | T |
| (303) 325-4616 | Closed Sundays, Thursdays |
| | Open Tuesday evenings |

Ouray is a delight of meticulously restored, tastefully painted Queen Anne, Victorian, Romanesque and Greek Revival buildings. It's about as close to a Swiss mountain village as you can get in America. The winter population is 600, but during the summer it reaches 4,500.

The library isn't large, but you can't miss it. The ground floor of the city hall/library building is Romanesque, the second floor Greek Revival and it's all topped by a clock tower with a gilded dome. The library is in the back of the city hall, and the lower floor used to be the holding cell for the jail. The library has lots of historical information, a children's section and a comfortable reading room downstairs. From every window you see rocky cliffs and snow-covered mountains. Not big, but comfortable.

Ouray's odorless public hot spring pool is 250 feet long and open year round. If you've gotten a little ragged from a four-wheel drive trip, or a bit uptight from a drive down the spectacular Million Dollar Drive toward Silverton, this is a great place for resting up.

## —— PUEBLO ——

### McClelland Public Library

| | |
|---|---|
| 100 East Abriendo Avenue<br>(719) 543-9604 | Closed Sundays |

    Pueblo, Colorado's third largest city outside the Denver area, is a major industrial center. The main public library, built in 1965, is plain and serviceable.
    This is not a library with fancy upholstered furniture; it's all solid wood. And with the heavy use it gets, it has to be.
    The main section of the library is on a plain rectangular plan. A wall of windows lets in a lot of light along one side and lets you see outdoor reading areas around the library as well as the center of the city.
    There are three working floors, with western research and genealogy upstairs, youth services downstairs. The library reflects the town: sturdy, and a little careworn, but serviceable and full of enthusiastic people.

## —— STEAMBOAT SPRINGS ——

### Bud Werner Memorial Library

| | |
|---|---|
| 1289 Lincoln Avenue<br>(303) 879-0240 | A, T<br>Open every day |

    Whether you're here to ski, relax in one of more than 150 local hot springs or visit the Strings in the Mountain music festival, this library on the banks of the Yampa River is well worth a visit. The library was built as a memorial to Bud Werner, a local skier of Olympic fame who died in an avalanche at the age of 29.
    The low-slung A-frame building is set off by stone columns at its entrance. The ceiling is arched, almost in chapel form, with curving dark laminated beams reaching from the floor to the peak of the arched ceiling. Clerestory windows add to the chapel-like feel of the building.
    This building is a tribute to what can be done with wood. Sections of ceiling are made of different types of wood, some light and knotty,

Steamboat Springs, CO
Bud Werner Memorial Library

others stained or varnished more darkly in differing patterns. Red oak used in some of the interior cabinet work contrasts nicely with the ivy growing in the library. The children's room looks out at a park and closes off completely from the main room with glass doors.

A mezzanine reading room, like a large pulpit, hangs in the middle of the library, but the space under the mezzanine is totally clear and useable. Climb up the flight of stairs and you're in a great secluded place to hide with a good book.

## —— TELLURIDE ——

### Wilkinson Public Library

| 134 South Spruce | A,T,H,V |
|---|---|
| (303) 728-4519 | Open every day |

The road into Telluride is heavenly. In summer you pass fields of wildflowers and see dark pines interspersed with deciduous trees with their lacy branches of light green leaves, in winter the glory of snow-covered mountains. Telluride itself, at an altitude of 8,774 feet, is nestled at the foot of mountains at the end of the street.

In 1976 a library was opened in a tiny building that used to be Telluride's jail. In 1986, Aspen architects Gibson and Reno created a jewel of an addition which more than tripled its size. The old jail was built out of rough-hewn sandstone. The entrance to the new library is built out of that same rock, while the extension is built of brick, carrying on the solid masonry feeling of the jail.

This small building has 148 windows, trimmed in white on the outside, in dark green inside (see cover photo). Every window seems to have a different view of the marvelous surroundings. It's not just one magnificent view—it's a series of different views. Light-colored wood trusses and angled bookshelves make this small library seem much bigger than it actually is. And children enjoy a children's section in what was the old city jail.

Telluride, a National Historic District with design and height restrictions, is well preserved and low key. The ski lifts come right down into the town and rise over 3,100 feet to the top of the mountain. You can take the lifts up the mountain and come down to the more resort-oriented Telluride Mountain Village.

# —— VAIL ——

## Vail Public Library

| | |
|---|---|
| 292 West Meadow Drive | A, T |
| (303) 479-2183 | Open every day |

As one might expect in this perfectly tailored and ideally located ski area, the library is perfectly tailored and well located. Surrounded by firs and aspens, it's opposite the Dobson Ice Arena, but so discreetly located next to Gore Creek that it's easy to miss. The design of local architects Snowdon and Hopkins makes copious use of native wood and stone. In a move to conserve as much energy as possible, this award-winning building is partially covered with a grass-lawn roof. This is a great place to relax if you get overloaded from Vail's hundreds of activities.

Low bookshelves in the main reading room allow you to see from one side of the room to the other. A large fireplace surrounded by some of the most comfortable leather chairs ever made is an outstanding feature of this building. There may be no better winter place to sit than in one of these chairs, on a Navajo rug, in front of a good fire, watching large snowflakes fall outside.

The lighting in the library tends toward specific "site" lighting, so that rather than uniform light throughout the building, it's supplied where it's needed by focused track lights.

## ——— WESTMINSTER ———

### Arabian Horse Trust Library

| | |
|---|---:|
| 12000 Zuni Street | A |
| (303) 450-4710 | Closed Saturdays, Sundays |

An absolute treasure trove for Arabian horse fanciers, this specialized library is about 20 miles north of Denver. The unique architecture of the center (by Hoffman/Reed of Denver) is developed around the Iwan arch, reflecting the Middle Eastern heritage of the Arabian horse.

The library, with its domestic and foreign stud books, is home to a number of private collections on Arabian horses and is also a museum with paintings, bronzes, Arabian saddles and weapons.

# · HAWAII ·

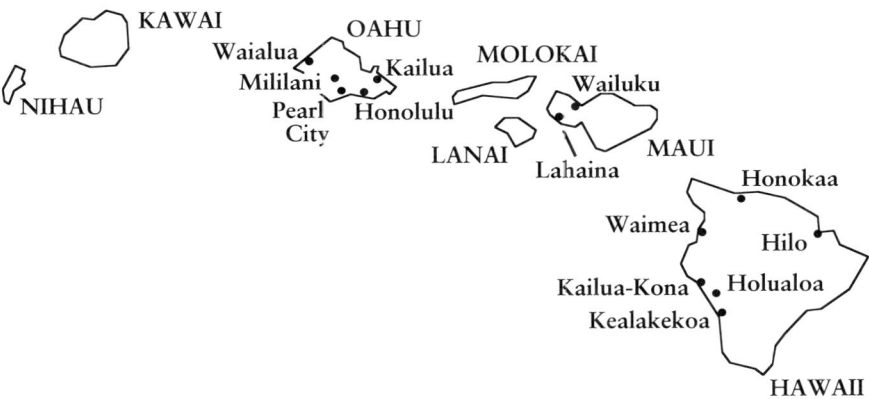

# ISLAND OF OAHU

## —— HAWAII KAI ——

### Hawaii Kai Public Library

249 Lunalilo Home Road
(808) 395-2310                                                Open every day

Near the great snorkeling beach at Hanauma Bay State Underwater Park, this library is conveniently across the street from the Koko Marina Shopping Center. The location is particularly good if you need a place to wait because you didn't notice that the beach is closed Wednesday morning, or if you need to rent snorkeling gear at the shopping center (there's none available at the beach).

It's a simple, modern, one-room facility with a large children's area to your left as you enter. The open, light main room is dominated by gigantic carp-shaped kites donated by a Japanese sister city.

## —— HONOLULU ——

### Hawaii State Library

478 South King Street                                                    A, T
(808) 586-3500                                                Closed Sundays

In 1879 the Honolulu Library and Reading Room opened to "... provide wholesome recreation in lieu of saloons frequented by men." It evolved into the State Library. The cornerstone of the present building was laid in 1911. It's wonderfully located near the Iolani Palace, the state capitol and most downtown sights. The building has undergone numerous expansions and renovations. The latest, designed by Aotani & Associates, was completed in 1992. Although the library's size was increased by a third, it's hard to tell which part is new and which is old.

Large trees grow on the library's expansive front lawn. Six massive columns dominate a grand entrance of two-story copper and glass

# Hawaii

Honolulu, HI
Hawaii State Library

arches. Dark arches and dark green roof contrast well with the off-white exterior. The old-fashioned, two-story-high lobby in this Colonial style building is quite elegant. Large globe lights hang over marble floors. The library is built around an open central patio where tropical plants grow around tables and chairs. The new furniture in the library is almost all wood—not much upholstered seating for lounging here. A unique feature of this building is that some of the bookshelves in the stacks are actually part of the steel that holds up the building—structural stacks, no less.

This is a major library, with 10 separate reference desks. Collections include a large Hawaii and Pacific section, an extensive sheet music collection and a genealogy collection. Natural light floods a children's room that has large murals painted by Juliette May Fraser in 1935.

Hawaii is the only one of the 50 states to have a single statewide library system. You can borrow a book in any Hawaiian library and return it to any other (even to branches on other islands). They are also generous in issuing library cards to visitors.

Waikiki, HI
Waikiki-Kapahulu Library

## Waikiki–Kapahulu Library

| | |
|---|---:|
| 400 Kapahulu Avenue | T, V |
| (808) 732-2777 | Closed Sundays |

About 60,000 tourists are liable to be in Waikiki at any given time, and its library is placed conveniently to serve them. Only a few minutes walk from Waikiki Beach, the library is at the Diamond Head end of the Ala Wai Canal which delineates one side of Waikiki. It's also only a few blocks from the Honolulu Zoo.

If you or your children would like to relax after too much sightseeing, this is a great place to visit. If you're staying in a condo with a kitchen, you might consider checking out one of their locally published cookbooks.

The library is also unique in the views it offers. From cathedral windows at one end you can see down the rows of high-rise hotels and condominiums on Ala Wai Boulevard, from the other end you see over Kapiolani Park to Diamond Head. The sandstone building has an outdoor reading area covered in bougainvillea. Seventy coconut palms grow on its grounds.

*Also of Note:*

## Bernice P. Bishop Museum Library

| | |
|---|---:|
| 1525 Bernice Street | H, T |
| (808) 847-3511 | Closed Sundays, Mondays |

This library, which is the only American library devoted exclusively to the Pacific region, is on the campus of the extraordinary Bishop Museum. You don't have to go to the museum to use the library. The library's holdings include the A.W.F. Fuller collection of books on the Pacific region, especially early voyage accounts; the George R. Carter collection of Hawaiian monographs, including works in the Hawaiian language and the Gressitt Entomology collection. The library also has a collection of hundreds of thousands of photographs. The library and its facilities are not architecturally outstanding, but the staff is exceedingly knowledgeable and helpful.

The Bishop Museum is marvelous. If you'd like an understanding of Hawaii and its peoples, this is a great place to start. For example, one major exhibit shows the influences on Hawaii of various immigrant groups, including Portuguese, Chinese, Korean, Filipino, Japanese, Polynesian, etc. There's a major exhibit on whales and whaling and a huge fascinating skeleton of a whale. Fortunately not all of the 187,000 artifacts or sixmillion shells, etc., are on exhibit at the same time.

The first Sunday in each month is Family Sunday, a particularly good time to visit if your children are with you, as there are lots of activities taking place on the lawns and in the museum buildings.

## —— KAILUA ——

### Kailua Public Library

239 Kuulei Road
(808) 261-4611                                              Closed Sundays

This is a medium-sized, one-room community library with a pleasant patio. The patio is beautifully maintained by the Windward Garden Club, and has a striking view of the hills.

Several walls of this high-ceilinged library have lava stone facings, which add to its warmth. Kailua, essentially a bedroom community for Honolulu, is best known for the sailboarding at Kailua Beach Park, and the library is a good relaxing place if there's either too much sun or too much rain.

## —— KANEOHE ——

### Kaneohe Public Library

| | |
|---|---|
| 45-829 Kamehameha Highway | V |
| (808) 247-6691 | Open every day |

Like so many of the Hawaii libraries, the Kaneohe library is surrounded by lush vegetation. Directly across the street is a striking ridge of sharply peaked mountains. While the peaks on Oahu are not very high, they are really craggy and seem alpine because they are so close. Should you be traveling by public transportation, Oahu's convenient TheBus system has a stop in front of the library.

On the wall at the main entrance is a tile construction representing the Koolau mountains. It was designed by Paul Nash in 1985, with the help of some student artists. You can peer up at craggy peaks of the wooded mountain range through high clerestory windows. It's as if some architects get so accustomed to a view that they see no need to highlight it. What a shame.

## —— MILILANI ——

### Mililani Public Library

| | |
|---|---|
| 95-450 Makaimoimo Street | |
| (808) 625-1388 | Open every day |

The library is on a grassy knoll, above street level and surrounded by greenery. Sculptor Han-Chew Hee's 1985 wall carvings flank the entrance. They have been sandblasted into Indian red granite and Taiwan marble. The island-born Hee studied with the famous French cubist painter, Fernand Leger. The main panel, *Golden Days of Hawaii*, is 19 feet wide by 8 feet high.

The library is anchored by a central, open atrium; you can see its greenery from anywhere in the library. A large children's room is decorated with lots of dolls and models hanging from the ceiling. Several reading areas provide comfortable seating.

About 20 miles northwest of Honolulu, this rapidly growing planned community is surrounded by mountains. The setting is quiet

Mililani, HI
Mililani Public Library

and you'll see few tourists here—that's what the residents like. The library is next to the Town Mall Shopping Center, one of two in this sprawling new suburb.

## —— PEARL CITY ——

### Pearl City Public Library

1138 Waimano Home Road
(808) 455-4134                                          Open every day

    The second busiest branch in the state system, like most of Hawaii's libraries, is not a visually exciting building. It's also the library closest to Pearl Harbor and the *USS Arizona* memorial. If someone's not up to the memorial, this is a good resting spot.
    A pleasant children's room is on your left as you enter. The media section has audiotapes in Korean, Japanese and Chinese as well as in English. The library also has a good-sized Hawaiiana collection.
    The library is not far from the famous Pearl City Tavern where you can have a drink and watch rhesus monkeys behind the bar (or get a really good meal).

## —— WAIALUA ——

### Waialua Public Library

67-068 Kealohanui Street
(808) 637-4876      Closed Sundays, Fridays

   This small, run-down library is located in a tiny off-the-beaten-path town. There is a huge, beautiful tree just outside the library. If you happen to be traveling by bus, the bus stop bench is just outside the library. (The 76 shuttle bus from the Kamehameha or "Kam" highway stops here.)
   The major attraction in this area is surfing, since the shore north of here is considered by many to be the surfing capital of the world.
   The library is directly across the street from the Sugar Bar, a fairly raucous surfer/biker hangout, in an old Bank of Hawaii building. Just down the street is a grotesquely beat up (but still working) sugar mill. Purely rural North Shore Oahu.

# ISLAND OF MAUI

## —— LAHAINA ——

### Lahaina Public Library

680 Wharf Street      V, T, H
(808) 661-0566      Closed Sundays, Fridays

   As romantic a setting as you'll find, in one of the most romantic cities this side of Venice, Italy. This library, next to the classically funky Pioneer Inn Hotel, Bar and Restaurant, sits right on the waterfront in the center of Lahaina. From the back look up and see mountains and from the front, out across the Pacific to the island of Lanai.
   The building is lava stone and stucco with a dark shake-shingle roof. The front lawn was once a taro patch, next to King Kamehameha's

Brick Palace. The building itself is plain, but marvelous light passes through windows, which offer wonderful views of the ocean past the *Carthaginian*, a three-masted, square-rigged brig berthed here.

The library is also within a block of sport fishing and whale-watching boats. The whale-watching trips take two and one-half hours, so this may be a good place to arrange to leave someone if they don't want to go on the trip (during the winter the sea can get pretty rough).

In addition to lots of historic buildings and shopping, Lahaina has memorable sunsets.

## —— WAILUKU ——

### Wailuku Public Library

| | |
|---|---:|
| 251 High Street | V |
| (808) 244-3945 | Closed Saturdays, Sundays |

This library is different in its external appearance from most other Hawaiian libraries. It's a large light orange building with a peaked red tile roof built in traditional Hawaiian style. As with many other Hawaiian libraries, there are fine views nearby—mountains at the back and expanses of green fields from the front entrance.

The library was designed by C. W. Dickey in 1929 with a high, steep roof for air circulation. In fact, it's still not air conditioned, and fans circulate the air on hot days. Although a Hawaiiana and music room were added in 1952, you get a feel for Hawaii's older institutional architecture here.

Although well-used, even worn, this is really a distinctive old building with its compartmented, beamed and trussed ceilings and fans. It's really the antithesis of the plain, flat-ceilinged rooms of most contemporary Hawaiian libraries.

# ISLAND OF HAWAII (THE BIG ISLAND)

## —— HILO ——

### Hilo Public Library

300 Waianuenue Avenue  
(808) 933-4650                                                                    Closed Sundays

The *malihini* (newly arrived) may be surprised to find a fireplace in a library in Hawaii, but this is the rainy side of the Big Island. Rainfall here can reach 150 inches a year, while on the opposite Kona coast annual rainfall is usually under 15 inches. During the rainy winter days, when it's not unusual to see snow on the nearby volcanic peaks, a cheery fire is a welcome sight. This is a good place to come and relax if you get caught in a rainstorm and don't want to drive Hawaii's sometimes curving roads in a downpour.

In front of the building are two large, black, historic stones, the Naha stone and the Pinao stone. The library has a handbook explaining their religious and historic significance.

This green-trimmed, lava-stone building is built around a large grassy atrium surrounded by tropical growth. A lanai, or veranda, runs around the patio to provide shelter from the rain. Reading chairs and tables are set all around. The wooden trellises are made of rare, hard Ohia wood. This wood is so highly resistant to termites it is said to be able to withstand eighty years in service as fence posts, even in termite-ridden ground.

This is a large, regional library, with a good-sized reference room. The service desks were recently rebuilt using beautiful (and also rare) Koa wood. A little north of the center of town, the library is on the road to both Honokaa and the Saddle Road turnoff.

# HOLUALOA

## Holualoa Public Library

75-138 Hualalai Road
(808) 324-1233                    Closed Sundays, Mondays, Wednesdays, Fridays

Just a few miles out of Kailua-Kona, this small, tin-roofed, half-timbered building sits in a tiny town. The library was built with Koa logs over a lava rock base.

The road to Holualoa rises steeply from the ocean and the views from the village are spectacular. Dominated by small art galleries, this quiet village is amazingly different from the busy shopping areas of upscale Kailua-Kona. It's home to a number of excellent contemporary artists. The library is just up the street from the Kona Art Center, an art training center and gallery.

Holualoa, HI
Holualoa Public Library

## —— HONOKAA ——

### Honokaa Public Library

45-3380 Mamane Street
(808) 775-7497                                              Closed Sundays

Sitting well above the ocean, this is another library in a splendid location. It also has a fireplace, Honokaa being in the rainy area of Hawaii.

There's a comfortable sitting area in front of the fireplace and a children's room to the right as you enter. There's no great view from the library, but from outside you can see past the small district courthouse down to the brilliant blue Pacific Ocean.

This might be a good place to drop someone off who absolutely couldn't resist the macadamia nuts on sale at the Hawaiian Holiday Macadamia Nut Company factory and gift shop a few miles from here.

## —— KAILUA–KONA ——

### Kailua–Kona Public Library

75-138 Hualalai Road                                                     A
(808) 329-2196                                        Closed Sundays, Mondays

Designed by local architect George Iwasaki, this branch, the newest of the libraries in the Hawaii state system, opened in 1992. A lime green tin roof covers an off-white concrete structure. The pleasant entryway is tiled in terra cotta and overhead clerestory windows reflect light off a wood-paneled ceiling. Although brand new, the square columns around the building evoke the colonial feeling that you see in the downtown Honolulu library.

The large children's department is almost a separate library, separate from the main library so noise won't drift into the main rooms. It has a number of stuffed dolls—the staff encourages children to read stories aloud to their favorite stuffed toys. There's a storytelling area and a paved terrace outside for noisy children's activities. A tiny "story corner" has just enough room for a rocking chair for a parent and chairs for a couple of children.

The young adult section is to your left as you enter, separated both from the children's and the adult's section. There's a lovely, stained-glass memorial to a previous librarian and a large prize-winning photograph of the solar eclipse that took place in Hawaii on July 11, 1991.

The adult reading and lounging area is close by the children's area. For coffee aficionados, the library has a small special collection on the history of Kona coffee.

There's actually a drive-up window at this library, not just to let you return books, but one at which you can pay fines, reserve a book or pick up one you have reserved.

## —— KEALAKEKUA ——

### Kealakekua Public Library

| | |
|---|---|
| Mamalahoa Highway | V |
| (808) 323-3653 | Closed Sundays |

This library is right by the side of the road on the way to Captain Cook, south out of Kailua-Kona. It's about 1,500 feet above the ocean, and there's an incredible panoramic view out of the back of this small library.

The building is lava stone and wood with a red tin roof. The most impressive thing is the view, but it really is outstanding.

## —— WAIMEA ——

### Thelma Parker Memorial Public & School Library

| | |
|---|---|
| 671209 Mamalahoa Highway | |
| (808) 885-4651 | Closed Sundays |

This combined public and school library is liable to be a bit noisy. Unfortunately there are no useable windows in the back of the library, otherwise there would be a fabulous view of Mauna Kea, towering almost 14,000 feet above the library in the distance. From outside the library you can see the astronomical observatories on the mountain (sometimes in fields of snow).

While wall space for books in libraries is important, so are aesthetics. It is unfortunate that this library and many of the other Hawaiian libraries make a mistake in not using the library to present and enhance the views of the nearby scenes.

# ·IDAHO·

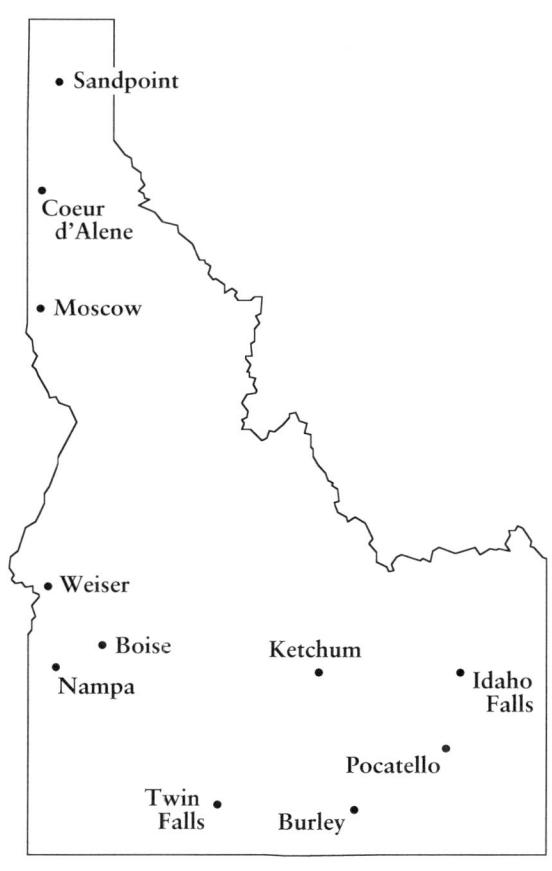

## ——— BOISE ———

### Boise Public Library

| | |
|---|---|
| 715 South Capitol Boulevard | A, T |
| (208) 384-4114 | Closed Sundays, summer |

Retailers say "location, location, location," and a retailer must have decided where to put this library. It's directly across Capitol Boulevard from the Art Museum, the State Historical Museum, a zoo, the Julia Davis Park and only a few blocks from the state capitol.

Inside, your major impression will be of lots and lots of space with a large, accessible collection. You can easily step back from a shelf and move around without having to worry about bumping into someone. Adding to the library's warmth are interior columns faced with brick. While the exterior of the building is plain, you'd never guess that it is a converted warehouse.

The huge children's room looks out into the park. It has both a changing room and a small "crying room." You can see through the room's soundproof windows into the auditorium where children's programs are presented.

This very contemporary library has a glassed-in section of microcomputers for patrons to use. A large collection of videotapes and compact discs is available for fast checkout at the "Entertainment Express," with its bright neon sign. On the third floor a closed Idaho collection is available for research.

Boise, ID
Boise Public Library

## Idaho State Library

325 West State Street  T
(208) 334-5124  Closed Saturdays, Sundays

A low, formal building just a few blocks from the capitol, the State Library is surrounded by state administrative buildings. It's set in a formal park with a fountain, a garden and a few picnic tables.

This is a reference library, not just for state legal matters, but a collection that includes medicine, geography, sports, construction, music, and so on. In fact, the reference collection is so eclectic it verges on the bizarre: sewing, horses, structural design, war and battles. There's a fine collection of art books (directly across from shelves of books on the "Properties of Hazardous Materials"). In the same building are the Idaho State Historical Society Archives. This would be a good place to start research on Idaho.

Structurally this library is the antithesis of the Boise Public Library. The shelves are extremely crowded and as close to each other as they could possibly be.

# —— BURLEY ——

## Burley Public Library

1300 Miller Avenue
(208) 678-7708  Closed Sundays

Burley is real small town America—a population of 9,000, kids on bicycles, people wheeling lots of babies. This is country to the point that on the road into town (in summer) you might see kids jumping off an overpass into a stream below. The major nearby attraction is the City of Rocks National Historic Reserve.

This an example of how the library in a small town can be a pleasant surprise. It's not a super library, it's not Twin Falls or Idaho Falls, but it is a comfortable place, built in the 1950s and expanded twice since then. This might be a good haven for a nonboater during the nearby power boat regatta in June, or for the nonskier while a companion skis at Mount Pomerelle.

## —— COEUR D'ALENE ——

### Coeur D'Alene Public Library

| | |
|---|---|
| 201 Harrison Avenue | T |
| (208) 769-2315 | Open every day |

This city of 25,000 is on the shore of one of America's most beautiful lakes, complete with a world-class vacation resort. Coeur D'Alene has lots to offer. In the summer tourists enjoy water sports while in the winter they go to nearby (45 minutes away) Silver Mountain Ski Area with the world's longest single-stage gondola.

The library is constructed of polished panels of rock aggregate. It has a permanent exhibit of current and historical color photographs of the area. They give you a good idea of the surroundings in different seasons.

The entrance is an internal bridge over a ramp which goes to the children's room, located by itself on a lower floor. There is also the Freedom Shrine with reproductions of famous American documents, the Bill of Rights, the Declaration of Independence, excerpts of presidential speeches, quotes from Martin Luther King, Jr. and more.

## —— IDAHO FALLS ——

### Idaho Falls Public Library

| | |
|---|---|
| 457 Broadway | A, E |
| (208) 529-1450 | Closed Sundays |

Even though Idaho Falls is the third largest city in Idaho, it still has fewer than 45,000 residents. This makes its exciting library a friendly surprise. At first glance it looks like a bank or a shopping center because of its sharp-edged brick and glass design. Broad concrete paths lead to the front entrance through a small forest of trees which screen the library so well that the building is hard to see from the street. Some library designs, such as in Boulder, Colorado, define a building by its entrance. Sundberg and Associates, who designed this building, hide the entrance and seem to say, "This is our building, these are our trees, come on in and see us."

*Idaho*

Idaho Falls, ID
Idaho Falls Public Library

Enter the library and you are greeted by three bright yellow stools. They're on a deep orange carpet, in front of a computer terminal near the information desk. You just know you're welcome to look things up (and there's a human nearby to help you).

The library is dominated by a central rotunda. From the entrance level one wide ramp leads upstairs and another spirals down, around dozens of trees, plants and ferns growing beneath the circular skylight. On the lower floor, wooden benches surround the planted area and form a huge conversation pit. (A large Christmas tree decorates this space during the holiday season.)

The upper level has lots of study space—obviously this community cares about its children's education. From the upper level you look down on large stacks of books and also out through the front windows and entrance.

The newly opened children's section on the lower level is like a separate library. You leave the main library and go through a hall to get into this enormous, well lit room full of study tables and small couches. The old children's library in the main library is now a spacious periodicals area.

## KETCHUM (SUN VALLEY)

### Community Library

| | |
|---|---|
| 415 Spruce Avenue North | A, T |
| (208) 726-3493 | Closed Sundays |

The library serving Sun Valley, the oldest and one of America's best known ski resorts, is everything you would expect.

From the floor-to-ceiling windows in the back of the library you can see the ski area a few miles away. If the cold winter weather (after all, the altitude here is almost 6,000 feet) is a little overwhelming, pull up one of the library's comfortable chairs in front of the huge, stone, double-sided fireplace.

Ernest Hemingway worked on *For Whom The Bell Tolls* while living in Sun Valley, and the library has a special collection of Hemingway's works.

Local buses are free and stop a block from the library, so if someone isn't skiing or visiting one of many art galleries or indulging in a hot spring, this is a great place to while away a day.

## MOSCOW

### Moscow–Latah County Library

| | |
|---|---|
| 110 South Jefferson | A |
| (208) 882-3925 | Closed Sundays in summer |

The library is a well-done expansion of a 1906 Carnegie library. The lines created by the large arched windows and semicircular rooms are extended to create angular shapes in the new area. This library is practically a textbook example of how well an expansion of a Carnegie can be done, making the expansion feel appropriate yet modern.

The old Carnegie is highlighted by brick arches, and the arch theme is carried out through the rest of the library. As you stand in either section, through arched connecting passageways you see more arched windows, all with half-circle sunburst tops. The old rooms have brightly polished, many-branched, globed lighting fixtures, hanging

Moscow, ID
Moscow–Latah County Library

from a paneled ceiling. There are lots of reading rooms and spaces with comfortable seating.

Moscow, home of the University of Idaho, is in beautiful country. In the spring and early summer it's brilliant with patches of yellow rapeseed blooming in emerald green farmland. The library is on the edge of the Fort Russell Historic Neighborhood, home to many turn-of-the-century mansions. It's an easy walk from the bookstores and restaurants of Main Street.

## —— NAMPA ——

### Nampa Public Library

101 South 11th Avenue
(208) 465-2264                                                  Closed Sundays

In 1966 Nampa's First Security Bank building, built in the Classical Revival style in 1919, was donated to the city for the library. The stained glass skylight in the main bank building is impressively formal. In 1985 the library expanded into a neighboring building which had been a printing plant. Much care was taken to mesh the two buildings.

Comfortably furnished mezzanines in each of the sections allow you to get away from the busier sections on the ground floor. This high, uncrowded library has lots of open space.

## —— SANDPOINT ——

### East Bonner County Library

| | |
|---|---|
| 419 North Second Avenue | T |
| (208) 263-6930 | Closed Sundays |

Sandpoint is another "sleeper" tourist area. Forty-five miles north of Coeur d'Alene, Sandpoint has a summertime white sand beach resort, a wintertime ski area that frequently gets 100 inches of powder snow and a library in a Spanish Colonial-style building.

The road to Sandpoint parallels 43-mile long Lake Pend Oreille, which you can't see until you come to a glorious wide expanse of water, with mountains in the background. Cross Long Bridge and you are in a small but comfortable resort town.

The library is a very formal twin-towered building which looks oddly familiar and governmental, until you realize you're looking at an old-fashioned post office building. A large archway decorates each of the towers. The building is raised on an embankment above the street. Adding to its general aura of oddity is a full-length statue of Abraham Lincoln in the main reading room.

The building is not very user-friendly, but it could be a temporary respite from an overdose of water skiing on the lake or snow skiing at Schweitzer Mountain, only 11 miles away. The library is only a block from the Cedar Street Bridge, with 15 shops and restaurants on a bridge crossing Sand Creek.

## —— TWIN FALLS ——

### Twin Falls Public Library

| | |
|---|---|
| 434 Second Street East | A |
| (208) 733-2965 | Closed Sundays |

The Twin Falls library is both an example of why you should check out small town libraries and of how a good building expansion is done. The expansion was done by Richardson Design Partnership of Salt Lake City in close collaboration with the local library staff. And, since

Twin Falls, ID
Twin Falls Public Library

there aren't any major towns for 120 miles in either direction, after seeing the 1,500-foot Perrine Bridge soaring almost 500 feet over the Snake River and exploring Shoshone Falls, this is a fine place to relax before getting back on the road.

The original library was replete with arched windows and the new, larger building uses that theme throughout. Twenty-foot arched windows in the old building are repeated as 30-foot arched windows in the new extension. The original building was built as a WPA project in 1936. It underwent a small expansion in 1976 and a larger one in 1991.

Inside, the first impression is of cool height. The floor is tile. The cool feeling is enhanced by interior colors of off-white and gray. The high ceiling is white, with large white and brass half-globe fixtures the length of the building.

The architects were careful to make movement from the older building to the new one easy. Arched passageways match the arches at each end of the building and brick-faced arches look down from mezzanines into the reading rooms.

## —— WEISER ——

### Weiser Public Library

628 East First Street
(208) 549-1243                    Closed Saturdays, Sundays in summer
                                  Closed Sundays, Mondays in winter

If you're heading north on route 95 toward Moscow or Coeur d'Alene, the plain but functional Weiser Public Library might be a good place to stop. Since you have about 250 miles to go before any major town, you could try their paperback exchange. Here, used paperbacks can be traded in for new ones to take on your trip. People who go through books like peanuts find this an effective way to recycle both books and car space.

# · MONTANA ·

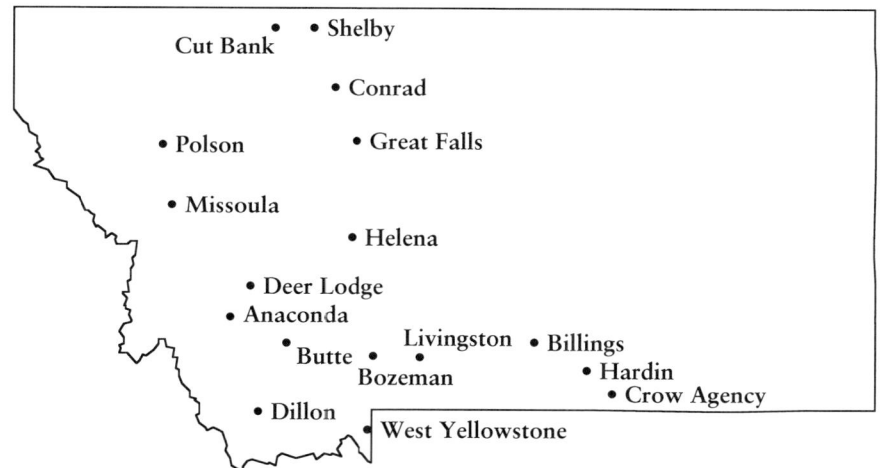

## —— ANACONDA ——

### Hearst Free Library

401 Main Street  
(406) 563-6932                    Closed Sundays, Mondays (not Accessible)

Andrew Carnegie was not the only turn-of-the-century benefactor of public libraries. Phoebe Hearst, mother of the famous newspaper publisher and castle builder William Randolph Hearst, donated this imposing building to Anaconda in 1898.

Inside and out, it still looks much as it did when it opened. Wide granite steps, massive granite columns and a dark copper cornice frame the stately brick building. The formal entrance is set off by brick arches which match the first floor's large arched windows. The furniture and interior decor of the library haven't changed much since 1898—it's well maintained and old-fashioned.

Straight up Main Street from the library is the marvelously ornate old Deer Lodge County Courthouse. It's worth the trip to see its copper-covered tower, rotunda and painted ceilings.

## —— BILLINGS ——

### Parmly Billings Library

510 North Broadway  
(406) 657-8257                                        Closed Sundays in summer

This multistory building is easily identified from the outside by a huge graphic proudly announcing the presence of the library and city offices. The library uses two floors of this four-story former furniture store. A wide and graceful spiral staircase connects the two floors of the library.

The Montana Room has an extraordinary collection of state history and a nationally renowned collection of works on the Battle at Little Big Horn.

## —— BOZEMAN ——

### Bozeman Public Library

| | |
|---|---|
| 220 East Lamme | A, T |
| (406) 586-4787 | Closed Sundays |

Bozeman is 16 miles south of the Bridger Bowl ski area and 45 miles north of Big Sky Ski Resort. It also has three museums. Not bad for a town of 24,000. You can enter its tree-shaded library by crossing a footbridge over a stream.

The entryway to this bright building leads to a two-story reading room with a wood-paneled ceiling. Some of the walls are light purple. A large skylight with adjustable shades lights the stairs to the mezzanine. On the mezzanine is the children's department with an adult reading area next to it. The nicely divided spaces on the mezzanine also include the small, quiet Montana Room which overlooks the ground floor.

There are some impressive hangings in this library. One three-part panel almost covers the eastern end of the main reading room. With many south-facing windows, the building makes good use of passive solar heating. The architects were Mattson and Prugh Lenon of Bozeman.

## —— BUTTE ——

### Butte–Silver Bow Public Library

| | |
|---|---|
| 226 West Broadway | |
| (406) 723-3361 | Closed Sundays |

Butte, once Montana's major metropolis, now has less than sixty percent of the population of Great Falls. It's trying though, and recently moved its library into a remodeled telephone exchange building. This is a plain remodel with its gray carpet, squarish mauve pillars and plain dropped ceilings. The most pleasant part of the library is a large children's section on the left as you enter, and the library does have an interesting collection of historical fishing books.

This square, three-story brick and concrete building is near the art center and historical district. Walking tours through ornate old buildings start a block from the library, which itself is only a block from the Copper King Mansion, a national historic place.

## —— CONRAD ——

### Conrad Public Library

15 4th Avenue Southwest
(406) 278-5751                                          Closed Saturdays, Sundays, Mondays

Should you be tired of driving and want a rest stop, the library in this 1916 City Hall building shows what can be done by a small community to re-use an older civic building. In the back, old jail cells are now used for more educational purposes.

From the outside you'd never guess that this formal two-story brick building with "CITY HALL" inscribed in granite across the front is a redesigned library extensively finished in wood. The second floor has been opened up in two places to allow mezzanines to overlook the main floor. Good carpeting and lighting combine with well-fashioned wooden banisters and rails to provide a welcoming aspect.

Near the entrance is a comfortable reading area with upholstered chairs and couches. In smaller towns like Conrad you don't have the wear and tear on the libraries that you do in bigger cities. It looks as if the woodwork (done by local craftsman Pete Hauer) was just finished, but in fact it's almost 15 years old.

## —— CROW AGENCY ——

### Little Big Horn College Archives and Library, Little Big Horn College

1 Forestry Lane                                                                H, T
(406) 638-2228                                          Closed Saturdays, Sundays

Tim Bernardus, this unique library's professionally trained librarian, is one of the most helpful, informative, welcoming people you can expect to meet. When it comes to local and Crow history he's fascinating, fascinated, almost fanatical (and he knows a hell of a lot). This library and archive are a tribute to him and to the Crow Indians who have organized to work with him.

The library at the Little Big Horn College is truly an example of what can be done with sweat, hard work and inspiration. This is not an elegant, comfortable library. The shelves and fixtures have been made mostly by the students or salvaged from other libraries, but it is an incredible example of how really dedicated people can get by on a minuscule budget.

The archive's aim is to preserve the history and culture of the Crow Indians through both historical and contemporary information. Records, papers, scrapbooks, family histories, photographs and individual histories, both written and oral, are all brought together. Here there are also works of non-Crow scholars on Crow Indian topics.

Crow Agency is only a few miles from the Custer Battlefield National Monument. The monument area and the outstanding visitor center are a notable tribute to the paradoxes of developing civilizations.

## —— CUT BANK ——

### Glacier County Library

21 First Avenue SE
(406) 873-4572                                    Closed Saturdays, Sundays

One whole wall of this small glass and brick library consists of windows. With low shelves near the windows and taller ones near the back, light floods the reading and studying space.

It's nothing fancy, but a good place to stop if you're tired. Look for a brick and glass building with a beautiful tall spruce tree at one end.

## —— DEER LODGE ——

### William K. Kohrs Memorial Library

501 Missouri Avenue
(408) 846-2622                    Closed Sundays, Mondays (not Accessible)

This granite and sandstone library hasn't changed much since 1902 when it was hailed as a "Corinthian Edifice" in the local newspapers. It fits well with the granite walls of the nearby prison and Deer Lodge's Victorian buildings. The old-fashioned main reading room has a dark oak counter and matching pigeon-hole desk. They sit in front of a splendid 6 foot by 9 foot stained glass window. Some of the iron bookshelves have been in place since the library opened.

In the basement of the building is a surprising collection of old magazines. If you want to see how *Cosmopolitan* has changed since 1891, take a look here; you'll also find *Scribners*, *Century*, *Harpers*, and *American Review* (back to 1908). Not a bad place to relax while somebody else tours the prison or the ranch.

Deer Lodge has some unique attractions. The threatening but fascinating Old Montana Prison and Law Enforcement Museum are open to the public. You can also visit the Towe Ford Museum's collection of over 100 antique Fords or the Grants-Kohrs Ranch National Historic Site. But don't look for gourmet food here. The lunch special is liable to be a grilled ham and cheese sandwich or a chili burger.

Deer Lodge, MT
William K. Kohrs
Memorial Library

Dillon, MT
Dillon City Library

## —— DILLON ——

### Dillon City Library

121 South Idaho
(406) 683-4544
Closed Sundays;
Closed Saturdays, Sundays in summer (not Accessible)

Dillon is just plain pleasant. Small, relaxed, with old buildings still in use, it's also full of young people from its college. The eclectic collection of architecture in Dillon includes an old county courthouse with a four-faced clock tower, a newspaper building with a pressed metal facade and an impressive late-nineteenth-century hotel building.

This native stone library, which looks much like a small church, is only a block from the county museum in Old Depot Park in the center of town. Even if there were no curved black iron sign over the arched doorway saying "Library" in bold letters, its sharply peaked roof and pointed tower would make it hard to miss. Look for the carved stone faces on the corners of the building.

While you're exploring Dillon, don't be surprised to see dust-covered people walking about. The local talc mine and mill are still in full operation and coat their workers in ghostly color.

## —— GREAT FALLS ——

### Great Falls Public Library

301 Second Avenue  A
(406) 453-0349  Closed Sundays in summer

One of the stellar attractions of this library is the big, comfortable Montana Room on the third floor. A delightful place in which to explore Montana history, it's inside the curved front of the building, looking out over the courtyard and fountain. Recently restored stained glass panels from an 1890 library hang in the floor-to-ceiling windows that form one of the walls of the room. This is a fine touch, bringing lovely parts of an old library into this newer structure.

The front of this unique curved building is a colonnaded walkway, with sheer glass walls on one side and a courtyard highlighted by a large fountain on the other. Concrete columns support an overhanging roof. Built in 1967, it still looks contemporary.

A mezzanine floor opens above the main floor entrance in a unique elliptical shape. A wide curved stairway leads to it from the ground floor. Soft recessed lights and good soundproofing add to the peaceful atmosphere.

Great Falls, MT
Great Falls Public Library

## Also of Note:

## Charles M. Russell Museum Library

| | |
|---|---|
| 400 13th Street North | T |
| (406) 727-8787 | Closed Fridays, Saturdays, Sundays |

This surprisingly large museum is much more than just a collection of the work of Charlie Russell, America's Cowboy Artist. It includes a wide variety of other Western American Art and artifacts, including a large firearms collection. In the E. S. Curtis Gallery you'll find a marvelous collection of Russell's letters, with wonderful pen, pencil and watercolor work as well as a collection of Curtis photographs of North American Indians. There are also changing exhibits of contemporary western art.

The library, like the museum, concentrates on Russell but has material on his contemporaries and on Western American Art in general. The library is just getting off the ground; in fact, the materials are not yet fully cataloged. However, if you're doing research on Western American artists, the American West, or on a particular artifact, the materials might be helpful. Appointments for use of the library are preferred; it will be expanded and more fully staffed in the future. The gift shop at the museum has a fine collection of reproductions.

# —— HARDIN ——

## Big Horn County Public Library

| | |
|---|---|
| 419 North Custer Avenue | T |
| (406) 665-1808 | Closed Sundays; |
| | Closed Saturdays, Sundays in summer |

A wonderful transformation of a Carnegie library. Unless you knew that there were old libraries being restored or enlarged, you simply wouldn't notice, either inside or out, that this is a major remodel. This is so even though Page-Werner Architects of Great Falls moved the main entrance from the front to the side of the building. The old entrance is now just an exit, the old library space a reading room.

High ceilings all around, good fluorescent lighting and contemporary furniture make this a bright and comfortable place. On the top floor you'll find a large paperback collection and comfortable upholstered chairs; even some rocking chairs. The children's room is in the basement.

Hardin is only 15 miles north of the Custer Battlefield National Monument.

## HELENA

### Lewis and Clark Library

| | |
|---|---|
| 120 South Last Chance Gulch | A, E, T |
| (406) 442-2380 | Closed Mondays |

For someone not familiar with Helena, the library's address—Last Chance Gulch—makes it sound as if it's somewhere out in the boondocks. On the contrary it sits in a parklike lawn at one end of the restored downtown section of Helena, a very popular upscale pedestrian mall.

The modern brick library is a sprawling two-story building. Its brick fits nicely with the old buildings of Last Chance Gulch. The gently sloping lawn in front is just right for children to roll on. As you look across the lawn at the library you see the hills up at the edge of the gulch.

This is one case where a first impression is almost overwhelming: open space, wood beams, brick columns, trees and ivy. A giant ceiling of wood panels with exposed wooden beams and trusses is crossed by exposed blue heating ducts. It's a beautiful contrast to the slender red

Helena, MT
Lewis and Clark Library

brick columns and light-colored wood trusses and ceiling. Both wooden stairs and an elevator go up to a mezzanine supported by more open wood trusses.

Over the brick floor of the entryway is a set of clerestory windows. Light from the windows adds to that coming from the black, six-sided fixtures hanging from the ceiling on black cables. Wherever you look you see potted trees. The wooden theme is carried over to the furniture, which is oak, upholstered in orange, purple and yellow.

Whether you stop here after exploring the shopping mall or eating at one of the nearby good restaurants, or if you just want to take a break in a large and delightful library, this is a good choice.

*Also of Note:*

## Montana Historical Society Library

| | |
|---|---|
| 225 North Roberts Street | V |
| (406) 444-4702 | Closed Saturdays, Sundays |

The Montana Historical Society Library and Museum are in a classic 1950s style government building directly across the street from the copper-domed state capitol. The museum is rightfully proud of its new Montana Homeland exhibit. The Last Chancer automotive train tour of Helena starts just outside the library during the summer.

The library consists of three sections: the library, the archives and the photographic archives.

The airy research room has two walls of windows, one looking out at the capitol, the other at the mountains across the high plains. Among other treasures, the library has copies of 95 percent of all the newspapers ever printed in Montana, band music scores from 1915 to 1940 and extensive material on the Lewis and Clark expedition. The photographic collection has over 250,000 items. This isn't a very good place for browsing, but researchers are always welcome here.

## LIVINGSTON

### Livingston Public Library

228 West Callender Street
(406) 293-2778   Closed Sundays

    Livingston is the northern gateway to Yellowstone Park, and while it's quieted down from its flamboyant past, it can still be a lot of fun.
    The old-fashioned Carnegie library with its huge columns might well be a haven for those who don't enjoy the intricacies of fly fishing. Incidentally, one of the best-known tourist attractions in town is Dan Bailey's Fly Shop at 209 West Park Street. It's a great source for the fly fisherman.

## MISSOULA

### Missoula Public Library

301 East Main Street
(406) 728-5900   Closed Sundays

    On the edge of the downtown area, this large, one-story building isn't fancy, but it's open and welcoming. Just inside the entryway are a green flowering garden, benches and trees. As you walk in you see across to windows and greenery on the other side of the building.
    The children's section, to your right as you enter, is also part of the main room, separated by bookshelves, not walls. The good-sized Montana collection (some open, some locked) has its own special room. In locked cabinets they have such treasures as the Deer Lodge *Weekly Independent Newspaper* from May 15, 1869–March 7, 1874.

## POLSON

### Polson City Library

21st Avenue East   A
(406) 883-4003   Closed Sundays

Polson is at the south end of Flathead Lake, the largest natural fresh-water lake west of the Mississippi. The new (1989) library is right next to the lake. Architect Jerry Balles from Missoula designed a lovely reading room that looks out from the library over the parking lot to the lake. During the winter when the leaves are off the trees you can see snow-covered mountains across the water.

In an unusual touch, the predominant colors in the library are various shades of green (including the bookshelves). The children's area has a huge tank of tropical fish. In the same building is a private, nonprofit art gallery and gift shop that displays and sells works of both local and other Montana artists. There is also a work area for classes and workshops in the arts.

Polson, while in popular recreation country, has a population of only 2,800. And yet here's a pleasant, bright building, with lots of activity. Any small community would be pleased to have this complex.

## —— SHELBY ——

### Toole County Free Library

| | |
|---|---:|
| 229 Maple Avenue | H |
| (406) 434-5411 | Closed Sundays |

The library has a beautiful and extensive collection of Native American artifacts—lots of arrowheads, pipes, hunting implements, skull crackers, blades, etc. These aren't just arrowheads from the local area but a truly national collection.

Shelby, MT
Toole County Free Library

As you walk up the grassy knoll to the library you'll see lots of bulletins and posters on the front windows and doors letting you know what's happening locally.

There's nothing spectacular to attract tourists to Shelby, but if you're looking for a stop as you cross Montana's Hi-Line country, try this pleasant library on a hill overlooking the Montana Plains. If you want to stop for the night, there's an inexpensive motel right across the street.

# WEST YELLOWSTONE

## West Yellowstone Public Library

100 Yellowstone Avenue
(406) 646-9017                           Closed Sundays (Not Accessible)

This small library is the only public library within a 90-mile radius. It's in one room of the 100-year-old Union Pacific Dining Hall building which is on the National Register of Historic Places. The building is owned by the Federation of Fly Fishers International, whose museum and library are in the same building.

This small, busy library has an active children's section. It's not a bad place to get away from the sometimes frenetic tourist activities of West Yellowstone.

*Also of Note:*

## International Fly Fishing Federation Library

200 Yellowstone Avenue                                              T
(406) 646-9541                                            Closed Sundays

In the same building as the West Yellowstone Public Library, this may be a fly fisher's version of heaven. A museum and exhibits on fly fishing, a small library about fly fishing, and staff who (like yourself, perhaps) live and breathe fly fishing. And of course there's great fly fishing all around here. To make it even better, the public library is just next door so those not interested in fly fishing won't be totally bored.

# · NEVADA ·

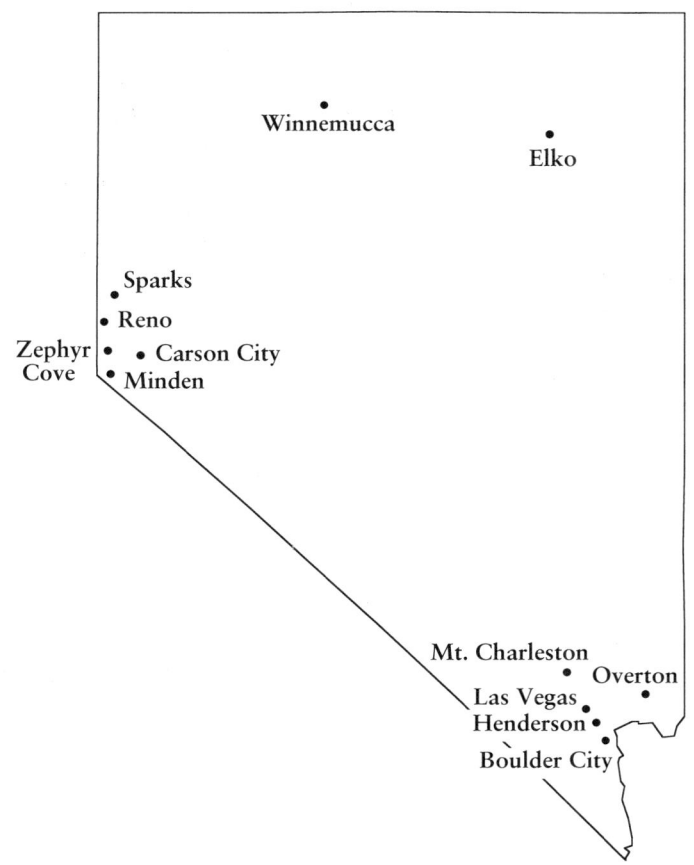

## BOULDER CITY

### Boulder City Library

| | |
|---|---|
| 813 Arizona Street | T |
| (702) 293-1281 | Closed Sundays |

An orange double door in a wall of shiny blue tiles contrasts with the rough adobe-like brick walls of the Boulder City Library. This modest, single-room building with wood-trimmed bookshelves has a pleasant view from its back reading area. Lots of light floods into the periodical reading room. A small children's room and art gallery are to your left as you enter.

The library is only a few blocks from Hotel Plaza, the center of town, with its pleasant park, shops and a small museum. Boulder City, the only city in Nevada to outlaw gambling, is just seven miles from Hoover Dam. If you want to take the guided tour of the dam or go on an hour-and-a-half flight over the Grand Canyon from nearby Boulder City Airport, this is a good place to drop off those with more sedentary interests.

The 7-mile drive from Boulder City to Lake Mead and the dam is fascinating. The road winds through barren, stark country. It's a well-marked mountain road, with guard walls at the side. At the bottom of this incredible canyon you actually drive over the dam.

## CARSON CITY

### Carson City Library

| | |
|---|---|
| 900 North Roop Street | |
| (702) 887-2247 | Closed Sundays |

This low-slung, white concrete building is so discreet it's easy to miss. Set back from the street, the building is surrounded by trees and bushes. The main reading room has leather and upholstered chairs, and windows looking out onto the street. A gray carpet adds to the coolness of the library, as does the spread out placement of the bookshelves. There's a lot of material here, but the library doesn't feel crowded.

The large children's room has a children's Nevada collection as well as a couple of pet rabbits. This is the type of children's room that has lots of things hanging around—plastic dinosaurs, puppets, etc.—that encourage children to think of reading as play.

*Also of Note:*

## Nevada State Library and Archives

| | |
|---|---:|
| 100 Stewart Street | A |
| (702) 687-5160 | Closed Fridays, Saturdays |

While the architecture of the new (1993) library is modern, architects DeLorenzo-Sticha of Las Vegas did a marvelous job of evoking the basic design elements of the 1886 state printing office to which it has been connected. The lower level of the old building is now used for exhibits.

The old building has sharply peaked roofs, and the new building carries these angles and other architectural elements into its design. From the Stewart Street entrance you see through the new building to a small park and the state capitol. At the back of the building is a campus-type arrangement of government buildings. The library is on the west side and the Capitol building on the east.

The library is only a few blocks from some large casinos—but then everything in this small state capital is only a few blocks from the casinos. The State Library and Archives building is a striking contrast to the 1888 Federal Post Office which it replaced.

Carson City, NV
Nevada State Library and Archives

## —— ELKO ——

### Elko County Library

720 Court Street
(702) 738-3066                                                                             Closed Sundays

This county library is surprisingly large with a large separate reference room at one end and a separate children's section at the other. This fairly crowded, no-frills library is a good stop if you're getting restless on the long drive across the Nevada desert.

The population of Elko is only 5,000 but the glitzy casinos and their attendant hotels and motels make the city seem larger.

## —— HENDERSON ——

### Green Valley Library, Las Vegas–Clark County Library District

2797 North Green Valley Parkway                                     A
(702) 435-1840                                                             Open every day

This large and interesting library sits up a small hill from a busy main intersection. The ocher building contrasts strongly with the green grass and palm and pine trees around it. The long walls of the building are broken up by tall narrow windows topped by tile patterns. The combination of decorative tile in a stucco wall makes for a gay, Southwest, Art Deco feeling. The main entrance, not visible from the street, is opposite the parking lot. It's a huge stucco canopy with a red tile roof.

The entryway opens to a delightful central octagonal rotunda with stained glass windows high on the walls around. The central desk of mottled gray stands on a green rug. Monumentally high halls lead from the center to reading and reference rooms. There are good signs, so you can see where you want to head from the central space. The colors are unique, with green carpets, peach on the lower walls with muted yellow above and high ceilings of bleached wood.

Reading areas in this spacious library are at the ends of the rooms away from the noise of the center. There are lots of upholstered chairs but nothing really luxurious. The children's room is large, bright and high with both a story room and story alcoves. The architect was Barbara Flammang.

Green Valley is a new, upscale, planned suburb of Las Vegas. It's in Henderson, on the route from Las Vegas to Boulder City and Lake Mead.

## Henderson District Public Library

280 Water Street
(702) 565-8402                                                                 Open every day

At first glance this formal building next to the striking Henderson Convention Center looks like it's built of large stone blocks. Actually, it's stucco, with panels ranging from off-white to pink to light blue. This is a small but innovative library with bright neon signs identifying book sections.

The entryway leads to a gray and white octagonal central room with pleasant hanging lights. There's a nice children's room and also a space technology and aerospace room. The library has a historic local photograph collection of about 5,000 items. Pictures start in 1941 when what is now a town of 65,000 was all desert.

# —— INCLINE VILLAGE ——

## Incline Branch Library, Washoe County Library System

846 Tahoe Boulevard
(702) 832-4130                                                                 Closed Sundays

The Incline Village library is on the main road that runs around Lake Tahoe. A half mile from the lake, the library is just south of Incline Village, a major ski and golf resort. The all-wood building has a "peek" view of the lake.

This crowded, plain, workable library is convenient if you want to take a break from the snow skiing, hiking, biking, water skiing and casino gambling that make this area so popular. The library is near lots of restaurants and shops.

# LAS VEGAS

## Las Vegas Library and Lied Discovery Children's Museum

| | |
|---|---|
| 833 Las Vegas Boulevard North | A, E, T, V |
| (702) 382-3493 | Open every day (Museum closed Mondays) |

Las Vegas libraries and museums firmly belie the popular image of this city as no more than a glitzy gambling capital. It is a glitzy gambling capital, but Las Vegas (and its surroundings) has a splendid collection of public libraries. Some were under construction as we wrote this. The West Charleston and Clark County buildings will be striking when they are finished.

The main library and Children's Discovery Museum are located on one end of Las Vegas Avenue (which becomes the fabulous "strip" at its other end). This unique building has a 93-foot cylindrical tower, a cone-shaped "birthday party room" and a sharply triangulated administrative section, along with some more conventional rectilinear shapes. Parts of the external walls are concrete, others quarried sandstone. The whole structure gives the impression of what children might do with a good set of building blocks. A small forest of palm trees sets off the front parking lot. The building was designed by Antoine Predock.

A polished flagstone entryway leads either to the Children's Discovery Museum to the left or to the library straight ahead. On the library's main floor rich blue carpets contrast with the light wooden framing of black bookshelves. Ceilings throughout are high with recessed lights, and the walls are blue and beige. There are views into various courtyards from the library's reading rooms.

A huge rotating globe dominates one end of the large reference room. You can get a more local perspective of the city by looking at an enormous 8-foot-square aerial photograph at the other end of the room. There is a special collection on gaming, both on how to do it and how to manage it as a business.

The young people's library occupies the mezzanine floor, with story rooms and low windows that allow children to see down into the main library and the museum. There's also a hands-on art and science gallery for children in this part of the library.

Las Vegas, NV
Las Vegas Library and Lied Museum
Photo courtesy Las Vegas Public Library

Worth a trip all by itself, the Lied Discovery Children's Museum, in the same building as the library (closed Mondays) is devoted to making art and science accessible to children through participation. Over 100 exhibits on two floors will excite almost every child who comes here. A big difference between this museum and other hands-on museums is the emphasis here on art and creative experience rather than just science. This is one of the largest children's museums in the country.

## Sunrise Branch Library

| | |
|---|---|
| 5400 Harris Avenue | A, V |
| (702) 453-1104 | Open every day |

On the east side of town in a calm residential area, light years away from the glitzy high-speed feel of the strip, this library looks up at a range of arid, tough mountains. The building is yellow stucco with a brown ceramic tile roof. Some external design details stand out. Windows divided into small panes are trimmed in blue and the entryway is paved in dark maroon tiles. Twin colonnades lead to two sets of double wooden entrance doors. The architect of this agreeable 1987 building is a local firm called Architronics.

Inside, strong concrete columns rise to high, angled ceiling sections above clerestory windows. Walls in desert pastels of lavender, teal and peach add to the lightness of the building. Above the central circulation desk is a four-part mural of nearby Sunrise Mountain. Hanging cylindrical light fixtures and banners delicate enough to move gently in the air conditioning add grace to the rooms. In the main section some quiet study rooms are glassed in on both sides. Readers can see out, and people in the main library can still see the view outside the library.

A small art gallery is used for both local artists and traveling exhibits. The fine children's department was carefully designed to maintain a feeling of coziness, but also has a large story room.

## West Las Vegas Branch Library

| | |
|---|---|
| 951 West Lake Mead Boulevard | A |
| (702) 647-2117 | Open every day |

Both inside and out, this building shows how imaginative use of materials creates atmosphere. This orange building with its copper roof separated from the walls by a band of turquoise really stands out. It's set off by a striking peaked entryway.

Banners and hanging sculptures enliven white rooms. Kitelike banners bring light, color and cheer. Skylights and clerestory windows add to fluorescent lighting which reflects from the white walls.

The children's room is decorated with lots of stuffed toys sitting on top of the bookshelves. It's a great place for kids. There is a small Black

Las Vegas, NV
West Las Vegas Library
Banners by Louise Kodis

history and culture section, as a significant portion of Las Vegas's minority population lives in this area.

The building was designed by Arturo Cambeiro and Associates and the banners, entitled *Secrets of My Garden*, are by Louise Kodis. A 300-seat theater is currently being built as an addition to the library.

## —— MINDEN ——

### Douglas County Public Library

| | |
|---|---|
| 1625 Library Lane | V |
| (702) 782-9841 | Closed Sundays |

In the Carson Valley near US 395, this stone and metal library has a sweeping orange metal roof contrasting with its stone walls. Enjoy a marvelous view of the east side of the Sierra Nevada Mountains from the periodicals section.

The overhanging front canopy is supported by exposed metal trusses, and these trusses carry through into the main library as visible supports for the ceiling.

Minden was originally settled by German farmers, and nearby Gardnerville was home to Basque sheep herders. The library has a significant collection of books in German, as well as a large amount of material on the Carson Valley. It is also home to Baker and Taylor, two library cats featured in advertisements by the library supply firm, Baker and Taylor.

## —— MOUNT CHARLESTON ——

### Mount Charleston Branch Library, Las Vegas–Clark County Library System

| 1252 Aspen Avenue | V |
| --- | --- |
| (702) 872-5585 | Closed Fridays, Sundays, weekday mornings |

If you want to get away from the desert, see the mountains and visit a pleasant library, try this drive. This small but modern library, about 40 miles north of Las Vegas, is directly across Route 157 from the Nevada Division of Forestry building. It has a tiled brick entryway, green carpets, a paneled wood ceiling with inset lights and comfortably upholstered furniture. A great location with a great view.

Taking the drive up toward Mt. Charleston gives you a chance to experience the high desert and mountains around Las Vegas, not on the freeway but on an easily handled road. You'll start in a cactus-dominated desert and end in the pine-covered mountains. Great location for a picnic or a hike.

## —— OVERTON ——

### Moapa Valley Branch Library, Las Vegas–Clark County Library System

| 350 Highway 169 | |
| --- | --- |
| (702) 397-2690 | Closed Sundays, Mondays |

This white stucco building with a sweeping red tiled roof has a large enclosed patio and a grassy area in back of the library for children's programs. Oddly enough for a library out in the Nevada desert, it has a rather extensive collection on Irish history.

This is a good stopping point for people exploring the rugged rocks and petroglyphs of the nearby Valley of Fire State Park (14 miles away) or the Lost City Museum of Archeology in Overton.

## —— RENO ——

### Washoe County Library

| | |
|---|---:|
| 301 South Center Street | A, E |
| (702) 785-4190 | Closed Saturdays, Sundays |

This outstanding library was one of the inspirations for this book. The authors have been visiting it on and off since 1966, just after it was built, and the Hewitt Wells design is as outstanding today as it was almost thirty years ago. Myth has it that when the library was unable to acquire park land, Wells decided to "put the park in the library since he couldn't put the library in a park." Hence, a library with over 1,300 plants.

You enter on a bridge to the main section of the building. The bridge is about twenty feet wide and fifty feet long, with lush green flower boxes along its length. Below, the lower section is a garden, with pond, rocks and planting beds with stepping stones. Comfortable chairs and tables let you enjoy sitting there.

Several podlike circular reading areas, supported from the ground floor and totally surrounded by plants, are reached by small bridges from the upper level of this three-story open library. As well as being architecturally outstanding, this is the largest public library between Salt Lake City and Sacramento.

The library has a gaming collection, both on how to do it and how to manage it as a business. Additionally, although the county's main children's collection is in the Sierra View Branch, this branch now has the Children's Circle section for children, downstairs and to the left of the main entrance.

Once you've been to this unforgettable library you'll begin to judge others against it. If you like libraries, or want to see how good architecture survives lots of use and some age, come here. Sadly, wonderful as the library is, budget cutbacks have forced it to close on weekends.

Reno, NV
Washoe County Library

## Sierra View Branch Library, Washoe County Library System

4001 South Virginia Street
(702) 827-3232                                                Open every day

This branch of the Washoe County Library is in the Old Town Mall on the south end of Reno. The roof of the mall is finished in shiny copper, and more copper is used inside the mall. Brick floors and columns add to the rich feel of the building.

You can't miss the green neon sign for the library in what was one of the larger stores in the mall. The library is rather plain, but since this is the central location for children's books in the county system, the children's collection is huge, and the mall location makes it very accessible.

## —— SPARKS ——

### Sparks Branch Library, Washoe County Library System

1125 Twelfth Street
(702) 785-4170                                              Closed Sundays

This moderately large, utilitarian library has several interesting special collections. There's a huge auto repair manual collection. Motor's, Chilton, Mitchell—a fantastic selection. The manuals are both at the professional and the do-it-yourself level. In addition, a large Nevada shelf lines one whole wall. There is also a complete selection of Nevada topographical maps.

While the library does have some tropical plants and a large children's room, it's neither luxurious nor overly comfortable. However, if you want to take a break from gambling, fix your car or find a topo map to tell you how to get someplace once you've got the car fixed, this is the place.

## —— WINNEMUCCA ——

### Humboldt County Library

85 East Fifth Street
(702) 623-6388                                              Closed Sundays

A billboard on Interstate 80 in Winnemucca (population 8,000) says "Winnemucca, one traffic jam every decade; exit now." That may well be the case, and if that's what you want, well, they do have a library here. In any case, the drive across Nevada can be pretty dull, and

Winnemucca is a possible rest stop (actually if you want to stop anyplace around here you'd better make it Winnemucca).

The library is a plain, low concrete building but not unattractive. Inside, concrete beams contrast with comfortable, overstuffed leather reading chairs in the middle of the library. It's an open, cool room. The reference area, at one end of the main room, is in its own raised section. The young adults' and children's sections are downstairs.

Be careful while driving through Winnemucca. Rather than speed bumps, there seem to be speed ditches. They're really for letting water run off during sudden rains, but raise hell on a car, especially if you're towing a trailer.

# —— ZEPHYR COVE ——

## Lake Tahoe Branch Library, Douglas County Library

233 Warrior Way
(702) 588-6411                                    Closed Sundays, Mondays

Just off Highway 50 in Zephyr Cove Park is a wooden building with a shake roof beautifully situated in a grove of large fir trees.

This is a plain but serviceable library. It's obviously had a lot of use, but it is comfortable. The windows look into groves of pines, and it's next to public tennis courts, a picnic ground and a playground. There's a good magazine rack where you will find, among other periodicals, *International Gaming and Wagering Business*, of interest to some of the local businessmen.

The playground is a special treat for young children, with imaginative bridges and other wooden play structures. Its surface is all sand. Next to the library is the start of a PAR exercise course for adults who would like to work out while their kids are in the playground or the library.

# ·NEW MEXICO·

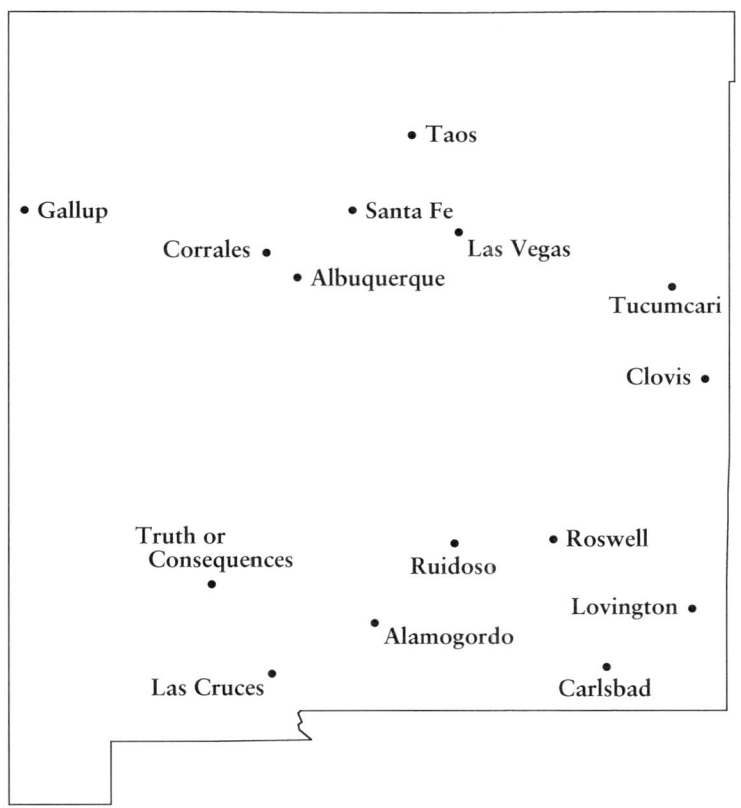

## —— ALAMOGORDO ——

### Alamogordo Public Library

920 Oregon Avenue  A, V
(505) 437-9058  Closed Sundays

This library's Eugene Manlove Rhodes collection, which has extensive material on the Tularosa Basin and on the Great Southwest, is much grander than many other New Mexico history collections. It occupies a large comfortable reading room with a working fireplace. Comfortable furniture and a bank teller's cage from 1909 built into one of the walls highlight the room.

Some libraries look good outside and plain inside; this one is the other way around. Slightly hidden by old deciduous trees, this is a simple building, but inside it is bright and comfortable. There's a huge children's room with a good view of the mountains. Brightly painted light fixtures and a storybook wall of children's tiles add to the cheeriness of the room.

The large, fairly low main room is well lit and has good directional signs. Gray carpet, walls in off-white, turquoise and pale blue, wood-trimmed blue shelves—all add to the cheery atmosphere. There's a double-sided fireplace, one side of which is in the Southwest Room, the other side in the main room. Check out the large community bulletin board. The 1960s design by architect John Reed has stood the test of time very well.

Alamogordo sits in the Tularosa Basin between the towering, rugged Sacramento mountains and the White Sands National Monument. The drive into the mountains (toward Ruidoso) is beautiful. It's also home to an International Space Hall of Fame, a Space Theater and the Chinese Star Restaurant which serves Chinese, American and Mexican food.

# ALBUQUERQUE

## Albuquerque Public Library

501 Copper Avenue Northwest
(505) 766-5100                                      Closed Sundays

    The main library is about a mile and a half from Old Town Plaza, Albuquerque's original settlement site, now turned into boutique heaven. This large, tan brick building opened almost 20 years ago and still works as well as ever. Obviously the architects (Stevens, Mallory, Pearl and Campbell) knew that libraries are constantly changing. There are no permanent walls in the full half-block expanses of the main building. Moveable walls enable the staff to remodel the library as needs change. Even the library's art gallery is built with moveable walls. This is not a beautiful or luxurious library, but it is extremely functional, and it's only a few blocks from the Albuquerque Convention Center.

    The children's room (with a large sunken story room and puppet theater) is on a lower level. There are lots of hanging cut-outs as well as children's toys. The library also has a large collection of sheet music from the years 1900–1950.

## San Pedro Branch Library

5600 Trumbull Avenue Southeast
(505) 256-2067                              Closed Sundays, Mondays

    This orange stucco building is housed in a pleasant neighborhood on the southeast side of Albuquerque. In keeping with the local architecture, it has few windows. The corners of the building are curved creating a soft, sensuous feeling. The interior walls are also stucco. A gently lit place, with a large children's room.

## South Valley Branch Library

3904 Isleta Boulevard Southwest                                    A
(505) 877-5170                                      Closed Sundays

    This well lit building has high, white ceilings with lots of clerestory windows. High bookshelves are spread out with lights directly over each set. Comfortably furnished reading areas around the sides of the library are next to windows on the enclosed grass patios. Purple, mauve and oak furniture rests on a gray carpet. The ceramic tile on supporting columns is a nice touch.

In the mode of many New Mexico buildings, this neighborhood library is enclosed by a protective stucco wall. The roof of the library is visible over it, and inside, patios surround the building.

The large children's section has cushioned alcoves built into the wall for small kids. Kids get to climb into a wall, sit and read. Each alcove has its own individual reading light. Outside the children's room there's a lovely trellis-covered grassy amphitheatre for storytelling. The building was designed by Jorge De La Torre of Albuquerque.

## Special Collections Branch Library

| | |
|---|---|
| 423 Central Avenue Northeast | A |
| (505) 848-1376 | Closed Sundays, Mondays |

Inside a handsome Pueblo style building, tall log posts support heavy beams above a dark red floor covered with handwoven rugs.

Albuquerque, NM
Special Collections Branch

Low adobe walls divide interior areas. Above two fireplaces and the south door are decorations signed by Gustav Bauman, Santa Fe's accomplished wood-block printer of the 1930s.

This was Albuquerque's main library from 1925 until 1975. Now it holds one of the largest genealogical collections in the Southwest and a very large New Mexico collection. The New Mexico section, off the main room, has handcrafted tables, chairs and wooden bookshelves.

As part of the locally funded Center for the Book there's an extensive display of various types of bookbinding. The project teaches children about printing, book binding, the history of books, writing, etc. Children in the program get to handle, look at and read old leather-bound books. Visitors to the library can see the replicas of the Ben Franklin Press and the Gutenberg Press used by the children in the program.

# —— CARLSBAD ——

## Carlsbad Public Library

101 South Halagueno T
(505) 885-6776 Open every day

This older library shares a building with the Carlsbad Municipal Museum and Art Center. An interesting Mission/Pueblo style building, it sits in the middle of a park-like block surrounded by live oaks. Built in the 1930s, the library has been enlarged several times.

This is a plain library, which has grown in fairly unplanned fashion. The children's section has a nice wooden floor with rugs around for kids to sit on. There's a good deal of reference material in the library on the Waste Isolation Pilot Plant (WIPP) low-level radioactive storage project that is being developed in this area. There's also an active genealogical section.

The museum is the Carlsbad Municipal Fine Arts Museum. One side is a fairly large collection of Native American and early pioneer artifacts; saddles, barbed wire, quilts. On the other side are both some good contemporary art and older photographs by Ray V. Davis and his old heavy duty view cameras. And there's a gallery of art for sale—mostly the works of Taos artists.

This complex is a good place for cooling off or resting while someone else explores Carlsbad Caverns National Park (twenty miles away) or the nearby Living Desert State Park.

## —— CLOVIS ——

### Clovis–Carver Public Library

701 North Main
(505) 769-7840   Closed Sundays

You'd never guess that this library, with its monumental front, is a converted Sears store. Completely remodeled, it opened as a library in 1992. The Curiosity Corner in the children's area is decorated to resemble a playground so new readers feel comfortable. Library usage has boomed since the new building was opened. As an extra added attraction, this surprising new library has a 400-year-old Latin bible.

Clovis isn't really on the way to anywhere, but it is a pleasant county seat. It was originally known as Riley's Switch, and now this agricultural center is best known as home to Cannon Air Force Base.

## —— CORRALES ——

### Corrales Community Library

84 La Entrada Road   A, E
(505) 897-0733   Closed Sundays

Just as a log cabin library fits perfectly in the mountain country of Jackson, Wyoming, this tiny Pueblo style building is perfect for a New Mexico town of 3,000. And this is indeed a small rural town: a fully saddled white horse tied up next door started to prance and neigh as we walked up. The neighborhood watch horse? Still, Corrales is just a few miles northwest of Albuquerque.

Typical of this style of architecture, the building is not striking from the outside. Inside, though, light floods into the building through a skylight illuminating brick floors, scattered handwoven rugs, hanging

Corrales, NM
Corrales Community Library

clay flower pots, clay bell light fixtures and a sunken goldfish pond surrounded by greenery.

The ceilings are wood planks, supported by viga beams, the stripped tree trunks of this type of architecture. The vigas were cut and stripped by local residents, as were the massive wooden lintels and door frames. In fact, this entire library was built by the townspeople.

The shelves are solid, old, dark wood, used not for aesthetic purposes but because that's what was available. A kivalike whitewalled southwestern room has delightful leather and wood chairs and couches and a corner fireplace. This is one of the warmest small libraries we've been in. It's a good way to see inside a particularly private style of architecture.

## —— GALLUP ——

### Octavia Fellin Public Library

115 West Hill
(505) 863-1291                                                        Closed Sundays

This is yet another of those New Mexico libraries that can fool you. You can't see much from the outside, but inside you'll find a significant collection of paintings from the federal projects of the 1930s, including the Works Projects Administration (WPA) and the Public Works of Art Project. The building is connected to a performing arts wing.

You can find both a good children's collection and an outstanding Southwest collection. There's not much between Flagstaff, Arizona, and Albuquerque, New Mexico, so this is a good place for a break. But be careful about driving in Gallup on weekends. Gallup supports a lot of serious drinkers; the library even has a special collection on alcoholism.

## —— LAS CRUCES ——

### Thomas Branigan Memorial Library

200 East Picacho Avenue
(505) 526-1047                                              Closed Sundays in summer

Chocolate brown is an unusual color for a library, and one shaped like the prow of a large boat is even more unusual. But that's what you'll find here, in a building that is also unique in having almost two-thirds of its public areas recessed into the ground.

The building has several levels in its main open space. Since much of the library was built underground to preserve energy, there are no outside views. But the building is large, and you get more of an open feeling as you get into the middle. In the center, the main room is two and one half stories high, with wood trim around the sides simulating a mezzanine. There are reading areas all around and in the center of the main room.

In the large children's room a marvelous doll house, The Adobe Hacienda, is in the Pueblo style so kids can relate to the local architecture. The room is divided into smaller spaces to be more comfortable for children.

A 1992 remodeling moved the administrative offices to a new upper floor, and opened up new space for the New Mexico and genealogical collections, as well as providing space for a well-equipped, public-use microcomputer room. Cat lovers might want to check out the library's sizeable feline collection (but for real feline fanatics, the place to go is the main public library in Glendale, California).

An old rolling ladder runs along a wall where hundreds of framed prints hang, available for circulation but also making a classic salon-style art display. There's a significant amount of art on permanent display, including *Refractor*, a mural by Glenn Schwaiger, made of 748 4-inch x 4-inch square mirrors.

Las Cruces, the second largest city in New Mexico, is only an hour north of the Mexican border, and like many cities in Mexico it has the very poor and the very rich, the old and the new. If all you've seen is historic districts and upscale shops, drive through some local barrios and you'll get a different feeling.

# —— LAS VEGAS ——

## Carnegie Public Library

500 National Avenue
(505) 454-1401                                                    Closed Mondays

A Neo-Classical Revival domed library modeled after Thomas Jefferson's home Monticello would be unusual enough anyplace, but to find it in the foothills of the Sangre de Cristo Mountains 65 miles east of Santa Fe, New Mexico, is amazing. Add to this a laid-back town of 16,000 with over 900 houses on the National Register of Historic Places and you get a real hidden treasure.

The Las Vegas Public Library is one of only three Carnegie libraries built in New Mexico, and the only one still functioning as a library. Pleasantly old-fashioned, it lets you see what a Carnegie library looked like in 1902. Obviously well maintained and cared for, it sits in the

Las Vegas, NM
Carnegie Public Library

middle of a park and so dominates the area that the walking tour around here is of the Carnegie District.

The children's room is downstairs. The library has a small Southwest collection in its own room, and a special collection on the *penitentes*, a sect which engages in self-flagellation.

Las Vegas is fascinating in its multiplicity of architectural styles and in the different way that the two halves of the city are laid out. When the railroad arrived in 1879, scores of Victorian, Italianente, and stone houses were built in contrast to the older parts of town with their more traditional New Mexican architecture. Make sure to visit the Chamber of Commerce and get a set of its illustrated walking tour guides, one of which contains a brief description of the library. You'll probably find at least one example of every type of house built in America between 1880 and 1940.

## —— LOVINGTON ——

### Lovington Public Library

115 Main Street
(505) 396-3144                                              Closed Sundays

Lovington may be most famous for its annual lizard race, but in fact it should get a lot of credit for an innovative reuse of an older building. In 1991 an old Ford dealership and garage was reopened as Lovington's new library, after a major renovation.

This is one more example of what you may find in out-of-the-way places. Lovington is in a desert area, much more involved in the oil industry than in the tourism business. In fact, the library's books on tape are often used by people driving out to the oil rigs.

## —— ROSWELL ——

### Roswell Public Library

| | |
|---|---:|
| 301 North Pennsylvania Avenue | A, E |
| (505) 622-7101 | Open every day |

This is the architecture of contrasts. Prominent vertical walls of randomly shaped flat New Mexico stone stand in striking angles to plain stucco walls. A roof of curved red tiles adds further contrast. Trees along a low stone wall line the walkway into the library.

Inside the angular wood and glass entryway, large laminated beams support a paneled ceiling in this bright, many-sided building. Even the bookshelves are bright. Some of them are blue, some maroon and some green. Occasional banners hang from the angled ceilings. There are remarkably few places in this library where two walls or the ceiling and a wall meet at right angles.

There are areas for relaxing in couches, and study areas with tables and straight chairs. In one corner there's a "quiet" area, in another part of the library a "teen" reading area. This segregation is suggested, not enforced, but it lets teens hang out with their friends, feel comfortable and not annoy older people or feel annoyed by them.

The children's room has a carpeted floor, lots of chairs and some mini-couches. Lots of papier-mâché figures add to its cheer, as do boxes of toys. This section accounts for almost 40 percent of the library's circulation. There's also a large Southwest collection. The original building was designed by Alley and Associates in 1978, with a recent addition by Dick Waggoner of Roswell.

## — RUIDOSO —

### Ruidoso Public Library

| | |
|---|---|
| Suddreth and Junction Road (505) 257-4335 | Closed Sundays |

This unassuming, pale yellow building is in a lovely site at the base of a hill. The library is friendly and inviting. Its bookshelves are framed in darker wood. There's gentle light throughout, some from a small barrel-vaulted skylight. In the reference section there's a good collection of pictures of Ruidoso before it was "discovered" and became a mountain tourist mecca.

The music section is equipped with a compact disc player and headset, so if you're tired out from skiing (or broke from going to the races at nearby Ruidoso Downs) you can relax here. The children's room also has a tape deck.

In Ruidoso you can go skiing or antique shopping or to the races. Try to get out of the center of town and drive along some of the smaller roads. There aren't big grandiose lodges, just cabins that look as if they belong here in the woods.

## — SANTA FE —

### Santa Fe Public Library

| | |
|---|---|
| 145 Washington Avenue (505) 984-6780 | Open every day |

A major attraction in this library is its very large Southwest collection. It's in a splendid reading room with a high beamed and paneled ceiling, parquet floor, solid wood tables and hand-carved chairs. Mexican-style chandeliers and black iron reading lamps on the individual tables make this a classic Southwest reading room.

In the heart of downtown Santa Fe, this former city hall is a block from the central plaza. Built in 1936 and extensively remodeled as a library in 1987, it looks like something you would expect to find in

Sante Fe, NM
Sante Fe Public Library

New Orleans. A covered balcony with white columns and balustrade seem a bit out of place in this town of Spanish Colonial and Pueblo style architecture.

The floor of the two-story entryway is tiled. Ahead is a wooden circulation desk and above, a barrel-vaulted skylight illuminates a semicircular mezzanine. The children's section is on the upper floor. There's a fireplace, in front of which are adult and children's rocking chairs. If you want to know what's going on in town, check out the huge bulletin boards.

*Also of Note:*

## History Library/Photo Archives

110 Washington Avenue
(505) 827-6470                                    Closed Saturdays, Sundays

Across the street from the Main Library, the Museum of New Mexico maintains both a photographic archive and a history library. These new quarters, which were being refinished at the time of this writing, are in the space that used to be occupied by the Main Library. These facilities welcome the general public, although they are oriented toward researchers.

The photographic archives are particularly outstanding, with over 450,000 items available. For those interested in researching the work of a particular photographer, the photographs are cross-indexed by artist. Naturally the History Library (an outgrowth of the State Historical Society), has an outstanding collection of New Mexico History.

## Laboratory of Anthropology Library

708 Camino Lejo
(505) 827-6344                                                    Closed Sundays

This is the library of the Museum of Indian Arts and Culture. It's one of four fascinating museum facilities side by side on Camino Lejo, just a few miles from the Plaza. The drive along Old Santa Fe Trail to Camino Lejo gets you away from the downtown scene, and you see that Pueblo Revival buildings with their gently rounded red-orange walls look even better when surrounded by desert brush.

The library is in a Pueblo Revival building next to the Museum of Arts and Culture. Some of the collection is in the museum's resource center, but if you want more information than you can get there, try the library. It's a well-staffed, noncirculating reference library. You can't browse the library shelves, but the collection is fully cataloged.

The museum itself is modern and monumental, tall with lots of open space, perhaps a little out of keeping with its collection of Native American artifacts. The high-rising main hall with huge laminated beams supporting a three story ceiling houses an outstanding collection of Native American Pottery. The museum's snack bar serves Native American dishes.

## The Library Bookstop

4250 Cerrillos Road (Villa Linda Mall)
(505) 473-7280                                        Open afternoons, every day

If you get tired of the small and crowded streets of downtown Santa Fe, come out to this huge shopping center on Cerrillos Road at the intersection with Rodeo Road. Inside, next to the entrance to J. C. Penney, is The Library Bookstop.

This plain, unassuming library with its mauve rug and blue walls is a useful place in which to rest your feet while shopping or to park a nonshopper in your party while you stock up for more of your trip.

## Museum of International Folk Art Library

705 Camino Lejo
(505) 827-6350                                        Closed Saturdays, Sundays
Also closed Mondays in January and February

This is the library of the world's largest museum of folk art. While the Hispanic Heritage Wing of the museum features Spanish Colonial New Mexico art, its collection has folk art from over 100 countries. All 12,000 volumes are in open stacks and available for browsing although they do not circulate. The staff is small but very helpful.

You will certainly find the *Handbook of North American Indians* in the library, but you'll also see books on Mexican cult figures, French folk art, China's crafts, the folk art of Japan, and a beautifully illustrated leather-bound copy of all 13 volumes of the limited edition *History of Egypt,* published at the turn of the century (and much, much more).

This is a major museum with over 125,000 artifacts in its collection. It's huge, and in contrast to the Museum of Indian Arts and Culture, its architecture is secondary to the exhibits, which are stunning in size and diversity.

## New Mexico State Library

325 Don Gaspar
(505) 827-3800                                              Closed Saturdays, Sundays

On Thursday and Friday afternoons you can do more than read about the Southwest—you can talk with a trained historian about the area's history. Go to the Southwest room on the third floor of the State Library, where there's also a good collection of material on New Mexico in handsome hand-carved bookcases. You'll be able to recognize the building by the white wooden columns of the colonnade along the front. It's only four blocks from the central plaza.

The rest of the library's collection is primarily focused on governmental affairs.

# —— TAOS ——

## Harwood Public Library

238 Ledoux Street                                                              H, T
(505) 758-3063                                                        Closed Sundays

If you get lost looking for this combined museum and library, just ask any resident for directions to the "Harwood." Part of this meandering adobe Pueblo Revival building is 170 years old; parts were built with WPA funds in the 1930s. The columns supporting the wood-

Taos, NM
Harwood Public Library

timbered ceilings are simple stripped tree trunks. The well-worn floors weren't made of wood strictly for aesthetics, but because that's what floors were made out of when the building was constructed.

The library winds from room to room, with massive wooden door frames and lintels. The furniture is classic, solid Southwest. The children's room is in a building next door to the main library. A large Southwest collection has its own special room. This is a well-worn library, in fact, it's kind of beat-up and funky, but it truly represents the Taos of the past, not some of the more modern and glitzy developments you'll see today. The library is used often, as befits a library in a town that has six bookstores (including the oldest one in the state).

The museum upstairs has truly classic Pueblo features, heavy dark wooden beams (vigas) that pierce the walls and can be seen outside, supporting a ceiling of stripped aspens (latillas). The collection features paintings, drawings, prints, sculptures and photographs by artists of Taos.

Amidst Taos's collection of galleries, shops, pueblos, museums, skiing and a slew of other tourist attractions, this is a nice place for a little quiet contemplation (or at least recuperation).

# ──── TRUTH OR CONSEQUENCES ────

## Truth or Consequences Public Library

325 Library Lane
(505) 894-3027                                              Closed Sundays

What stands out about this library is its generous size in a town of only 5,000. (In case you haven't heard, local usage for the town's name is "T or C.") The children's room has a toy-lending library as well as fuzzy toys for kids to play with in the library. Naturally, there's a special collection of Southwestern and genealogical materials. There's also a set of computers available for public use.

The library is the only new building in a school complex that has been converted to general municipal use. It's near a senior citizens' building; the seniors were very influential in helping get this facility constructed. The complex sits just below a water tank vividly painted with a mural commemorating a Native American peace treaty. The mural, supported by local citizens who formed Water Tanks Inc., was painted by Tony Pennock, a Las Cruces artist who specializes in water tank murals.

Surprisingly, many of the recreational opportunities in this desert area are water-oriented: hot springs in town and water sports at the Elephant Butte Reservoir. North along the Rio Grande is the Bosque del Apache Wildlife Refuge. The library can be a refuge from the outdoors, if you would like some inside recreation. Construction of public tennis courts is planned for an area next to it.

# —— TUCUMCARI ——

## Kenneth Schlientz Memorial Library

602 South Second Street
(505) 461-0295                                                    Closed Sundays

Tucumcari is about halfway between Albuquerque and Amarillo. Its library looks as if it were made out of concrete blocks standing on end. There are also some unique copper decorations along one side of the building.

On your right as you come in is a children's room with brightly colored wall panels; on your left is the main library room with comfortable upholstered chairs and couches.

Tucumcari is in the middle of nowhere and a long way from anywhere (except for Conchas Lake State Park, 31 miles north) so it's a good place for a driving break.

# —— ALBANY ——

## Albany Public Library

| | |
|---|---|
| 1390 Waverly Drive Southeast | T |
| (503) 967-4304 | Closed Sundays |

 This contemporary pink stucco building is several miles from Albany's three separate historic districts, where you can find 150 historic buildings, including beautifully preserved examples of every major architectural style popular in the United States since 1850.

 The library is only a few blocks from the freeway and right around the corner from a major shopping center. Angled ceilings allow for clerestory windows that let in a lot of light. Laminated trusses (supported by laminated columns) cross the ceiling. Windows look out to enclosed gardens and there is a small outdoor children's story area with mushroomlike concrete benches. A good place for someone to stay who is not interested in accompanying you as you walk, bike or drive through old Albany.

## Downtown Branch Library

| | |
|---|---|
| 302 South Ferry Street | T, H |
| (503) 967-4308 | Closed Saturdays, Sundays, Mondays (not Accesible) |

 This is an old Carnegie library in Albany's downtown historic district. Local authorities wanted to close it after the new branch was opened, but citizens raised enough money (and hell) to keep it open. Unfortunately, it's not wheelchair accessible and only open four days a week. It is a good place to stop, though, if you get overloaded from looking at Federal, Classic Revival, Gothic Revival, Italianate, French Second Empire, Stick and Eastlake, Colonial Revival, Queen Anne, Craftsman, American Renaissance and Bungalow houses, all well preserved in Albany.

 Or, you might get lucky, and someone will be as kind to you as Bill Bush, the owner of Marshall House, was to us. He invited two tired authors to sit on his porch and rest up before pressing on to explore more libraries.

# ASHLAND

## Ashland Branch Library, Jackson County Library System

410 Siskiyou Boulevard  
(503) 482-1197

T  
Closed Sundays

This solid old Carnegie has not changed much since it was built in 1912. Directly outside the side entrance is a quiet grassy area with benches for relaxed outdoor reading. The library is only a few blocks from the three theaters that house the famous Oregon Shakespeare Festival.

The library has a large drama collection, along with a large Oregon collection. Its Shakespeare selection is good, but the collection of rare and unusual Shakespearean works has been transferred to a nearby college library.

One way of getting tickets to the often sold-out plays is to hang out in Shakespeare Plaza and try to buy them from people who have changed their minds or who have not picked up their tickets from the box office. This may take a couple of hours, so someone might wish to wait in the library (unless, of course they choose to relax in beautiful Lithia Park). This is also a good place to shelter if the ski conditions at nearby Mt. Ashland get rough.

# ASTORIA

## Astoria Public Library

450 Tenth Street  
(503) 325-7323

Closed Sundays in summer

Never judge a book by its cover—and don't judge libraries just by their outside appearance. Once you get past this one's dull exterior, you'll find a welcoming, useable library.

There's a significant Scandinavian influence in Astoria, and its library has a modest collection of Norwegian and Finnish books. For instance, on the open shelves there is an 1898 leather-bound edition of

Henrik Ibsen in Norwegian. On the main floor of the library there is a local history collection as well as general material on the Northwest.

Astoria is an interesting old working port, with attractions like the Columbia River Maritime Museum. The Victorian buildings haven't been restored as much as well maintained in use since they were built. Besides exercise, the Astoria Column (164 steps lead to the top of this 125-foot tower on top of 569-foot Coxcomb Hill) provides a spectacular aerial view of the Columbia River Bar and its environs.

## —— CANNON BEACH ——

### Cannon Beach Library

| | |
|---|---|
| 131 North Hemlock | T |
| No telephone | Closed Sundays in summer |
| Closed Sundays, Mondays, Wednesdays, Fridays in winter | |

Shop, shop, shop—sun, sun, sun—beach, beach, beach, and when you get done, come into the library to rest up. This lovely gray building, with its vertical wood planks and a shingled roof, fits right into the scene of the busy tourist facilities of Cannon Beach.

The library is cozy and comfortable with a stone fireplace and mantel taking up most of the wall at one end—the answer to tired feet or empty pockets. The library gets no tax support but is totally supported and staffed by local volunteers and the money they raise and contribute.

Only two hours from Portland (79 miles on US 26) Cannon beach is no longer a quiet artist colony. Its 7 miles of white sand beach spread out from a collection of boutiques, galleries, resorts and restaurants.

## —— COOS BAY ——

### Coos Bay Public Library

| | |
|---|---|
| 525 West Anderson | |
| (503) 269-1101 | Closed Sundays |

This is another building more pleasing internally than externally. Outside, the building is dark and plain—inside, while rather crowded, the high central ceiling and hanging globe lights add lots of warmth. Windows from the reading room look out into a pleasant planted area. The Helene Stack Bower Oregon Collection is a large collection on Oregon—some of it open, other parts closed.

Coos Bay is at the southern end of the Oregon Dunes National Recreation Area, which extends 41 miles north to Florence. This is only one of many parks surrounding this area. Don't miss the beautiful formal gardens in Shore Acres State Park. There are also a surprising number of museums and theaters around here.

# —— CORVALLIS ——

## Corvallis–Benton County Public Library

645 Northwest Monroe Avenue  A
(503) 757-6927  Open every day

This splendid library is within walking distance of the beautiful 500-acre campus of Oregon State University. It faces Central Park, an idyllic setting complete with rose garden, lawns, gazebo and children's playground. Across the Park are the First Christian Church and the Corvallis Art Center.

Corvallis, OR
Corvallis-Benton County Public Library

The original building, designed by Pietro Belluschi in 1932, was 5,200 square feet. Enlarged to 22,000 square feet in 1965, it just reopened after a topflight expansion to 57,000 square feet designed by Cardwell/Thomas Associates of Seattle. The original brick chapel-like structure of the Belluschi design with its grand entrance and leaded windows is so well integrated into the newer structures that it's hard to tell where one stops and the other begins.

After a rather austere foyer, you enter the main library under a 20-foot-square skylight pouring light past a mezzanine floor above. On your right is a huge children's and young adult room, separated from the main adult reading room by a long windowed wall. The children's section has a number of alcoves and storytelling areas along with a generous sprinkling of computers.

The ground floor reading room is comfortable and useable with white and chrome art nouveau light fixtures hanging from the ceiling. The original 1935 library is now just a reading room, but what a room! A beautiful dark wood paneled ceiling arches over a space with lots and lots of upholstered wing chairs, wooden bookcases along the sides and soft light filtering in through leaded glass windows.

On the second floor the peaked metal corrugated roof in the main room, supported by metal trusses, is a total contrast to the materials used in the old library, but an evocation of its shape. Oddly enough, it works, even though the materials used are so different.

## —— EUGENE ——

### Eugene Public Library

100 West 13th Avenue
(503) 341-5805                                         Closed Sundays in summer

This plain 1959 building, typical of institutional architecture of that period, is so busy that one of the librarians says he now gets bored when he visits more sedate institutions. It's so crowded that the upstairs art gallery is also used as a reading room. Books, shelves, art—everything is crammed on top of everything else. A friendly, top-notch staff, also.

In Eugene's downtown area, this is a good place to come and either get more information about the incredible choice of activities around here, or to rest up from participating in so many of them. The library is about a mile from the campus of the University of Oregon, with its fascinating old art museum and magnificent trees.

## —— FLORENCE ——

### Siuslaw Public Library

| | |
|---|---:|
| 1460 9th Street | A |
| (503) 997-3132 | Closed Sundays |

    This pleasant, new, low-slung wood and tile building is topped by a cupola reminiscent of some of the lighthouses you see along the coast. A black tile roof sets off gray and white walls. Residents of Florence are so proud (and rightfully so) of this library (designed by Richard Turi of North Bend, Oregon) that they bring visitors here when showing them the local sights.

    The open, main reading room has a unique ceiling—while the dark truss structure is peaked, the white ceiling carries on upwards on one side to provide for a significant bank of clerestory windows. Other lighting is provided by sconce lights bouncing light off the white ceilings.

    Oak and fir are used heavily; the bookshelves (not just the end panels) are light wood. Shades and chairs are raspberry colored, in contrast to the mauve tops of the wooden tables. Wooden ceiling sections and lowered panels are used to break up the feeling of one large

Florence, OR
Siuslaw Public Library

room. The ceiling of the children's room was further lowered to help isolate sound.

Florence was temporarily home to the late Frank Herbert, author of the *Dune* science fiction series. Herbert developed the concept for his series while studying the ecology of the huge sand dunes that stretch south of Florence and make this a popular tourist area. The library has a separate room for its special collection of over a thousand volumes from Herbert's private reference library.

## —— GRESHAM ——

### Gresham Branch Library, Library Association of Portland

385 Northwest Miller Avenue
(503) 248-5387                                               Closed Mondays

    This large, unusual building is off-white with blue and turquoise trim. It's a contemporary version of an Art Deco building. Two of the window walls have cantilevered sections reaching out over truncated glassed-in corners that let in light and also let you see into the library. Tiles in the entryway are blue and off white, matching the white walls and blue and turquoise exterior trim. The building's architect was SERA Architects of Portland, Oregon.

    The library is essentially one room with a large reading area with upholstered chairs and reading tables in the center. In front of a window at the back is a bronze sculpture of a woman reading. The quality of the lighting is outstanding; banks of inverted fluorescent lights run under the white ceiling in huge squares, reflecting bright light into the library. Two large skylights provide additional light.

    The old Gresham Carnegie library, built in 1913, is nearby at the corner of Main and Northeast Fourth street. Now a museum, it's a Tudor half-timbered building with lovely drooping trees out in front. It has lots of leaded glass windows and intricately patterned brickwork walls.

Hood River, OR
Hood River County Library

## —— HOOD RIVER ——

### Hood River County Library

| | |
|---|---|
| 502 State Street | V |
| (503) 386-2535 | Closed Sundays |

Hood River has a Carnegie library that was built in 1923 and remodeled in 1969. It features a large rectangular room with a high white ceiling supported by dark trusses. A set of angled arches along the sides form a colonnade within the room.

On the north wall leaded windows look out over the Columbia River. So many people sailboard out in the river that on a summer day when you look through the trees it looks as if the river has fleas.

The library is at the top of a steeply sloped grassy park—a great place for kids to roll on lawns. During the summer every other car that goes by has a sailboard or a bicycle on top, some both. Lots of stores sell sailboarding equipment, from frames to sails to clothes to boards. The library would certainly be a good place for someone in the party who doesn't sailboard.

## —— KLAMATH FALLS ——

### Klamath County Library

| 126 South Third Street<br>(503) 882-8894 | Closed Saturdays, Sundays in summer<br>Closed Sundays, Mondays in winter |
|---|---|

Several reading areas in this two-story, block-long building look out on gardens. All of the public services are located on the first floor. Aspiring writers might be interested in checking out the library's sizeable Small Press Collection.

While this area is struggling economically, there is a lot to do, whether it's walking to the nearby Favell Museum of Western Art and Indian Artifacts (to view a collection of thousands of arrowheads) or taking the fairly adventurous drive north 55 miles to Crater Lake.

## —— LAKE OSWEGO ——

### Lake Oswego Public Library

| 706 Fourth Street<br>(503) 636-7628 | Closed Sundays in summer |
|---|---|

This suburban library is inconspicuously tucked behind a lot of large leafy trees in the middle of a residential neighborhood. It's really a good example of suburban Portland life.

You'll enter a brick patio in this two-story, brown, wooden building. The second floor, part of which creates a mezzanine around the main downstairs area, is very open. Clerestory windows in a sawtooth ceiling let in lots of natural light. There are many windowside reading nooks and bay window sections with comfortable chairs.

The children's room (with a good storytelling section) and the main reading room with more comfortable chairs and its large periodical collection are on the main floor.

# MANZANITA

## Manzanita Branch Library, Tillamook County Library System

571 Laneda Avenue  
(503) 368-6665

A  
Closed Sundays

Manzanita, 21 miles south of bustling Cannon Beach, is low key and residentially oriented. The library is just off Highway 101, built right into the pines. It's a shingle building with wooden bracing all around. The posts, the supports and all the hardware show careful, hand-crafted woodwork.

Outside one of the reading room areas of this small library is an enclosed exterior reading area. Inside, upholstered chairs sit next to the windows, some looking out at pine trees, others at a small garden landscaped in Japanese style.

Although the library is small, it's divided into several sitting areas. Light wood, gray carpets, and maroon and yellow walls lend a feeling of creative care to the design. Wood ceilings contrast well with these strong colors. Go on down the road past the library and you get to a beautiful stretch of uncrowded beach.

# MCMINNVILLE

## McMinnville Public Library

225 North Adams  
(503) 434-7308

Closed Sundays, April through December

The McMinnville Public Library reflects its town, solid, peaceful—and a little old. An ivy-covered brick building, this 1912 Carnegie (remodeled in 1982) sits in a park near huge spreading trees.

McMinnville is the center of Oregon's wine country. The library might serve as a temporary resting place if you've visited one winery too many.

# MOUNT ANGEL

## Mount Angel Abbey Library

Mount Angel Abbey, St. Benedict  
(503) 845-3317

A, E  
Open every day

The Mount Angel Abbey and Library is in truck farming country in the Willamette Valley, one mile outside of Mount Angel. Up a 300-foot hill on a parklike road is a large, formal quadrangle of buildings on a huge lawn. The public is welcome at the abbey and the library.

This outstanding library was designed by the late Finnish architect Alvar Aalto. The entrance is on an upper floor. When you enter, you face a large curving section of bookshelves, and then as you move forward and look down, you see a curving mezzanine and then a further, lower, curving section of bookshelves. The mezzanine and balcony have long, black-topped, uninterrupted reading desks with individual lights for each reader. High clerestory windows spread gentle light throughout.

Mount Angel, OR  
Mount Angel Abbey Library  
Curved study desks with lamps

The furnishings, the reading desks, lights, stools and chairs were all designed by the architect. Blond wood contrasts beautifully with white walls, gray carpets and black desk tops.

The Fall Rare Book Room displays a portion of the library's 5,000-volume antiquarian theology collection. The general collection is not solely devoted to religious and philosophic works, and you may find the latest issues of the computer magazine *Byte* next to works of a French religious scholar printed in 1865. The library also has a large collection of material on the American Civil War, and its periodical room has current issues of 600 publications, mostly of religious or philosophical content.

# NEWPORT

## Newport Public Library

35 Northwest Nye Street
(503) 265-2153                                                   Open every day

Near the Performing and Visual Arts Centers, this 1985 library stands out with its walls of brown tile and gray-green wood. The same tile is used inside.

This is one of those buildings that looks larger once you enter, especially since you don't at first realize that you are entering on an upper level and that there is a full lower floor to the rear and below. The reference room and a friendly children's room are on the lower level.

Comfortable chairs sit in front of a fireplace painted with Northwest Indian designs in the bright main reading room. Oak furniture with blue upholstery goes well with blue carpets. One of the two cats in residence is Marian the Librarian; the other is Benjamin Franklin.

*Also of Note:*

## Hatfield Marine Science Center

2030 Marine Science Drive
(503) 867-0100                                            Closed Saturdays, Sundays

This huge research library is not part of the spectacular Northwest Coast Aquarium just off Highway 101 South of Newport. It's in the back of another fascinating aquarium, this one at Oregon State University's Hatfield Marine Science Center about a half mile from the Northwest Coast aquarium.

If you want any more information on marine subjects after having exhausted the nearby aquariums this would be the place to come. This huge facility is a plain modern structure with laminated beams and high clerestory windows, and its rows of shelves seem to go on for as far as you can see.

## —— NORTH BEND ——

### North Bend Public Library

1800 Sherman Avenue
(503) 756-0400                                                  Closed Sundays

It's hard to believe that this brick building with its dark tinted windows was designed by Richard Turi (of North Bend) who created the light, wooden library in Florence, Oregon. This building has a much sterner and more institutional feeling. Its all brick structure is highlighted by curved windows on the corners and a large transparent barrel vault at the entrance. The curved windows are much more pleasing from inside the building.

It is also an interesting difference in design from the library at Boulder, Colorado, where large expanses of clear glass were used to invite passersby to see the activity inside. Here you have no idea what's going on inside.

The tile and brick entrance under the clear barrel vault displays bright banners announcing local tourist attractions. Inside, while there is a nicely separated children's section, you are almost overwhelmed by crowds of bookshelves. The library has an extensive Oregon collection.

Portland, OR
Multnomah County Library

## —— PORTLAND ——

### Multnomah County Library

| | |
|---|---|
| 801 Southwest Tenth Avenue | T, H |
| (503) 248-5123 | Open every day |

Slow down for a moment before you enter this grand old building and take time to read some of the three hundred names of notable historic characters carved into its stone panels. Admire the other carvings in limestone friezes and sculptured balustrades. This lovely Georgian building, built in 1912, deserves its place in the National Register of Historic Places.

Inside, marble columns support the entry hall ceiling, and a splendid marble staircase goes all the way up to the fifth floor. The reading room on the ground floor suffers from heavy use by not particularly careful clients, but the John Wilson Room on the second floor houses a 6,000-volume rare book collection. The second floor also has large reading rooms for literature and history, government documents, and business. The rooms are classically tall, with high windows and off-white walls. Currently the rooms are somewhat obscured by scaffolding as a protection against structural weaknesses that have been found in the building.

The Friends Gallery under a lovely cupola on the third floor has fascinating exhibits ranging from Blues Memorabilia to Women Printmakers to Audubon's Animals and Birds.

As well as being only a few blocks from the main cultural centers in downtown Portland, the library is diagonally across from The Real Mother Goose, one of the finest art and gift shops around.

## North Portland Branch Library

| | |
|---|---:|
| 512 North Killingsworth Street | A |
| (503) 248-5394 | Closed Sundays, Mondays, Fridays |

This lovingly restored half-timbered period Carnegie was originally built in 1913. One section of the chapel-like interior has a high ceiling supported by dark arched beams with carvings of famous authors in the brackets supporting them. Some rooms have coffered plaster ceilings with fluorescent lights reflecting from them.

The building is reminiscent of a Gothic church, both in terms of the arches and its crosslike layout, with the large main room going from front to rear, while the children's room is to one side and a general reading room is on the other.

The library has a Black resources collection, fittingly, as this area of Portland has the highest percentage of African-American residents.

Portland, OR
North Portland Branch

*Also of Note:*

## Oregon Historical Society Library

1230 Southwest Park Avenue
(503) 222-1741                               Closed Sundays, Mondays

This is a wonderful library, in the heart of Portland's cultural district. The Portland Art Museum is directly across the street. The Performing Arts Center and the Schnitzer Concert Hall are next door. The library, on the third floor of the Oregon Historical Society building, is a fabulous research facility, specializing in Oregon and Northwest history. The museum alone is well worth a visit.

The library has over 100,000 volumes in its collection, including pamphlets and rare books, newspaper clippings on 4,000 subjects, 8,500 linear feet of original documents and manuscripts, 20,000 maps and over 2,500,000 items in its photograph collection.

The photograph collection is well cataloged and cross-indexed. Name the subject, go to the card catalog (oversized) and you can probably find a picture of the subject that interests you. There are small copies of the photos attached to the card file, and prints can be purchased at nominal prices.

## —— SALEM ——

### Salem Public Library

| | |
|---|---|
| 585 Liberty Street Southeast | A |
| (503) 558-6071 | Closed Sundays in summer |

This large, recently remodeled library sits across a wide plaza from City Hall Salem Civic Center. In the plaza, the 1988 Peace Wall is engraved with marvelous quotations:
"An eye for an eye makes the whole world blind."

Salem, OR
Salem Public Library

"Peace is not a season, it's a way of life."
"Our goal must be not peace in our time but peace for all time."
"The only thing necessary for the triumph of evil is for good men to do nothing."

Walk by the fountain in the plaza and listen to the lovely thrum of water hitting bronze walls. On the ground floor of the library there's a coffee shop and, in good weather, tables out front. Get a book and a cup of coffee and relax in the plaza.

The library is elegant. Local architects Settecase, Smith, Doss did a splendid remodeling and expansion. Expanses of dark green carpet, concrete walls, wooden banisters, good upholstered wooden furniture and wood-trimmed bookshelves all have a clean contemporary look. So many works of art have been placed in the library that there is a special brochure describing them.

The high ceiling of the spacious main reading room is supported by slender concrete columns. This is a remarkably open and friendly place with mezzanines and windows all around. Several of the reading areas look over the plaza toward City Hall. Glassed-in private reading rooms allow visitors to get away from the main library's activity. The library is hugely popular and invariably busy. The formally furnished Salem Heritage Room is a quiet place to bone up on the city's history.

Children's and young adults' areas are on the second floor. In the center of the large children's room is a circular light well under a skylit cupola. It's a skylight both for the checkout desk below and the children's section. Splendid etched glass panels totally enclose the light well so light goes down but the children's noise stays above. The children's area is replete with catalog and educational computers. The Discovery Room has interactive exhibits for children.

*Also of Note:*

## Oregon State Library

Summer and Court Streets  T
(503) 378-4243  Closed Saturdays, Sundays

The Oregon State Library is in a quadrangle headed by the Oregon State Capitol and bordered by massive granite buildings. The Capitol dome is topped by a gilded 23-foot tall statue of the "Oregon Pioneer." Diagonally across from the capitol, the solid 1930s style library is decorated with bronze medallions. It's a formal building, beautifully set off by fountains and lawns.

This is primarily a legislative reference library. The reading room on the second floor is a calm, quiet, high and fully wood-paneled room. It has solid wood reading tables and chairs, and lots of reference materials. While open to the public, you'll find little light reading here outside of newspapers and periodicals. The library is also a patent depository and a national cartographic center of the U. S. Geological Society.

Outside the reading room is the Oregon Index, a beautiful room-size information index. In an era when card catalogs are being replaced by computers, this is a beautiful (if anachronistic) example of what libraries' card catalogs used to look like.

## —— SISTERS ——

### Sisters Public Library, Deschutes County Library System

164 East Main Street
(503) 549-2921                                          Closed Saturdays, Sundays

At the foothills of its namesake mountains, Sisters has a population of 700. Since 1970 building codes have required that new public and commercial buildings reflect an 1880s "western style." The town's wooden boardwalks and facades sit naturally with 10,000-foot peaks in the background.

The 2,500-square-foot library proves how, if well done, this type of design review can work. The Neal Huston Architectural firm of nearby Bend, Oregon, came up with a simple, open design in a wooden building that truly reflects the building style of early western America without being cute.

There's family skiing at nearby Hoodoo Ski Bowl and a llama herd at the Patterson ranch on the edge of town.

Sisters, OR
Sisters Library
Photo by Neal Huston, Architect

## —— THE DALLES ——

### The Dalles City–Wasco County Library

| | |
|---|---:|
| 722 Court Street | V |
| (503) 296-2815 | Closed Sundays |

There's a 150-year-old sycamore tree growing through the deck in front of this library. It keeps the deck shady during the summer, and it's made even more enjoyable by the cedar sculptures of a bear family at the tree's base. Actually it's probably more accurate to say that the library grows around the tree.

The public areas are all in one main room. A number of windowed alcoves provide well lit reading areas with pleasant views. You can see the Columbia River, Washington and Mount Adams through the trees outside the north windows.

## —— WILSONVILLE ——

### Wilsonville Public Library

8200 Southwest Wilsonville Road
(503) 682-2744                                    Closed Thursdays and Sundays

Wilsonville is a fast-growing town of 9,000 20 miles south of Portland. The library and nearby city hall are not more than a half mile from the freeway.

A brick walled building with a sweeping roof, much of the library is devoted to a large community meeting room. This is one of those buildings that looks bigger from the outside than from the inside.

There's a pleasant corner reading room for adults and a good separate children's room. This might be a convenient stop before entering or just after leaving Portland. The library is just across the street from a good sized shopping center.

# · TEXAS ·

## ABILENE

### Abilene Public Library

202 Cedar Street
(915) 677-2474       Closed Sundays

One of the nicer buildings in downtown Abilene, this multistory library has large windows and lots of light. It's about 40 years old, and is showing its age, partly because of the crowding on all of its floors. However, potted plants, trees and interesting sculptures are scattered throughout the library and there's a large aquarium in the entrance. The basement holds an extensive genealogy collection.

Abilene, with three religious colleges, has been called the "Buckle of the Bible Belt." It's also in the middle of Texas's Prairies section, not the most scenic drive in the world.

## ALPINE

### Alpine Public Library

203 North Seventh Street
(915) 837-2621       Closed Sundays

This plain library is easy to miss. It's simply two family houses joined together, and at first glance it looks like every other single-family house in the neighborhood. The city of Alpine itself is also fairly easy to miss, even though its population of 7,000 makes it the largest town in Texas's largest county. In any case, look for the sheriff's office—the library is right across the street. The rooms are all small, and you get a really private feeling as you wander from one to the next. There are several small children's rooms.

Even if you're not interested in going all the way south to Big Bend National Park, taking Interstate 10 south to the tri-city area of Alpine,

Marfa and Fort Davis is an interesting detour. The area is still range country, but you get much closer to the local mountains than if you just drive along Interstate 10. There aren't many trees here, but the scenery is varied. The drive from Interstate 10 to Fort Davis on Wild Rose Pass is glorious, even when the roses are not in season. This is classic Southwestern country, with steep rock escarpments and longhorn cattle on the range.

"Star-Date" radio program fans might note that the program is broadcast from the McDonald observatory that, with its visitor center, is just north of here outside of Fort Davis.

If this library isn't funky enough for you, drive 26 miles to Marfa, where the library is in a worn adobe building that used to be a laundromat.

# —— AMARILLO ——

## Amarillo Public Library

413 East Fourth Street  
(806) 378-3054                                              Open every day

This large two-story building has some very special collections. The William Henry Bush collection on Southwest history and the Laurence J. FitzSimon collection on the part played in Southwest history by the Catholic church are both impressive. They're in a set of formal rooms separated from the library by windowed walls and doors. This is not an open collection, but arrangements can be made with the librarians for its use.

Many of the beams along the inner sections of the library are decorated with an attractive abstract desert scene. The rows and rows of bookshelves are interspersed with comfortable reading areas. It's like walking through a forest and coming to a clearing.

The children's department takes up about half of the second floor of this large library. Marvelous soft sculptures hang from the ceiling and stuffed dinosaurs sit on top of bookshelves. The other half of the second floor is devoted to fiction.

*Also of Note:*

## American Quarter Horse Foundation Museum and Library

2601 Interstate 40 East
(806) 376-5181            Closed Saturdays, Sundays

Built in 1991, this large, modern, brick and glass building has displays and a library devoted to quarter horses. The sheer scale (along with good contemporary architecture) is amazing. The research (noncirculating) library has stud books, racing chart books, books on equine history, and it subscribes to over 250 equine periodicals. In addition, it has a significant local history collection.

# —— AUSTIN ——

## Austin Public Library

800 Guadalupe Street            A
(512) 499-7300            Open every day

Large dark-tinted windows recessed in a concrete structure give this building the look of a municipal garage, but it's actually a fine, four-story library. It used to be located next door in the building that now houses the Austin Historic Society.

Entering the library you'll be greeted by an inviting 20-foot-wide stairway to the second floor. The large concrete support columns have had their corners cut back to form planes, so the columns are almost octagonal. A large children's library is at the back of the main floor.

Past the wide stairs you can see all the way to the back of the library—and this is a long, long library. Three walls are almost all windows, and the bookshelves are low enough so the light comes in over them throughout the floor. Special collections include an outstanding map collection and genealogical collection.

Texas 227

The library's hill location gives you good views of the city from comfortable seating areas. The best view of the state capitol is from the third floor. Just in back of the library there are marvelously preserved Victorian buildings, some used as private homes and some as businesses. The library is convenient to the two main tourist areas in Austin, the upscale business area on Congress Avenue and the Sixth Street night club and country music area.

*Also of Note:*

## Austin History Center

810 Guadalupe Street  
(512) 499-7480                                                           Open every day

Housing more than 1 million items the Austin History Center (a division of the Austin Public Library) has an extensive collection of personal and family archives, local biographies, books, photographs, maps, newspapers, etc., documenting the history of Austin and Travis County. The photography archive alone has over 600,000 images.

The limestone Italian Renaissance Revival style building was built in 1932. Local craftsmen were employed to do elaborate woodwork,

Austin, TX  
Austin History Center

ornamental wrought-iron and frescoes. An impressive grand entrance has three arches with complex caps, three sets of double doors and fresco tracings.

The high-ceilinged lobby (with large chandeliers and constantly changing exhibits) and the reading room are the only public areas in the building. The reading room is formally impressive. The staff is most helpful in finding materials in the large collection. Across the street is Wooldridge Park, one of four public squares originally designated in a city plan developed in the 1880s.

## O. Henry Museum and (sort of) Library

| | |
|---|---:|
| 409 East Fifth Street | H, T |
| (512) 472-1903 | Closed Mondays, Tuesdays |

Most people don't know that the author O. Henry was actually William S. Porter, who began to use his pen name while serving a prison term (in the pen?) for embezzling from the bank where he worked in Austin. He lived in this tiny Victorian style building between 1894 and 1895. Today, modern office buildings rise just behind it.

This is a moderately well preserved little green wood house with a balcony and white trim. It opened as a museum in 1934, and while it has more memorabilia and documentation than literary works, it is of interest to O. Henry fans from around the world. The curator/librarian is extremely knowledgeable about O. Henry and willing to help you with reference requests.

## Lyndon Baines Johnson Library and Museum

| | |
|---|---:|
| 2313 Red River Street | H, T |
| (512) 482-5137 | Museum open every day; |
| | Library closed Saturdays, Sundays |

This huge, eight-story, white stone building, with a checkered stone plaza and fountain out front, looks like a giant mausoleum. It's on the campus of the University of Texas at Austin. The library houses 40 million pages of manuscripts, used primarily by scholars, and the museum has fascinating exhibits open to the general public.

The archives are kept in closed stacks. Ask for an archivist at the information desk, and someone will escort you to the reading room and help you find what you need. If you're looking for some-

Austin, TX
Lyndon Baines Johnson Library and Museum
Now these are archives!

thing specific, call first and discuss your needs with the reading room staff.

To get a feeling for the size of the collection, go up to the 8,500-square-foot Great Hall on the second floor. From there you can look up at a four-story expanse of red and gold file boxes showing through the windows of the archives above. The display, while almost overwhelming in size, invites you to explore.

The first, second and eighth floor of the building are used for fascinating museum exhibits. One of the interesting exhibits on the eighth floor is a life-size replica of the Oval Office.

## Elisabet Ney Museum and Library

304 East 44th Street
(512) 458-2255                                   Closed Mondays, Tuesdays

This fortresslike stone building resembles a tiny European castle, with cut limestone walls, a square tower and large wooden doors. The first section of the building was built in 1892, the second in 1902. You can walk up a wooden staircase to the second floor past massive cedar posts and banisters, and then go up even further into the square tower by climbing a particularly steep and narrow spiral iron staircase.

Elisabet Ney was a well-known German-born sculptor who moved to Texas in the late 19th century. This was her studio for a time, and it still holds a remarkable collection of her sculpture. There is information on her in the museum, but if anyone wants more, the tiny corner library collects material not only on Ney, but on sculpture in general.

## Texas State Library

1201 Brazos
(512) 463-5463
Closed Saturdays, Sundays;
Genealogy closed Sundays, Mondays

Just east of the largest state capitol in the country you'll find this monumental granite building, with huge columns rising the length of the building. The capitol grounds, at the foot of Congress Avenue, are large and park-like with lots of statues and greenery.

A 45-foot-wide mural dominates the lobby of the building portraying significant elements of Texas history, from Stephen B. Austin to Sam Houston, Davy Crockett and Jim Bowie. Coverage extends to everyone involved in Texas history from Spanish conquistadors to Texas oil men.

The collection is primarily state and other government records, from colonial times to the present. In addition, the library has a significant genealogical collection, including the Archives of Nuevo Leon (in Spanish), with materials dating back to 1776.

# —— BEAUMONT ——

## Beaumont Public Library

801 Pearl Street
(409) 838-6606
A
Open every day

Beaumont, strongly influenced by Cajun and African-American culture, is a "sleeper" city. In addition to good libraries, it's home to the Spindletop/Gladys City Boomtown Monument, the Art Museum

Beaumont, TX
Beaumont Public Library

of Southeast Texas, the Texas State Fire Museum, the Texas Energy Museum, the Edison Power Museum, the Babe Didrikson Zaharias Museum, the John Jay French Museum and a bundle of other interesting sights—all only about 25 miles from Louisiana.

The main entrance to the library has two sets of large double wooden doors. The doors are big enough by themselves, but their slanted planks are carried on as a frame another 15 feet above them to the top of the building. They create a truly monumental entrance.

At 20,000 square feet, the main library may have the largest single room of any we have visited. And yet, because of the room's great height and all-around floor-to-ceiling bronzed windows, it seems neither cavernous nor dark. You can see out to trees growing all around on the library's block.

Banners hang from the coffered concrete ceiling and modify the immensity of the room. Touches such as upholstered lounge chairs, a crib in the reading room and supermarket handbaskets for gathering books make it quite personal.

There are comfortable and inviting reading areas, both in the center of the library and along the walls of windows. An unusual lending collection here is a large selection of dress patterns.

Beaumont, TX
Tyrrell Historical Branch Library

## Tyrrell Historical Branch Library

695 Pearl Street
(409) 833-2759                                              Closed Sundays, Mondays

Only two blocks from the Beaumont Public Library, the all stone Romanesque Revival style Tyrrell Public Library was built in 1903 as the First Baptist Church. It has four towers with conical peaks and a square bell tower. The towers have stone balconies, and there are stained windows galore. A library since 1926, the building underwent a major renovation in 1990.

The library houses collections in genealogy, history and fine art. The main seating area of the church is now a reading room filled with desks. The room is surrounded by brilliantly colored stained glass. Of course this keeps any natural light from coming in, but it's a fair trade and an interesting contrast with the light-flooded main library nearby. In any case, each of the desks has its own reading lights.

In front of one section of stained glass is a set of comfortable overstuffed leather couches and chairs with ottomans. Naturally there are dark brown bookshelves built into the walls, and throughout the library there are solid writing and studying desks. Wooden spiral staircases go up the corners of the room to a balcony reading area from which you can look down into the main reading room. This is a "hide from the world" place!

# BOERNE

## Boerne Public Library

400 East Blanco Street
(512) 249-3053                                                     Closed Sundays

A plaque on the Joseph Dienger building, now the Boerne Public Library, says, "This limestone commercial structure was built for Joseph Dienger, 1859–1950, shortly after he purchased the site in 1884. The ground floor housed his grocery and the second floor provided living quarters for his family. A later addition was used for the dry goods store of Dienger's sisters, Lina and Louise. It was owned by family members until 1967. The double galleried building uses Victorian styling with German influences."

Architects Wagner and Klein did a splendid conversion of the building in 1990. They have left the interesting shell, saved some artifacts and totally redesigned the space into a modern, comfortable library. The lighting is good, enhanced by a lighthouse-like skylight,

Boerne, TX
Boerne Public Library

the shelves are new and modern, and the doors are trimmed in oak. All in all it's a pleasant surprise.

The library has a German bible printed in 1614 whose cover bears the coat of arms of Augustus, Duke of Saxony, who authorized the printing. There were only six of these bibles printed. There's also a good local history room. Boerne is about 35 miles northwest of San Antonio. It's a tourist center with a number of antique shops and not far from the Fiesta Texas Race Track.

Although contemporary in style, the library is reputedly haunted by Dienger's ghost. In benign fashion he has been haunting the building's occupants since 1968. The librarians will tell you more about it if you ask.

# —— BONHAM ——

## Sam Rayburn Foundation Library and Museum

| 800 West Sam Rayburn | T, H |
|---|---|
| (903) 583-2455 | Open every day |

The Sam Rayburn Library pays homage to the man who may have been the most powerful person ever to serve in the U.S. House of Representatives. He served as Speaker of the House for over seventeen years. This fascinating, formal building contains exhibits, photographs, letters, furniture and personal memorabilia as well as some original furnishings from the White House and the Capitol Building in Washington, D.C. There's even a replica of the formal Office of the Speaker with a chandelier that once hung in the White House.

The originals of most of Rayburn's papers are now stored in the Center for American History at the University of Texas at Austin, but they are available on microfilm in the library here.

## —— CANYON ——

### Panhandle–Plains Historical Museum Library

2401 4th Avenue  
(806) 656-2260

T  
Closed Saturdays, Sundays;  
Museum open every day

This is an outgrowth of the collection of the Panhandle–Plains Historical Society. The building is owned by the state and the collection by the society. This surprisingly large library, open to the public, is on the third floor of the museum. As large as the reading rooms are, only about a third of the materials are on open shelves, with the rest in stacks in the basement. The main room is 120 feet long by 75 feet wide.

The museum collection is large (300,000 square feet) and includes an interesting display of ranching, automobiles, paleontology, Native American artifacts, oil well drilling, wagons and buggies. There's even a whole section of a 1920s oil drilling rig. Kids will enjoy the Pioneer Town display of rooms and cabins. Canyon is only 18 miles from Palo Duro State Park, one of the most fascinating parts of the Texas Panhandle.

Among other collections in the library is the Bob Wills Archive of Popular Music (remember Bob Wills and his Texas Playboys?). There's a collection of Western periodicals, Western pulp fiction series (*Mammoth Western, New Western, Masked Rider Western, Max Brand's Westerns*) and a big collection of cowboy music, along with a significant collection of books on the art of the Southwest.

## —— CORRIGAN ——

### Mickey Reily Public Library

502 South Mathews  
(409) 398-4156

Closed Saturdays, Sundays

To the traveller, Corrigan (population 2,000) is not much more than a way-station on a north-south road in East Texas between Houston and Shreveport, Louisiana. However, this town does have a surprising library.

At the intersection of Texas Route 287 and State 59, just south of Diboll, is a modern, tan brick structure. Built in 1986, this small library with its blue and gray tiled floor and pleasant children's room is a nice highway break. The library was named after a past mayor, whose wife is a former librarian.

# DALLAS

## J. Erik Jonsson Central Library

| | |
|---|---:|
| 1515 Young Street | A, E |
| (214) 670-1400 | Open every day |

This is a library that matches its city's psyche. The main library in Dallas could be nothing less than huge—and it is. The entrance lobby could hold whole small-town libraries. Just a few blocks from the Dallas Convention Center, this eight-story, terraced library is so big it has four elevators. There's a parking garage under the library, which is right across the street from City Hall Plaza and City Hall.

The library has far more special collections than we have room to note, ranging from Dallas Black History to a Bergdoff Goodman fashion collection. In the large children's section on the second floor is the Kahn Pavilion, an amphitheater for shows and storytelling. There's also a computer learning center for children where they learn the basics and can then use the PAC (Public Access Catalog) computers to find books or regular computers to play games. Some of the bookshelves are

Dallas, TX
J. Erik Jonsson Central Library

shaped like castles. It's a treat to watch children sitting on the floor in front of castle walls full of books.

A good way to explore this giant is to take an elevator to the top and walk down. Open stairways from several floors lead down to two-story reading rooms on the floor below, which in turn open up to outdoor terraces. On the top (eighth) floor is an enormous genealogy collection, the beautiful McDermott collection of framed Native American blankets and also the history and social science collection.

The seventh floor has Dallas and Texas history, as well as rare books and a photograph collection—a treasure trove of unedited history. It's well-indexed, too. The sixth floor has an innovative Urban Information Center. The reading spaces on these floors are large, calm and spacious. And on the fifth and third floors there are balconies for outdoor reading in pleasant weather.

The library has four art galleries and an excellent fine art collection on the fourth floor. There's also a gift shop.

## Fretz Park Branch Library

6990 Belt Line Road
(214) 670-6421                                                   Closed Thursdays, Sundays

In a substantial residential neighborhood in the north of Dallas this large, low brick building sits up on a wide lawn, surrounded by trees. It's next to the Fretz Park recreation area where there are public tennis courts and a swimming pool.

The warmth of brick is carried over inside—even the service counters are brick. The carpet is a warm deep orange, and some of the wall sections, between brick columns, have also been carpeted. Screened fluorescent lights and a clerestory window over the entryway (that looks like it was made from a steel bridge truss) help with the light.

In the children's room papier-mâché dolls, dinosaurs and their friends sit on top of shelves. As you wander through the shelves you find comfortable chairs and see more clerestory windows at the back. Large ceramic tiles in parts of the floor set off the brickwork in this very attractive library.

## North Oak Cliff Branch Library

| | |
|---|---:|
| 302 West Tenth Street | A |
| (214) 670-7555 | Closed Thursdays, Sundays |

Dallas doesn't just spend its money downtown. This attractive library in the Oak Cliff neighborhood serves a mixed African-American and Hispanic population, as well as those living in a nearby historic pioneer district.

A long, high, skylit canopy extends well out in front of the building. Inside, the canopy carries on as a skylight down the library's full length. Dallas architects Good, Hass and Fulton seem to have emulated the "longhouse" approach of the Pacific Northwest. Your eye follows the skylight all the way to a set of windows on the back wall. This library gets lots of light.

The different areas of the library are well marked with clear signs along the passageway under the skylight (unfortunately the signs are printed only on the side facing you as you walk in—not quite as useful as if they had been printed on both sides).

The spacious reading areas along the windowed walls are furnished in cool tones of gray and green, an interesting contrast to the use of black metal shelves with wood-trimmed ends. A good-sized children's room is to your left as you enter.

## Skyline Branch Library

| | |
|---|---:|
| 6006 Everglade Road | V |
| (214) 670-0938 | Closed Fridays, Sundays |

This neighborhood library provides a good view of the Dallas skyline from the east, but its unique mix of architecture should also be noted. It's tempting to describe it as a Mexican ski lodge. The shake-shingled roofs of two intersecting sections are so sharply peaked that they look like alpine A-frames, but the interior stucco walls and gently curved arches look like New Mexican Pueblo architecture. Adding to the architectural confusion are large external chimneys for the library's two fireplaces.

The library was built in 1976 and is set back in the trees of Everglade Park in a surprisingly woodsy section of this urban community. The central section is charming, if somewhat confusing. Here, where the two wings meet, a skylight, mezzanine, staircase and high-peaked roofs connect at odd angles. The original roof was clay tile, but because the skylights leaked the roof was replaced with shake shingles.

Inner stucco walls have a comfortable irregular pattern that emphasize the library's warm feel. The large inner spaces are broken up by gently curving archways. There is a public pool directly across the street, so this might be a good stopping place in the summer.

## —— EL PASO ——

### El Paso Public Library

501 North Oregon Street
(915) 543-5433                                              Closed Sundays

Built in 1954 and showing its age, this well-used institution is more for work than for relaxing. Two floors of the library are above ground and two more are underground. The 1950s Modern Southwest style of the library is enlivened by a number of murals and pictographs.

The staff at the reference desk at the library entrance can direct you to the large El Paso and Southwest history collection on the first floor. Some of the stacks are open, some closed. There's also an interesting photographic collection on the 1910–1920 Mexican Revolution. The children's room is on the second floor.

The genealogy collection is down in the bowels of the library in a second basement, sort of a cross between a battleship and a prison. A maze of gray pipes and pillars support the low ceilings.

The library is only a block from historic San Jacinto Plaza and two blocks from the Tourist Center and the departure point of the trolleys to Ciudad Juarez (across the Mexican border). Across the street, Le Baron's Primitive Indian Artifacts store has a good selection of international folk art. If you want to leave someone in a library while you visit Mexico for a few hours, they might be more comfortable in the Armijo branch (see below).

If you want to see some really unique architecture influenced by Himalayan buildings, visit the campus of the University of Texas at El Paso.

## Armijo Branch Library

| | |
|---|---|
| 710 East Seventh Avenue | A |
| (915) 533-1333 | Closed Sundays, Mondays |

This 1992 building is in a neighborhood that will give you a taste of the prevalence of the Mexican-American population of El Paso. Here, English seems much more like a foreign language than Spanish. Colorful murals decorate walls throughout the neighborhood, and the friendly bilingual library staff is developing a guide to them. A significant part of the library's collection is in Spanish.

Inside this high-walled building you'll find cool gray carpet, oak furniture with mauve upholstery and gray, plastic-topped computer shelves. Alvidrez Associates of El Paso designed this library with clerestory windows at the top of the high walls and a skylight to let in lots of light.

The library is only a few blocks from parts of the main business area. Here, just five blocks down Campbell Street from the city and county building at San Antonio Avenue, is a different world.

# —— FORT STOCKTON ——

## Fort Stockton Public Library

| | |
|---|---|
| 500 North Water Street | |
| (915) 336-3374 | Closed Sundays |

Fort Stockton is 243 miles from El Paso and 321 miles from San Antonio, so it is a useful freeway stop. While it has several historic sites, it's perhaps best known for its 10-foot-high "Paisano Pete" statue of a roadrunner.

The library is remarkably large for a town of 10,000. The single high, bright room is welcoming and homey; a tall tan room with many of the walls covered in grass cloth. The comfortable children's section takes up about half of the space. On the left is a periodical reading area with both leather and upholstered furniture. There's a fairly large Southwest collection. The architects were Huckabee and Donham of Andrews, Texas.

# —— FORT WORTH ——

## Fort Worth Public Library

300 Taylor Street
(817) 870-7700                                    Closed Sundays, Mondays

    The Fort Worth library is one of the country's largest underground libraries. In the heart of downtown Fort Worth, it's within a few blocks of some of Fort Worth's outstanding skyscrapers. The skylit entrance is like the entryway to a conference center or a large museum—very tall, with windows all around and lots of chairs where people meet and chat.
    A wide staircase leads down to the main room. This very large, very bright library goes on and on underground. It's one block wide, two blocks long and carpeted in deep orange. In the rear some natural light comes in through clerestory windows. There's a nice quiet children's room with an excellent story room.
    The large genealogy and local history sections are impressive as is the extensive sheet music collection that features silent and sound film music from the late 19th century through the first half of the 20th century.

## Northside Branch Library

601 Park Street                                                        V
(817) 626-8241                                    Closed Sundays, Mondays

    This neighborhood and its medium sized one-room library are significantly different from glitzy, downtown Fort Worth with its modern high rise office buildings. The Northside branch is an undistinguished white building at the top of a hill in a park, but it has a splendid view of the city's skyline rising from the plains. It's particularly nice late in the day to see the sinking sun reflecting gold off the tall buildings, or to see the downtown lights after dark.
    The drive to the branch, in northwest Fort Worth, takes you through neighborhoods of small one-family houses, an older section with a largely Mexican-American population. Large parts of both the adult and children's collection are in Spanish.

Fort Worth, TX
Southwest Regional Library

## Southwest Regional Library

| 4001 Library Lane | A |
| --- | --- |
| (817) 782-9853 | Closed Sundays, Mondays |

This striking contemporary building is a curved brick structure, trimmed in green. Bands of white stone course along the front of a library dominated by a three-story tower. Sections of glass brick windows give the library an Art Deco look.

The entrance is beneath a peaked skylight that runs the width of the building. Ahead you see a sweeping curved expanse of glass brick wall at the back. The center section is clear, and light flows into a comfortably furnished reading area with ferns and other greenery growing around the chairs. The carpets are a pleasant gray-green. This library is a real success; local staff say it circulates almost as many books as the main library downtown.

The building was originally designed by CRSS Architects as a regional reference library, but the residents of this upscale neighborhood have developed it into a general community library.

# —— FRANKSTON ——

## Frankston Depot Library

| Town Square, South | H, T |
| --- | --- |
| (903) 876-4463 | Closed Mondays, Wednesdays, Fridays, Sundays |

Frankston, about 80 miles southeast of Dallas, isn't very exciting, but the library is charming. It looks just like the old railroad depot it used to be. The tracks are gone, but the right-of-way still runs off into the woods in back of the building. It seems as though a train might arrive at any minute, even though the Texas and New Orleans Railroad depot was built in 1906 and trains stopped running in 1964.

The library is only open three days a week, but it's worth a look at any time. It has yellow planking with dark brown pillars. Carved wood brackets angle out to help hold up the roof overhang.

If you're fortunate enough to be here when it's open, you'll enter a long, narrow library with narrow vertical wood paneling and hanging incandescent light fixtures. The children's room takes up almost half of the library. It has little old school desks for reading tables. Naturally, there's a wooden floor. In the summer the library sponsors a Stories in the Park program in the nearby square.

People move to this backcountry east Texas area to get away from the hustle and bustle of bigger cities. The library, which opened in 1985, is an excellent example of what can be accomplished by community involvement in a small town (population 1,200).

## —— GALVESTON ——

### Rosenberg Library and Museum

| | |
|---|---|
| 2310 Sealy Avenue | T, H, E |
| (409) 763-8854 | Closed Sundays, June through August |

Galveston, TX
Rosenberg Library
and Museum

It's hard to believe that Galveston, an historically oriented island community of 60,000 (with over 550 structures on the National Register of Historic Places), is only 50 miles from the brash 4 million-strong metropolitan Houston area. Maybe it's just another Texas contradiction.

One of the typically nice things about coming into Galveston is that as you drive in you can't miss the sights or the attractions, not because you can see them all, but because of the marvelous direction signs on Broadway to all the museums and historic houses.

The Rosenberg Library also serves as a museum for the City of Galveston. The museum part has over 5,000 art works and artifacts that chronicle the city's history, while the library has over 2 million manuscript items in its Galveston and Texas History Center. The reading room for the history collection is quiet and spacious.

In the museum the Lykes Maritime Gallery, with its displays of ship models, ships' wheels, paintings and nautical artifacts, highlights the history of Gulf Coast shipping. A number of lovely galleries house travelling collections. The Fox Rare Book Room at one end of the museum is elegant, with carved wooden columns, walls papered with floral patterns and Victorian furnishings from the home of the room's donor.

On the second floor you simply walk from the museum at one end to the library at the other end. It's quite a switch to move from the formal older building right into the modern community library. A circular staircase goes down to the ground floor of the library, almost all of which is taken up by the large children's department.

The Rosenberg library is an excellent first stop where travelers can get a feeling for the history of the area. History buffs will want to explore the museum, while others can use the regular library facilities in the same building.

Galveston is a Gulf Coast resort city, with 32 miles of beaches. The Strand, the old financial district, is nicely funky, with restored iron-front New Orleans-type buildings, complete with balconies. On the Strand you're near the Texas Seaport Museum and only a block from the still-working main port/waterfront. At the waterfront you might be able to see one of the immense oil drilling rigs up close, as they come into harbor here.

There are many historic places to see here, but don't miss touring the impressive 24-room Bishop's Palace.

Houston, TX
Houston Public Library

## ——— HOUSTON ———

### Houston Public Library

| | |
|---|---|
| 500 McKinney Avenue | A |
| (713) 236-1313 | Open every day |

    In the heart of downtown, Houston's main library and the nearby Ideson Building that holds the Texas and Local History Library are flanked by huge glass skyscrapers. Yet, this area is on the edge of the city's oldest park, Sam Houston Park.
    The six-story library is built right out over a large plaza. The walls of the library facing the plaza are glass; as you approach you see the plaza's brick paving continuing inside the library as its floor. The second and third floors are set back inside, so their mezzanines look out into the immense lobby space below and through the glass out into the plaza. The bookshelves and patrons moving about or sitting and reading are also highly visible from the outside—there is no doubt whatsoever about the function of this huge building.

Generous reading areas abound. The decor is subdued, with white walls and light rose carpets. The first floor holds the humanities collection and the huge reference section, and the second floor is devoted to business at one end and art at the other. The library also has exceptionally fine collections of art and sheet music. The basement contains the brightly lit children's room, with bright blue steel shelves sitting on a gray rug. Children have access to both educational and Public Access Catalog (PAC) computers.

## Clayton Library, Center for Genealogical Research

5300 Caroline
(713) 524-0101                                                                Closed Sundays

This stolid 1988 building is the center for genealogical research in the Houston library system. It's among the five largest libraries in the United States devoted solely to genealogy, with an international collection. It outgrew the old brick building next door that is closed now, but which someday will be used to expand the genealogical collection even more.

The staff is wonderfully friendly and helpful. If you are a beginning researcher, they will furnish you with a guidebook on genealogical research, and also get you started by giving you a tour of the library. There's even a current registry so you can see if anyone else is researching the same family you are. The second floor has almost 100 microfilm readers. Only the center of the floor is well lit; the banks of readers are off to the sides in a much more dimly lit space.

Knowing that people doing genealogical research spend a lot of time at it, the designers installed lockers where patrons can store a snack and a lunch room where they can heat it up.

## Julia B. Ideson Building—Archives and Texas Room

500 McKinney Avenue                                                                    A, H
(713) 236-1313                                           Archives closed Saturdays, Sundays
                                                                   Texas Room closed Sundays

Built in 1926 in Spanish Renaissance Revival style, this fine old classic was the city's main library until 1976. It was restored to its original beauty in 1979. A quiet, dignified building, it looks as if it would be at home in Spain. The collection is devoted to Texas and Houston history and archives, with four thousand linear feet of files and thirty thousand volumes. Houston's genealogy collection is at the Clayton branch library.

As a tourist spot this is really fun, even though the second floor reading and catalog room is the only room open to the public. The lovely old children's room and other reading rooms on the first floor are museum-like, lovely to look at, but you just can't get in.

The open reading room upstairs is attractive, with its high, arched windows. Carved plaster columns and brackets decorate the ceiling. More arches lead to a side room, and there's a fancifully carved and gilt entryway to the main landing of the second floor. Lovely marble pillars with intricately carved caps support a carved ceiling. Make sure you walk up to the balcony above the second floor landing and look down. The tiles are beautiful—highly polished in attractive angled patterns.

## Montrose Branch Library

| | |
|---|---|
| 4100 Montrose | A |
| (713) 520-5487 | Closed Sundays |

In 1946, this brick building was designed as a Central Church of Christ to emulate an Italian Romanesque church building. In 1988 it was converted to a library after an extensive remodel designed by Houston's Ray Bailey Architects.

Some church buildings, when redesigned for library use, simply reuse the existing space. This is different. A long mezzanine was installed as a second floor above the sanctuary, increasing usable space from 9,000 to 16,000 square feet. From the mezzanine you can look down at the ground floor, at the tall old windows along the side of the building, out the narrow cathedral windows at the front of the building and at the bookcases below.

The furniture is dark brown wood with green upholstery that contrasts well with the gray rug and white walls. The reading tables have individual lights.

The library is on one corner of a small shopping center, the Campanile complex, dominated by a 68-foot-tall brick bell tower. The library building is connected by a brick covered breezeway to Cyrano's Coffee Roastery and Cafe, and is close to the Black Labrador Restaurant and to a piano bar. This is a relaxing little area—a nice place to come and spend some time. The old church building and the land it sits on were donated to the Houston library system by John Hansen.

## Judson W. Robinson, Jr. Westchase Branch Library

| | |
|---|---:|
| 3223 Wilcrest Drive | A |
| (713) 784-0987 | Closed Sundays |

On a major thoroughfare in a rapidly growing residential and commercial section of southwest Houston, this 1992 library is a vivid advertisement for library services. Its vari-colored brick structure is a pleasant contrast to nearby glass-fronted office and manufacturing buildings. The windows on the street side are set back in alcoves, which allows the use of clear glass so people passing by can see what's happening inside.

A 4-foot high row of tiles all around the base of the building sets off broad bands of pale yellow and light orange brick above. A startling bright blue metal roof has four pyramid-shaped sections. One of the pyramids is supported by huge brick columns at the entrance of the building on the side facing away from the street.

Inside, white shelves and lots of bright light create a high-tech atmosphere. White walls, blue carpets and white-on-blue direction signs carry out the look. Under the roof's pyramids are raised white ceiling sections. Each periodical bookcase has its own built-in lights. The feeling of the library matches the offices around it. You can see shiny new office buildings across the street from the comfortably upholstered oak chairs in front of the back windows.

The library has a large, bright children's section. One of the walls is covered with carpet so it's easy to display children's drawings. Although primarily a community library, there is a good reference section for the nearby small businesses. This striking library was designed by The White Budd Van Ness Partnership.

*Also of Note:*

## American Productivity Library

| | |
|---|---:|
| 123 North Post Oak Lane | A |
| (713) 685-4660 | Closed Saturdays, Sundays |

On the grounds of The Houstonian Hotel and Resort, the American Productivity & Quality of Work Life Center is a nonprofit organization that works with business, labor, government and academia to improve productivity, quality and quality of work life. The library is used by a whole range of people—businesspeople, students and consulting firms.

The library, which is open to the public, focuses on productivity in both manufacturing and service industries. The well-informed staff prefer that you have an appointment, but if you're here without one they are very helpful. The library has about 3,000 books, but what is unique is an indexed collection of 13,000 articles on productivity and quality.

# KERRVILLE

## Butt–Holdsworth Memorial Library

| 505 Water Street | A, V, T |
|---|---:|
| (512) 257-8422 | Closed Sundays |

Although built in 1967, this bright, two-story, circular library is a tribute to the staying power of good contemporary architecture. Inside, in nearly perfect symmetry, one stairway goes up to the mezzanine to the left and one to the right. This spacious mezzanine extends around the circumference of the building, creating a wide variety of reading and shelf spaces. Windows surround the space.

A charming quilt with images of a number of Kerrville's historic buildings hangs in one of the reading rooms on the mezzanine.

Several outdoor reading areas, some shaded by trees, others on a broad cement terrace, create a parklike atmosphere. An outdoor amphitheater for children's story hours has tiles of children's books in the seats with a mosaic wall of characters from a number of children's classics. This active library is used for all sorts of community events including children's sleepouts and Chamber of Commerce receptions.

Kerrville is in the Hill Country resort area overlooking the Guadalupe River; it's about a thousand feet higher than the surrounding area and 10 degrees cooler. From the library an elevated wooden riverwalk takes you past hackberry trees, through live oak trees and past a stand of fairly rare river cypress. The view is lovely.

*Also of Note:*

## Cowboy Artists of America Museum Library

| | |
|---|---|
| 1550 Bandera Highway | |
| (210) 896-2553 | Closed Mondays |

This is more than just an attractive museum. It's an association of active Western artists who create work on cowboy and Western themes. Artists work and lead workshops here. The Southwest Regional style of the building, with brick domes over mesquite floors, adds to the Western ambiance.

The books in the library, primarily Western American art and history, are on display in glass cabinets, but access is limited, depending on the number of volunteers in attendance. You're more likely to be able to look at the books you need if you make an appointment in advance, or if you see a book and ask if you can come back to study it. The collection has a number of rare books on Western history and ranch life.

# —— KILGORE ——

## Kilgore Public Library

| | |
|---|---|
| 301 Henderson Boulevard | E, A, H |
| (903) 984-1520 | Closed Sundays |

Kilgore is only 5 miles south of Interstate 20 (between Shreveport and Dallas), and the library is worth the short trip. Since Kilgore was home to one of the biggest oil fields ever found, it's not surprising to find the East Texas Oil Museum in Kilgore. What is truly surprising is the public library.

This unexpected and magical building was built in 1939 with WPA help. It's a French Provincial building, complete with arched doors, cut stone, leaded glass windows, dark woodwork, carved plaster ceilings and a sharply peaked shingle roof. It looks like a stone witch's cottage with its turret and huge chimney surrounded by tall trees.

The lobby is a small octagonal room, with dark brick walls and pointed arches. One archway leads to the community room, another to the main library and still another to the children's room. The floor

Kilgore, TX
Kilgore Public Library

is of blue, green and gray slate, irregular in both size and surface. Dark beams lead to the top of the carved, conical ceiling, from which hangs a dark, wrought iron chandelier.

The children's room has a domelike patterned plaster ceiling, squares embellished with curlicues all around the room. There are couches at the side of the room as well as children's furniture. Iron sconces illuminate this interesting ceiling, and there is a small fireplace. A separate special collections room has collections in local history, genealogy and geology.

The library was designed in 1929 by George N. Marble and expanded in 1978 in a fine effort by Leland Guinn. From the outside it's almost impossible to tell where the addition begins. Inside, you can tell you are in an addition, but the basic design elements have been carried through to the new section. This was a make-believe antique building to start with, and the expansion continued that delightful fantasy. The library is next to the Kilgore City Park's swimming pool and tennis courts.

Texas Highway 31 is a picturesque two-lane road between Tyler and Kilgore that wanders through pine and deciduous forests. You'll think you are in New England. It's almost parklike and certainly a break from the huge, thundering traffic of Interstate 20.

## —— LA GRANGE ——

### Fayette Public Library

855 South Jefferson  
(409) 968-3765 — Closed Mondays

Ten miles north of Interstate 10, halfway between Houston and San Antonio, La Grange makes quite an effort to maintain its Czech/German heritage. In keeping with that feeling, the small library/museum building was built to resemble a German barn.

Built in 1978, it serves as a history museum and archive center as well as a community public library. La Grange is also home to the Kreische Brewery State Park and a number of other historic sites.

## —— LIBERTY ——

### Sam Houston Regional Library and Research Center

Farm Road 1011, 3 miles North of Liberty — T  
(409) 336-8821 — Open every day

This all-white Greek Revival building is primarily a research library. It's surprising, to say the least, to find such an elegant and specialized library in a town of 8,000, but Texans (particularly in the southeast part of the state) are especially conscious of their history. Liberty is about 30 miles Northeast of Houston.

The library sits on 114 acres of grounds with a number of historic houses. The collection documents the history of Southeast Texas with records, manuscripts, artifacts, etc. The museum displays memorabilia and photographs from a diverse set of historical characters, including both General Sam Houston and the French pirate, Jean Laffite. Genealogists make extensive use of the library.

## —— LOCKHART ——

### Dr. Eugene Clark Library

217 South Main Street
(512) 398-3223 ................................................ Closed Sundays

The 1899 library is a two-story red brick and limestone structure, modeled after the Villa Rotunda, in Vicenza, Italy. Ornate stained glass, twin spiral staircases and some of the original furnishings make it fun to explore.

Lockhart is loaded with old buildings, a fanciful courthouse with domes and turrets (nicely lit at night), a fortlike old jail, historic homes and the oldest continuously used public library in the state.

Don't leave town without trying some local barbecue. *Texas Monthly* has named Lockhart the barbecue capital of Texas. Black's Barbecue has been up the street at 215 North Main since 1932 and claims to be the oldest barbecue restaurant in Texas operated by a single family since its opening.

## —— LUBBOCK ——

### Lubbock City–County Library

1306 Ninth Street
(806) 767-2828 ................................................ Open every day

Lubbock is best known as the birthplace of famous rock music innovator Buddy Holly. In fact the Buddy Holly Monument and Walk of Fame are only a five-minute walk from the library. Given the Buddy Holly Statue, Prairie Dog Town and an isolated location, Lubbock is the butt of a lot of jokes, but its library is no laughing matter.

This very large stone aggregate building is shaded by graceful overhangs, cantilevered out over slender rock-covered pylons. Both the sidewalk and some of the inner walls are made of the same aggregate material. Light floods in through clear windows cut sharply in the stone walls. There are large, comfortably furnished, bright reading rooms in two corners of the library.

A mezzanine office floor in the center of the library breaks up space that would otherwise seem immense. There's a large children's room at the rear. The reference section has a significant Texas history and genealogy section and its own large reading area.

## —— MCGREGOR ——

### McGinley Memorial Library

| | |
|---|---:|
| 317 South Main | T, H |
| (817) 840-3732 | Closed Sundays, Mondays |

The remnants of an old movie marquee still hang in front of this library. Sometimes the librarians are not too busy and will take patrons upstairs to the projection booth of the old Ritz Theater which operated here from 1936 to 1958. The building was donated to the city by the owner of the theater for use as a library, and the library was built within the shell of the old auditorium.

This is a good example of what local effort can achieve. Some bookshelves are homemade, some donated by local stores. The theater had a little glassed-in crying-room for children who were fussing, and it's been turned into a quiet, one-person study room.

The projection room still has all of the implements of the trade—huge arc light projectors with the ash inside from the last time the carbon arcs were burning, the rewind mechanisms, the splicing machines, even the beat up old chair the projectionist sat in.

In front of the projection room are the old balcony seats (over the library shell). One staircase leads to each side of the balcony, which was strictly segregated in the bad old days. Downstairs, the box office is used for storage, and the old dialless phone is still hanging on its hook; when it was used there was an operator in town, no dials or pushbuttons.

Peaceful McGregor, a town of 5,000, is only 20 miles from much more cosmopolitan Waco, with its population of over 100,000. Church bells ring in the quiet air and you could stop for a cold one in a bar named He Ain't Here.

# —— MISSOURI CITY ——

## Missouri City Branch Library, Fort Bend County Library System

| | |
|---|---|
| 1530 Texas Parkway | A |
| (713) 499-4100 | Closed Sundays |

This sprawling new building is in an upscale, growing commuter community south of Houston. Designed by Hall/Merriman of Houston, it opened in 1991. Striking concrete beams extend the walls across the approach road to this modern one-story library. Expanses of lightly tinted windows display the activity and books inside. In 1992 this library, which was built for an ultimate collection of 80,000 volumes, held only 30,000—plenty of room to grow.

The barrel-vaulted entrance to the library is striking. Above the inner entrance is a bright kinetic sculpture by Jaraslav Belik. One wall has large windowed alcoves looking into the children's room, and the equally bright children's room has a fun, pathlike stripe on its blue-purple carpet, as well as rocking chairs for adults and kids.

The furniture is comfortable, some chrome and leather, some upholstered. One corner of the library has been truncated and its five windowed bays have created a quiet, pleasant reading area. Both entrances lead to a central desk that monitors the wings of the library.

# —— PALESTINE ——

## Palestine Public Library

| | |
|---|---|
| 1101 North Cedar Street | A, E |
| (903) 729-4121 | Closed Sundays |

Palestine lies about 40 extra miles off the road from Dallas to Houston, but it's worth the trip to visit what the American Library Trustees Association declared The Outstanding Small Library for 1992. (If you get lost, make sure to ask directions to "Palesteen" so local folks will know what city you're talking about.)

Palestine, TX
Palestine Public Library

The two-story brick ex-schoolhouse with additions on each side isn't exciting from the outside, but inside it sparkles ... both with good looks and activities. The conversion was designed in 1986 by architects Morgan, O'Neal, Hill and Sutton of Lufkin, Texas.

The difference between the staid exterior and striking interior is startling. A bluff-sided lobby with a curved wooden overhead leads you to a wooden service desk under exposed steel "I" beams and a shiny many-branched chandelier. Above the beams are shaded clerestory widows. Turquoise and teal predominate.

When new wings were added, the old brick school walls were left uncovered and became warm parts of the interior. Seats in front of large windows in the wings provide sunlit reading areas. In one wing the large children's room has a rocking chair for storytellers and a marvelous built-in puppet theater. Bookcase ends have been covered with muted colored fabrics in orange, turquoise, and blue-gray. The other wing houses a glass-walled special collections room with extensive genealogy, Texas history and Civil War collections.

You can check a first edition of the *Official Records of the War of the Rebellion of the Union and Confederate Armies* published shortly after the Civil War. You'll find, among thousands of other letters, such documentation as, "Sir, the skirmish lines of my troops, both on the right and left of Crawford are out one and three quarter miles. May 31, 1864 8:30 A.M. Signed L. Cutler." This goes on and on in great and fascinating detail and is a remarkable tie-in of history and genealogy.

Palestine has many older homes and office buildings. Every house seems to have a porch or overhang held up by oversized columns. In the middle of town, the 1914 Anderson County Courthouse is a huge Neo-Classical monolith with four porticoes supported by Ionic columns. Also, Palestine is one terminus of the 50-mile round trip you can take behind a steam engine at the Texas State Railroad Historical Park.

# RICHMOND

## George Memorial Library, Fort Bend County Library System

1001 Golfview  
(713) 342-4455                                                    Open every day

    Since Richmond only has a population of about 10,000, its huge George Memorial Library, fronted by an enormous arched canopy, is quite a surprise. Rough granite panels form the front of a 40-foot tall arch, while the outer structure of the library is polished pink granite. The library looks like one you might expect to see downtown in a state capital. Opened in 1988, the library still has half of one floor empty with lots of room for expansion. It was donated by the George family, a wealthy oil and ranching dynasty.

    The three-story window walls on the front of the building are tinted so darkly that you can't see through, but when you enter you discover that the barrel arch above the entry goes through to the back of the building, where there is a 750-seat outdoor auditorium flanked by an intricate fountain.

    On the first floor is a lovely children's area, with soft seating for kids, contrasting with all the highly polished stone in the building (even the tops of the check-out counters and low bookshelves are polished stone). There's a good story room and a toy lending section. Computers have both an online catalog and games for kids.

    A calm, quiet genealogy and history section is closed off from the rest of the library. The library has large expanses of rose colored carpeting and matching pale rose furniture in the lobby. Watch out for tornadoes, though. On the radio in this area a bad storm coming is announced as being in the "wooly bugger" category. The library also has a kind staff who fed a weary traveler freshly made blueberry cake.

Richmond, southwest of Houston, is one of the older cities in Texas, but it's an area that is growing rapidly.

# —— SAN ANTONIO ——

## San Antonio Public Library

203 South St. Mary's Street
(210) 299-7790     Closed Sundays

A new $28 million San Antonio main library is being built at Navarro Plaza, but it won't open until 1995. When it opens it will be one more attraction for what many people consider their favorite city in Texas.

Like many other things in downtown San Antonio, the present main library has a river canal running right next to it. You have your choice of looking at the river through the library's windows or checking out a book, walking down an outside staircase and going to read by the water. In addition, the basement boasts a marina for the riverboat barges that ply San Antonio's famous River Walk canals.

The library is a pleasant four-story brick building with wide arches facing the river. Clear windows are recessed inside the arches. Direction signs in the library are clear, and they are also in both Spanish and English, a reflection of the great number of Spanish-speaking patrons. The large children's room is on the third floor. The collection of videotapes is as large as some rental stores, there are lots of books on tape and a good collection of compact discs.

The library is within walking distance of the main downtown areas, three blocks from the Hertzberg Circus Museum and Library and just another three blocks from the Alamo.

## Landa Branch Library

233 Bushnell Avenue
(512) 732-8369     Closed Sundays

This branch library, which was a private residence, gives you a personal experience of San Antonio houses. Built in 1928, it's a large house in the Monte Vista Historical District, not far from the San

Antonio Zoo. The building is on several acres of grass and gardens and the houses surrounding it are still family dwellings.

A Spanish Colonial building, it has a dramatic arched and painted ceiling in its foyer over a black and white marble floor with a balcony above. You can easily imagine this as a grand entrance for a private home. Splendid marble fireplaces are at each end of the building. The thickness of the walls shows at the windows, as they are almost tunnels to the outside with scallop-shaped lintels above. The rooms have heavily beamed ceilings and small windows look down onto the ground floor.

This is not the type of library in which designers tear out the inside of an old building and remodel the inside. Here, someone just brought bookshelves, desks and library furniture into an old house as best they could. This, in fact, may be one of the few libraries around that has bathtubs in the bathrooms.

*Also of Note:*

## Daughters of the Republic of Texas Library

| On the grounds of The Alamo | T, H |
|---|---|
| (210) 225-1071 | Closed Sundays |

Most questions about the Alamo, the Texas Republic and the early history of this territory can be answered by the incredibly well-informed guides at the Alamo shrine next door. If they can't help you, this library is the place to come. Both the library and shrine are staffed and maintained by the Daughters of the Republic of Texas. Although the library was constructed in 1950 and expanded twice since then, its

San Antonio, TX
Daughters of the
Republic of Texas Library

stained, rough-hewn stone facade makes it look as old as the Alamo buildings themselves.

Modern and comfortable inside, this facility is a noncirculating research library with closed stacks, but the friendly and well-qualified staff will be glad to bring you material you find indexed in their comprehensive catalog. The emphasis of the collection is on the Texas Republic between 1836 and 1846, as well as San Antonio from its earliest history to the present.

This library shows how well San Antonio has been able to preserve its history and architectural integrity. It's still a modern, clean city, but on a more human scale than some of Texas's other giant cities (and certainly easier to get around in).

## Hertzberg Circus Collection Museum and Library

210 Market Street  
(512) 299-7810  

H, T  
Open every day in summer  
Closed Sundays in winter

The Circus Museum and Library isn't hard to find—just look for two brightly painted elephant statues on the sidewalk. From 1930 to 1968 this building housed San Antonio's main library. Harry Hertzberg, an inveterate circus buff, donated his collection of circus books and memorabilia to the San Antonio library when he died in 1946.

The collection has both open and closed stacks. Sheet music, route books, early copies of *Billboard* magazine, rare books and a spectacular collection of original circus posters going back to the 1880s make this a world-famous collection. Mostly a reference collection, the library has a very helpful staff.

The fanciful museum collection is quite a contrast to the old Carnegie library. A somber carved ceiling and dark balcony rise above bright costumes and flashy circus displays. Part of the 7,000-item circus collection includes Tom Thumb's violin and rifle, a brightly painted ticket wagon and a detailed model of an old animal drawn circus train that's more than 30 feet long. This place is great fun, both as a museum and as a library.

# Marion Koogler McNay Art Museum Library

6000 North New Braunfels Avenue
(210) 824-5369 Closed Saturdays, Sundays, Mondays

In a city famous for the quality and variety of its museums, some feel that this is not only one of the best locally, but one of the finest in the Southwest. The collection, the buildings and the gardens are magnificent.

A spiral staircase joins the two floors of the pleasant research library, that, like the museum, focuses on late 19th and 20th century art. Additionally, the Tobin Collection details the history of theater, costume and stage design from the 1500s to the present.

# San Antonio Conservation Foundation Society Library

107 King William Street
(512) 224-6163 Closed Wednesdays through Sundays

This small library is in the headquarters of the Conservation Society, which assists in the preservation of San Antonio and its architectural history. You can get lots of information about older San Antonio here including an illustrated brochure that guides you on a walking tour of this historic King William area and its dozens of restored late 19th century houses.

Headquartered in the historic Anton Wulff house, an 1876 limestone house with an Italianesque stone tower on pleasant grassy grounds, the library has a marvelous collection of files on individual buildings, with ownership records, drawings, pictures and even some building plans. These records are invaluable if an architect or owner wants to recreate a deteriorated or damaged building. Information is indexed by building and address—a treasure trove of material!

Library collections also include general information on historic preservation and restoration. There's an extensive photo collection, including some old glass negative plates. If you've bought an older house and want to restore it, not just build over it, there is a wealth of information here.

In any case the King William district is a marvelous area to explore. There is access from the River Walk at Gunther Mill Park and the Johnson Street Bridge.

## —— TEMPLE ——

### Slavonic Benevolent Order of Texas Museum and Library

| | |
|---|---|
| 520 North Main Street | T, H |
| (817) 773-1575 | Closed Saturdays, Sundays |

Just about halfway between Dallas and San Antonio, this surprising library has a collection of 18,000 books in Czech (out of a total collection of 23,000). The library and a museum collection of pioneer artifacts celebrating the history of Czechoslovakian immigrants are in the home office building of the Czech Fraternal Life Insurance Company.

As you'll find out here, the third most frequently spoken language in Texas (after English and Spanish) is Czech. The first wave of Czech immigrants arrived in the 1830s, with many more between 1850 and 1860. In addition to the Czech books and original documents, there are also translations of books originally written in English. You'll even find cowboy novels by Zane Grey translated into Czech. Naturally there are Czech cookbooks, in both Czech and English.

The museum is wonderful, with a myriad of items used by the Czech settlers: sausage stuffers, churns, dolls, uniforms, gramophones, and an 1853 music box. A pioneer museum with the added charm of Czech influence.

## —— TYLER ——

### Tyler Public Library

| | |
|---|---|
| 201 South College | A |
| (903) 593-7323 | Open every day |

If you like bricks or roses, Tyler is a good place to stop. Roses because Tyler nurseries raise about a third of the commercially grown rose bushes in America. The Tyler Municipal Rose Garden is the nation's largest. Bricks because the Tyler Public Library has huge expanses of brick, both inside and outside.

The open ground floor of this large, three-story building is set off by a striking, brick-faced mezzanine above. The columns supporting the mezzanine and going all the way to the high ceiling are also brick. Bright banners hang from the ceiling, giving additional color to the room. Light flows in from angled glass windows along one side of the main floor.

The top floor has a good local history and genealogy collection. The view to the active main floor from the mezzanine is striking because of the generous expanses of brick. Built in 1980, the library still has lots of room for expansion.

## ── WACO ──

### Waco–McLennan County Library

| | |
|---|---|
| 1717 Austin Avenue | T |
| (817) 750-5941 | Open every day |

Waco, on the Brazos River, is one of Texas's more diversified midsized communities. Let's face it, a town that contains the Texas Sports Hall of Fame Museum, Baylor University (the world's largest Baptist University) with a library and museum devoted to Robert and Elizabeth Barrett Browning, the Texas Ranger Hall of Fame and Museum, a suspension bridge completed in 1870 (the world's longest at that time) and the Dr. Pepper Museum and Free Enterprise Institute has got to be classified as eclectic. It also surfaced in 1993 as the home of the infamous Branch Davidians.

The library is like the city—full of interesting things. But it's also plain and overcrowded. A badly needed expansion is in the planning stage. Downstairs, closed but available, is the Schumacher Room, a private room with the library's small but well cataloged collection of rare books, and also a collection of Chinese porcelain dolls and sculptures. There's also a remarkable genealogy collection for a library this size. The children's room is on the main floor, and there's an outdoor reading area next to the parking lot.

Surrounding one of the reading areas on the main floor are display cases of fine Chinese jade (some dating back to 960 A.D.) and some ivory Japanese carvings. It's surprising to find a museum-quality collection in this plain public library.

## Also of Note:

## Texas Ranger Museum and Hall of Fame Library

| | |
|---|---|
| Fort Fisher Park, | |
| Interstate-35 and University Parks, Exit 335B | H, T |
| (817) 750-5986 | Closed Saturdays, Sundays |

This is another example of how to extend just plain fun into some slightly more specific intellectual pursuits. Most people will end up feeling that they have learned everything they want to know about the history of the Texas Rangers and law enforcement in the frontier days after visiting this museum and talking to its staff.

If you want even more information, particularly about a specific Texas Ranger or ranch, ask if you can visit the library. It has rosters and biographical information on Rangers as well 1,500 books on Texas history, the Mexican War and the Civil War. The library also has a photo collection, audiotapes and videotapes.

# —— WAXAHACHIE ——

## Nicholas P. Sims Library

| | |
|---|---|
| 515 West Main | H, T |
| (214) 937-2671 | Closed Sundays, Mondays |

Waxahachie is a marvelous step back into the past. About 30 miles south of ultra-modern Dallas, this city of 15,000 has hundreds of houses on the National Register of Historic Places, a huge and melodramatic 1896 county courthouse and a classic 1905 library. On the other end of the time spectrum, Waxahachie is also the site of the superconducting supercollider, the nation's most advanced nuclear research facility. (If you want to sound more or less local, pronounce the name of the town WACHS-ahatchee, not WAX-ahatchee.)

Four massive Doric columns flank the entrance to this classic Renaissance library. There are copper cornices above the windows, a complex lintel over the door and an even more complex copper cap at the top of the building. Inside, tiled floors and marble columns add up

Waxahachie, TX
Nicholas P. Sims Library

to a very formal entrance. On the other hand, a comfortable children's room is just to the right of the lobby.

The ceilings are pressed tin, plastered and painted white—that's how they got those fancy patterns. The library was expanded in 1958, 1965 and 1990, but the additions were so well done you don't spot them right away.

Upstairs a lyceum, or auditorium, built with the library in 1905 still looks much as it did originally. The proscenium arch over the stage is wonderfully intricate—seven carved plaster arches, one inside the other, all covered in gold leaf. The original bronze light fixtures hang from another pressed-tin roof. The floor and the seats are original (with an original wire hat rack under each seat). The staff will take you up the double-wide marble staircase and show you the room.

Waxahachie is doubly remarkable for its willingness to preserve the past, compared to its big neighbor, Dallas, where the municipal hobby seems to have been to pull down anything old enough to need a new coat of paint.

## WEATHERFORD

### Weatherford Public Library

1214 Charles Street  
(817) 594-2767

T  
Closed Sundays

Weatherford's library may contain the town's most notable tourist attraction. Thirty miles from Fort Worth, this is the birthplace of actress Mary Martin. As well as a full-size bronze sculpture of Ms. Martin as Peter Pan, the library is home to the Mary Martin Collection of documents and museum items.

The display, in the library's Heritage Room, will be a treat to Mary Martin fans. It has a rotating collection of articles, pictures, videotapes, memorabilia, sculptures, costumes, etc. Visitors can even buy Mary Martin prints and souvenirs. The balance of this contemporary stone-faced library is bright and comfortable, so there's lots to see and do for those less interested in Ms. Martin.

# —— WOODVILLE ——

## Allan Shivers Library and Museum

| 302 North Charlton | T |
| (409) 283-3709 | Closed Sundays |

This plain community library is attached to the Allan Shivers museum next door and administered by the same people. Shivers was governor of Texas from 1949–1957. The library is connected to the museum by a passageway through a patio between the two buildings, and tours of the museum start there.

The building housing the museum was built in 1851, and remodeled and moved to this spot in 1963, when the library was built. If you really want to get a feeling for politics in the 1940s and 1950s this collection of memorabilia ia a gold mine. The librarian is a gentle, elderly woman who is incredibly informative and knowledgeable.

# ·UTAH·

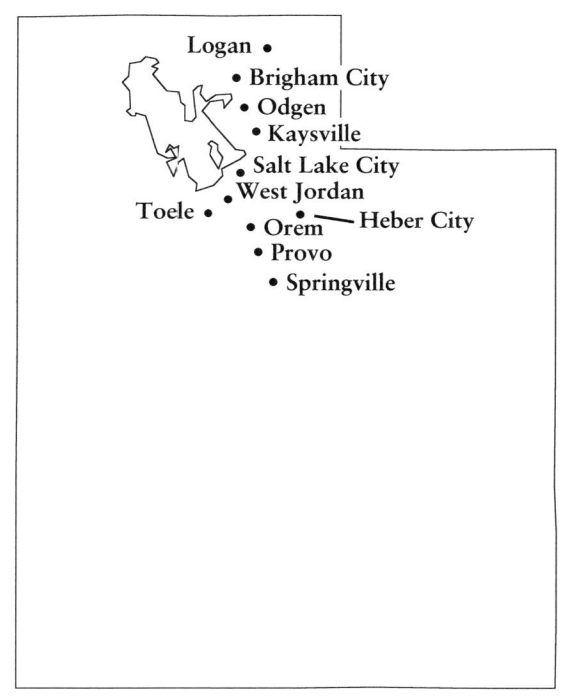

## BRIGHAM CITY

### Brigham City Library

26 East Forest
(801) 723-5850                                              Closed Sundays

    This solid brick building is the result of a large 1977 addition grafted onto a 1915 Carnegie library. Architects Edwards and Daniels Associates created bright new rooms, especially in the children's area. They maintained the original space as a quiet reading room, however, with wooden bookshelves and soft light from tinted glass windows.

    One interior wall of the bright children's area is the old outer brick wall of the Carnegie building. Above, a slanted glass skylight serves as a roof connecting the two buildings. Another of the old outer walls serves as an inner wall for the new section's main reading room. Quite an effort has been made in decorating this comfortable library.

    Brigham City is home to the gothic style Box Elder Tabernacle, considered by many to be Utah's most beautiful building.

## HEBER CITY

### Wasatch County Library

188 South Main Street
(801) 654-1511                                              Closed Sundays

    This pleasantly restored old stone library is like Heber City, pretty laid back. The actual entrance is at the back of the building, opposite the original entrance with "LIBRARY" imposingly carved in its stone lintel. You have to look carefully to see where the old stone blocks stop and newer ones start. The bookshelves are old and wooden and fit this old-fashioned library.

    The scenic trip on the nearby Heber Creeper historic railroad takes about three and one-half hours. Travelers not enthralled with the idea of open-sided railroad car rides might prefer some quiet time in the library.

# KAYSVILLE

## Kaysville City Library

44 North Main Street  
(801) 544-2826

A  
Closed Sundays

This surprising library might be the main reason for a stop in Kaysville. A varicolored rock building, it sits in a grassy plaza next to a similarly designed municipal building. The Wasatch Mountains provide a scenic backdrop. The designer was Babcock/Pace of Salt Lake City.

Inside is a gallery devoted to the paintings of LeConte Stewart, a nationally known local landscape artist. The gallery is designed and furnished in a fascinating interpretation of American Arts and Crafts style. Gustav Stickley chairs, a Spanish style light fixture, Craftsman furniture and a working fireplace lend to the character of the room.

The children's section of this library is not tucked away. It's in the middle of the main room on a raised section surrounded by bookcases. Along the side of the main room are glassed-in reading rooms. There are pictures on the walls, portraits of the American presidents, posters, kids' drawings—wherever you look there's a sign that somebody is doing something. It's an active, well-used library.

Perhaps to compensate for the children's area in the center of the library, there's a quiet and inviting reading room for those 21 and older at one end of the library. It has a couch, leather chairs, a rocking chair and other antiques comfortably placed on a mauve rug.

# LOGAN

## Logan Library

225 North Main Street  
(801) 750-9870

Closed Sundays

The Logan Library totally belies its past. You'd never guess that this cool (almost cold) building was a turn-of-the century dance hall and then a Sears store before it became home to the Logan City Offices and Library.

A long, formal hall leads past city offices and council chambers to the library. The main library room is long and modern with gray partitions—very office-like. The children's section is similarly decorated but it has smaller furniture.

The lighting in this long library is excellent. Sets of inconspicuous clerestory windows bounce light off angled panels, and cleverly recessed fluorescents add brilliance to the room.

# OGDEN

## Weber County Library

2464 Jefferson Avenue
(801) 627-6913                                                           Open every day

The Weber County Library sits in a grassy park among large trees, and from the second floor you can see up into the Wasatch Mountains. The two-story beige brick walls are divided by full height window bays. Each end of the library is illuminated by floor-to-ceiling windows. Raised central ceilings add to the feeling of inner space in the library. Hanging globe lights complement recessed fluorescent lighting. It has the second largest public library collection in the state.

Ogden was active in the heyday of railroading, and, as befits a town with formidable railroad museums (in the restored Union Station), the library has an impressive railroad history collection. Most of the railroad books are in a closed collection in a special and elegant reading room in the basement. They are cataloged, though, and the friendly reference librarians will be glad to help you if you're interested. Ogden is railroad-buff heaven!

## —— OREM ——

### Orem Public Library

| | |
|---|---|
| 58 North State Street | A |
| (801) 224-7050 | Closed Sundays |

This attractive, large building is red brick, inside and out. It's connected to the Orem City Hall by a breezeway and set on a lawn with flower beds in a campuslike setting.

Curving inner brick walls are segmented by floor-to-ceiling windows, impressive in a main room over two stories high. Large circular light fixtures in the high ceiling add to copious light from the tall windows. Inner support columns are unique—brick, with curved corners. The contrast between the warm textures of this building and the stark modernity of both Salt Lake City's new Sandy library and the nearby Provo library is startling.

Sculptures sit on many of the bookshelves. In some places wood-trimmed mauve panels have been attached to the brick walls to make it easier to hang paintings and posters. The brick walls are trimmed in varnished wood, and wherever you look you see paintings. Even the elevator is framed in brick with a wood-paneled door. It is also glassed in so you can see into the library as you ride up to the mezzanine reading room.

The collection of about 5,000 videotapes, 5,000 compact disks and 10,000 audiotapes makes this one of the best audiovisual collections in the state. The audiovisual room looks like a huge music store. The

Orem, UT
Orem Public Library

comfortable children's room (with happy cut-outs of dinosaurs and dragons on the ceiling) will be replaced by a large addition that should open in 1994. Hopefully the same informal friendliness of the old room will be continued in the new one—it's being designed by Scott, Louie and Browning who designed the Sandy Library in Salt Lake City.

## —— PARK CITY ——

### Park City Library

| 1255 Park Avenue | H, T |
| --- | --- |
| (801) 645-5140 | Open every day |

From 1982 until 1993 the library was housed in the 1904 Miners' Hospital building at 1354 Park Avenue, rightfully known as "one of the most beautiful small town libraries anywhere." As well as serving as a hospital for 50 years, the building had housed a bar, restaurant, dentist's office and skier's dormitory before being moved to this site and restored as a library in 1982.

As this was being written the 1928 brick Park City High School building was being restored to house expanded library facilities. If it's even close to the previous library in charm, it will be well worth a visit. As well as being accessible for those with permanent disabilities and for skiing's walking wounded, the restored school will have much more room, and it also will not be spread out on four small floors.

Try to visit the old building; current plans are to use it for some public purpose. It's a great example of how an older building designed for something else can be turned into a library. The designers restored the original oak window frames, doors and banisters. They added fluorescent lights in inverted tubes reflecting bright light on light brown carpets to create a relaxed reading environment.

Utah

# —— PROVO ——

## Provo City Public Library

425 West Center Street
(801) 379-6650                                    Closed Sundays

Downtown Provo is a little schizophrenic. Its huge, old, brick tabernacle contrasts sharply against the glass-skinned Newskin International's glitzy skyscraper. The library is just as contradictory. From the street it looks plain, almost dowdy. From the rear or the sides you discover a unique structure.

It's a triangle with the long leg on Center Street. At the rear, curved stairs next to a broad, grassy terraced slope lead up a low hill to an entrance on street level. A veritable grove of young trees has been planted on the slope, and in a few years they will provide a shady place to sit.

There are windows on every side of this large library. The shelves in the center of the main reading room are no more than 4 feet high, allowing clear views all around. On the west wall are study carrels. On the south side, a large reading room has a splendid mountain view.

The ceiling is not just a plain, flat expanse. It's raised in varying shapes in a number of places, and the architects (Richards and Associates) also used windows of differing shapes.

Downstairs is an inviting children's room. Mobile structures hang from the walls and ceiling, and there's a nice story pit with comfortably carpeted floor and little awnings hanging over the windows. The library lends toys as well as educational videotapes. Next to the children's room is a Parent Education Resource Center with materials on all aspects of parenting. One of those rare places that gives parents how-to information.

Salt Lake City, UT
Salt Lake City Public Library
City and County Building at rear

## —— SALT LAKE CITY ——

### Salt Lake City Public Library

| | |
|---|---:|
| 209 East Fifth South | A, V |
| (801) 524-8200 | Closed Sundays |

If Salt Lake City's street numbering system confuses you and you want to find the main library, watch for the clock in the tall stone main tower of the Richardsonian Romanesque city and county building. The library is right across the street.

This large, four-story, cast-stone library, designed by Edwards and Daniels, was built in 1964. The entrance is dominated by a huge cast cement frieze by Jo Roper. There is art throughout the library.

A 14-foot by 27-foot mural, escalators and a young adult browsing area dominate the spacious main floor. Windows all around add to the roomy feel. There's a very large children's room on the second floor complete with its own parakeet. The carpet is deep orange and lots of adult-size chairs are scattered around so you can stay and read while kids enjoy themselves.

The rest of the second floor has quiet study rooms around the sides, utilitarian reading tables and chrome and black leather couches. A large central balcony looks down into the first floor.

The lovely atrium gallery on the top floor hosts 10 art exhibits every year. From this floor there are fabulous views of the city and the mountains around the city. A sculpture garden in the center opens to the sky. The art and media room is also on this floor with a huge collection of books on art and a good picture file.

## Anderson Branch Library

| | |
|---|---|
| 1125 South 2100 East | A |
| (801) 524-8278 | Closed Sundays |

On the west side of town, this library is in an upscale neighborhood at the foot of the mountains. Brick, lots of glass and a shake-shingle roof make the exterior quite attractive. A small concrete amphitheater on the south side is available for story hours, group meetings or just relaxing with a book.

Inner brick walls, beautifully grained light oak service desks, wooden furniture with blue and brown cushions and a blue-gray carpet are all inviting. As in most Utah libraries, there's a large children's section.

This is a good example of how to plan for expansion. Two building "pods" were built in 1985 and two more were added in 1991–1992, so seamlessly that you can't see where the new section starts.

The Edwards and Daniels design makes use of loftlike raised ceilings, giving this modest library an expansive feel. It also keeps noise from going from one section to another. Metal strips that encourage the librarians to hang a variety of art are permanently attached around the brick walls.

The Foothill Village Shopping Center is further down Foothill Boulevard, making this a good spot to rest while someone else does some serious shopping.

## Avenues Branch Library

| | |
|---|---|
| 455 F Street | A, V |
| (801) 524-8276 | Closed Sundays |

The library is in an attractive, quiet neighborhood with lots of Victorian style houses in various stages of preservation and renovation. Accordingly, it has a good collection of books on architectural restoration.

This is basically the same modular design used in the Anderson Foothill branch noted above. The third and fourth "pods" were to be added in late 1993. The elevated site makes for splendid views of the Salt Lake Valley, Wasatch Mountains to the east and the Oquirrh range to the west.

Once again, internal brick walls, oak furnishings, some tile on the floor, dramatic carpeting, provision for local art and comfortable furniture are successfully merged in a small library. Like the Anderson Valley library it has regular displays of local artists' work.

## Chapman Branch Library

| | |
|---|---|
| 577 South 9th West | |
| (801) 524-8285 | Closed Sundays |

A Carnegie library, this dark red brick building was constructed in 1917. Curved concrete stairs lead to four solid columns framing arched wooden doors. Inside, dark polished wooden columns support dark beams across gentle arches. Walls of arched windows light the entire library. Old-fashioned and pleasing.

The library has identical wings at right angles to each other that meet at the service desk just inside the entrance. The design lets in much more light than you would expect in a 75-year-old brick building.

In this oldest of Salt Lake City's libraries, there's surprising testimony to the growing diversity of users. The library has a sizeable collection of books in Asian languages to support new needs.

## Sprague Branch Library

| | |
|---|---|
| 2131 South 11th East | |
| (801) 524-8280 | Closed Sundays, April through October |

In 1935 The American Library Association selected this high-gabled Tudor style building as "the most beautiful branch library in the country." Built in 1928, it might not get that rating today, but it still looks like the library you'd hope to find in an English village.

Hanging bronze bowls throw light up at a plastered cathedral-like ceiling and the light is gently reflected down into the library. There's a working fireplace in one reading room.

Leaded glass windows illuminate the rooms. The building is attractive in an old-fashioned, Charles Dickens sort of way, but not really as inviting as some more modern structures. The children's section is not large, probably because the area in which the library is located is an older, established residential area.

*Also of Note:*

## Family History Library

| | |
|---|---|
| 35 North West Temple Street | T, H, E |
| (801) 240-2331 | Closed Sundays |

The largest Family History Library in the world, across from Temple Square, should be a part of everyone's visit to Salt Lake City. Without a doubt this fascinating place is mecca for anyone even remotely interested in family history.

This place has to be seen to be believed. It has rank upon rank of computers and microfilm indexes, and shelf after shelf of books and microfilmed records. It has over 700 microfilm readers, 1.7 million rolls of microfilm and 235,000 books. In the individual family histories you might find *Three Hundred and Fifty Years of Bickfords in New Hampshire*, and then, in another section one volume of carefully retyped records of the deaths recorded in Kentucky for the year 1880.

These records are not just of Mormon family histories. They come from all over the world; they date mostly from 1550 to 1910. Two floors are devoted to the United States and Canada, one to the British Isles and one to Europe, Scandinavia, Latin America and other countries.

If you're not a genealogist but just want to do a little research, come in and look around. It's fun to play here, and the friendly staff will help and, in fact, train you in genealogical research. Actually, it's almost impossible to come here and resist the temptation to look up your family on the user-friendly computer system.

While Mormons do genealogical research for religious purposes, non-Mormons are genuinely welcome to use this facility.

## Utah State Historical Society Library

| | |
|---|---:|
| 300 Rio Grande | T, H |
| (801) 533-5808 | Closed Sundays |

The library concentrates on Utah history (not LDS Church history) with a smaller collection of works on surrounding western states. The photo library is easy to use, with large reproductions of the images. If you're interested in pictures of mines or flowers or schools or animals just come up here and browse. It's all indexed and the staff is very helpful. This is a fascinating trail into the mysteries of local history.

The Historical Society and its library are in the historic Denver & Rio Grande Railroad Depot. The stately old waiting room is now a museum and the library is just off the mezzanine. One part of the building is still in use for Amtrak passengers. There's a startling contrast between the grand old waiting room, with its glorious 30-foot-high windows, and the Amtrak waiting room, that has all the plastic ambience of a bus depot. The museum's bookstore has a very good selection of Utah history and travel.

A block or so north of the building are the local rescue missions, and a block or so southwest on Pierpoint Avenue is an artists' community with live-work spaces, studios and interesting galleries. This looks like the frequent pattern of artists' spaces following low rents; in this area the creative spaces were funded in part by federal money.

Salt Lake City, UT
Utah State Historical Society Library

Sandy, UT
Sandy Branch Library,
Salt Lake County
Library System

## —— SANDY ——

### Sandy Branch Library, Salt Lake County Library System

| | |
|---|---:|
| 10100 South Petunia Way | A, V |
| (801) 943-4636 | Closed Sundays |

This striking new library (designed by Scott, Louie and Browning of Salt Lake City) serves a growing community just south of Salt Lake City. The library is a good base camp for nonskiers whose parties are going to the slopes at Alta, Solitude or Brighton. It's located in the foothills of the mountains at the base of Little Cottonwood Canyon. From one side of the library you see the Wasatch Mountains looming over new housing developments. From the other side you have a fabulous view of the entire valley.

A large multipeaked entryway stands out as you approach this symmetrical, one-story building. Even before you enter you can see clear through and out the other side of the building. The peaked entryway becomes a brilliantly skylit ceiling across the building.

A large children's and fiction wing is to the left, reference and nonfiction to the right. Around the west wall there are several reading rooms with good views and lots of natural light. Unfortunately, there's not much art or other informal display to break up the symmetry of the building.

# SPRINGVILLE

## Springville Public Library

50 South Main Street
(801) 489-2720
Closed Sundays

The library in the north end of the Civic Center Building sits in a municipal park surrounded by lovely trees and walkways lined with brightly colored flower beds. The dark tinted windows of the stone aggregate library are an interesting contrast to the flowers.

This friendly one-room library with wooden chairs and tables might be a good place to recuperate after an hour or so of museum or gallery sight-seeing (see next entry). If you're interested in municipal government, see if the city council is in session across the hall (it was when we visited).

*Also of Note:*

## Springville Museum of Art Library and Archives

126 East 400 South
(801) 489-2727
A, E
Closed Mondays
Closed last two weeks in March

This surprising museum of Utah art is in a large Spanish Colonial Revival style building. It has lovely polished ceramic tile floors and Moroccan arches leading from one large gallery to another. Some of

Springville, UT
Springville Museum of Art
Library and Archives
One of many museum galleries

the exhibits are in courtyard-like galleries, others are salon style exhibits in hallway galleries. A WPA project, the museum was completed in 1937. It's filled with an eclectic collection of work by Utah artists and work about Utah.

The library collection is devoted primarily to Utah artists and is basically a research library. It may be the largest research library for any single state's art west of the Mississippi River. There are thousands of mounted photographs of work by Utah artists, and by itinerant artists who have done work on Utah. The staff would prefer that you make an appointment to use the library. It's a small library in an interesting attic room.

If you're interested in Utah art, you might read *Utah Art* published by Peregrine Smith Books, edited by Vern Swanson (curator of the museum), Robert Olpin and William Seifert. Springville is small and mainly a bedroom community for Provo and Salt Lake City, but its museum should in no way be prejudged as a dry and dusty little place. Seven miles south of Provo, it's a nice excursion from Provo or Salt Lake City.

In addition to the Springville Museum of Art there are so many art galleries in this town of 12,000 that it's sometimes referred to as Art City. The city also has a significant number of high-tech buildings and factories.

## —— TOOELE ——

### Tooele Public Library

47 East Vine Street
(801) 882-2182                                    Closed Sundays, Mondays

This is a small, pleasant community library in a small pleasant country town. Tooele (pronounced tu-ILL-uh) has a number of museums and small historic buildings from the turn of the century and before.

The library, located in the heart of town, has a tiny but pleasant children's section. The present building has been in use since 1973, when the library moved from a Carnegie library building next door (now a museum).

If you're a little adventurous and sure of yourself on mountain roads, you can continue up Vine Street to an incredible overlook over

Kennecott's huge Bingham Canyon open pit copper mine. This isn't the visitor center with its gift shops and displays; you get there through Copperton by way of Magna or West Jordan.

You can't do this trip in an RV or towing a large trailer. The last 4 miles are dirt and a bit tricky. But the view of most of northern and western Utah from the Oquirrh overlook, just under 11 miles from the library, is worth it. Don't do this in the rain and don't even think about it in the snow. If someone's a little queasy about the prospect, the library would be a good alternative for an hour while the rest of the party goes up the mountain.

## —— WEST JORDAN ——

### West Jordan Branch, Salt Lake County Library System

| | |
|---|---|
| 1970 West 7800 South | A,T |
| (801) 943-4636 | Closed Sundays, Mondays |

The color scheme in this strikingly modern triangular library puts mauve and purple on the walls, while the pedestals for the computers are deep purple and navy blue. The seats are upholstered in blue. It's unusual, but it works.

Richardson Design Partnership of Salt Lake City produced the striking modern design for this large, single-story library. Above, as you walk in, is a row of solid triangular trusses with large circular cut-outs. The room is almost completely surrounded by windows. The views are great and there is a tremendous amount of light.

West Jordan is a good stop on the way out of Salt Lake City to the visitor center at Kennecott Copper's Bingham Canyon Mine. For construction watchers the working open pit mine is next to heaven. Trucks as big as a house with a capacity of 190 tons work in a man-made hole twice as deep as the height of the Sears Tower in Chicago. And it's worth the drive just to get the famous view back across the valley to the Wasatch Mountains behind Salt Lake City.

# ·WASHINGTON·

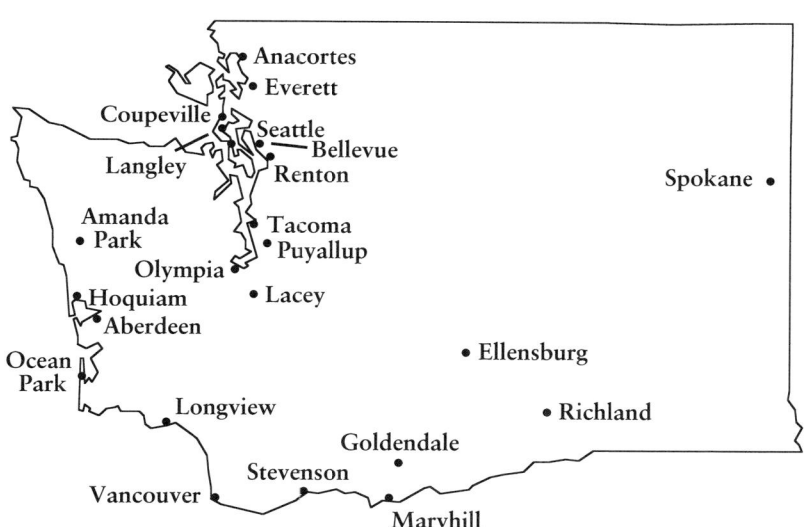

## —— AMANDA PARK ——

### Amanda Park Branch Library, Timberland Regional Library System

| | |
|---|---|
| 6118 US Highway 101 | A |
| (206) 288-2725 | Closed Mondays, Wednesdays, Fridays, Sundays |

The value of jewels often comes from their being found in out-of-the-way places. Add the Amanda Park branch of the Timberland library system to that collection. On Highway 101, which loops around the Olympic Peninsula, the library is on the Quinalt Indian Reservation at the southwest corner of the Olympic National Park.

This unique design by Clint Pherson of Seattle reflects the Northwest Coastal Indian "Plank House" tradition and other ideas of Quinalt cultural and spiritual life. The long, narrow building sits above the ground so as not to disturb Mother Earth. A bare framework projects past the front of the building, with a partial covering ultimately blending into the structure of the library.

Glass walls and decks at each end of the library frame dense woodlands. This tiny building proves the old saying that good things come in small packages.

## —— ABERDEEN ——

### Aberdeen Branch Library, Timberland Regional Library System

| | |
|---|---|
| 121 East Market | T |
| (206) 533-2360 | Closed Sundays |

Aberdeen, in Grays Harbor County, is in an attractive tourist area, especially for those interested in maritime activities, from clam digging to demonstrations of tall boat construction.

The Aberdeen library's arched windows are, oddly, wider than they are tall. The dark red brick walls of the library have been textured by the extrusion of various pieces of brick from the wall—some brick ends, some sides and some irregular shapes. The exterior design enlivens the placid shape of this square two-story building. Inside a mezzanine overlooks a large general reading area.

## ANACORTES

### Anacortes Public Library

| | |
|---|---|
| 1209 9th Street | T |
| (206) 293-1910 | Open every day |

Anacortes is on the north end of Fidalgo Island. The library, a blue-gray shingled building, is in a grassy square with a grove of cherry trees, four blocks from a marina with berths for 1,100 pleasure boats.

It's a good place to wait before you take a ferry from this gateway to the San Juan Islands or Sidney, British Columbia, or if you can't sail from the harbor until the weather clears up. Boaters will find a good collection of books on sailing and shipbuilding. There are twisting slides, sandboxes and other children's playthings in a little playground in the library block.

The marina is also worth seeing with its brand new harbor master's building next to shops and restaurants. Connecting Fidalgo island to Whidbey Island to the south is the Deception Pass Bridge, in a beautiful fjordlike area, with lots of pine trees and black boulders next to the road. The wooded country near Deception Pass State Park is worth a special trip.

## BAINBRIDGE ISLAND

### Bainbridge Island Branch Library, Kitsap Regional Library System

| | |
|---|---|
| 1270 Madison Avenue North | |
| (206) 842-4162 | Closed Sundays |

Bainbridge Island is just a 35-minute ferry ride from downtown Seattle, but the difference in atmosphere is startling. If you'd like to leave your car behind for a while, just get on the ferry on the mainland side and walk off into downtown Winslow.

After visiting some of the stores and the Steamliner Diner for some good basic food, it's less than a half mile to the Bainbridge Island Library. This airy, low-slung building with a sweeping shake-shingle roof is surrounded by azaleas, rhododendrons and evergreens.

## —— BELLEVUE ——

### Bellevue Branch Library, King County Library System

| | |
|---|---|
| 1111 110th Street Northeast | A |
| (206) 462-9600 | Open every day |

On the map, Bellevue looks like just another small town outside Seattle, due east across Lake Washington. In reality, it's Silicon Valley north, home to a dazzling gaggle of glitzy new office buildings. This is a wealthy, rapidly developing suburb of technologically modern Seattle.

The new library (opened in the summer of 1993) is the largest in the King County Library System. Designed by the Zimmer Gunsul Frasca Partnership of Seattle, it includes a 10,000-square-foot children's area and an exceptionally large reference collection.

Sides of the library facing downtown feature large expanses of clear glass windows, exposed concrete columns and red sandstone walls. Shedlike roofs over second floor windows provide copious indirect light. Naturally, in this timber oriented area, the ceilings are of natural wood.

Bellevue, WA
Bellevue Branch Library
Model, new Bellevue Library
Photo copyright © 1991
Strode Eckert Photographic

# BONNEY LAKE

## Bonney Lake Branch Library, Pierce County Library System

| | |
|---|---|
| 18501 90th Street East | A |
| (206) 863-5867 | Closed Sundays, Mondays |

A hidden jewel, this tiny building is tucked well back into the woods. With its shake-shingle roof and meeting room with a wood-burning stove, the little gray wood building is perfect for a library in the woods.

Like the libraries in Arizona, where you step from the library into the desert, here you walk from the library into the forest. You won't get lost (right away) but you will have a genuine feeling of forest around you.

Off State Route 410, at 184th Avenue East, go 50 yards to 90th Street to find the library. This is a great example of how to do a lot in a little space.

# BOTHELL

## Bothell Branch Library, King County Library System

| | |
|---|---|
| 9654 Northeast 182nd Street | |
| (206) 486-7811 | Open every day |

Bothell is a quiet, suburban community on Lake Washington, just northeast of downtown Seattle.

The pleasant community library is a circular building with a network of wooden trusses reaching out from its center. It's a little off the main road, but not too hard to find. If you are lucky enough to be here during April or May you'll be dazzled by the proliferation of rhododendrons around the building.

## —— COUPEVILLE ——

### Coupeville Branch Library, Sno-Isle Regional Library System

| | |
|---|---|
| 788 Northwest Alexander | V |
| (206) 678-4911 | Closed Thursdays, Sundays |

This workmanlike new library sits on a hill that gives it a fine view of Saratoga Passage and Skagit Bay to the east. The design, by architects Lewis/Nelson, matches the plain buildings of Coupeville. It has a comfortably carpeted children's room.

The Coupeville Art Center, headquartered in Coupeville, conducts two-day to week-long seminars and workshops in subjects ranging from painting to needlework. It has no central facility, using various community venues.

The area between here and Anacortes is bucolic—green trees, ponds, coves, harbors, mountains off in the distance (and the occasional jet plane from the Whidbey Naval Air Station roaring overhead). There also are state parks the length of Whidbey Island.

## —— ELLENSBURG ——

### Ellensburg Public Library

| | |
|---|---|
| 209 North Ruby Street | |
| (509) 962-7250 | Open every day |

A good rest stop on the road between Spokane and Seattle, Ellensburg's historical business district is being preserved and restored. There's a small children's activity center and museum at 4th and Main in the heart of downtown Ellensburg.

The library, faced in rough stone, is set off from the street by bushes and trees. As you approach you see a pleasant stained glass mural in the front window. The stone work is carried out inside, with interior columns of the same rounded stones.

Even though it's not very big, there are several small, distinct bays and reading rooms. This library is pleasant, open and user-friendly, with striking use of orange carpet and large ceramic floor tiles. There's a big arts and crafts collection here.

## —— EVERETT ——

### Everett Public Library

| | |
|---|---|
| 2702 Hoyt Avenue | A, E ,T, V |
| (206) 259-8010 | Open every day |

This is a don't-miss-it library! Looking out over Puget Sound, the building has Art Deco brick and terra cotta walls, with brushed aluminum windows, door frames and decorations. Inside, the original WPA style beaten-metal sculptures, bas reliefs and paintings from the 1934 design by prominent Northwestern Architect Carl Gould have been preserved and combined with more contemporary art works. A recent restoration by architects Cardwell/Thomas successfully enhances the original design. It also uncovered much of the original artwork that had been hidden by a less successful 1965 renovation.

Everett, WA
Everett Public Library

The central point of the recent restoration and addition is a splendid barrel-vaulted reading room with a high ceiling of naturally finished bent-maple paneling. The light flowing into this room is magnificent, even on an overcast day. On the second floor, quiet, private, almost secluded reading areas overlook both the main reading room and Possession Sound. Locally manufactured furniture carries out the period feeling of the building.

Boeing has an aircraft manufacturing facility on the road from Everett to the ferry to Whidbey Island. The Boeing tours tend to fill up in the morning, so if you get there for the morning tour and it's full, pick up a ticket for an afternoon tour and spend the morning at the library. The contrast between the restored handcrafted art work at the library and Boeing's 100-acre main assembly building is striking.

## —— GOLDENDALE ——

### Goldendale Community Library, Fort Vancouver Regional Library System

| | |
|---|---|
| 131 West Burgen | A |
| (509) 773-4487 | Closed Sundays |

In order to preserve the original design and calm symmetrical character of this rural community's 1914 Carnegie library, wings in the same style as the original building were added to each end of the library. The library is now four times the size of the original building and looks brand new.

The architects for the expansion, Callan & Willson of Portland, Oregon, designed extensions that are joined to the old building by glass-enclosed passageways. A bay window the size of a small greenhouse in one of the extensions looks out over a small outdoor amphitheater. The extension at the other end has a deck on the second level. A loft reading room runs the full length of the combined building. It has lots of light and lots of comfortable easy chairs.

Inside, the library is contemporary and warm. There are wooden bookshelves, white walls and arched doorways leading through exposed interior brick walls. The bay window is in the children's section and lets in light for the kids and for the plants growing just inside.

Hoquiam, WA
Hoquiam Branch Library

## ——— HOQUIAM ———

### Hoquiam Branch Library, Timberland Regional Library System

| | |
|---|---|
| 621 K Street | A, T |
| (206) 532-1710 | Closed Sundays |

The Hoquiam library was designed by a friend of architect Frank Lloyd Wright. The sedate interior of this Prairie Style building has lots of dark oak verticals, contrasting with planes of light let in through clerestory windows and rectangular skylights.

A beautiful wooden staircase at the entrance leads up to the main floor. Dark oak rails and banisters establish a formal feeling, but copious amounts of natural light keep it from being oppressive. The information and reference desks are dark oak, with green tops. Even though the children's circulation desk carries out the same formal design, the whole desk has been constructed on a low level for smaller people.

A 1991 restoration by Tonkin/Storch Architects of Seattle has more than doubled the library's size. The restoration was so good that you can hardly tell where the remodeling stopped and the old library begins.

Hoquiam is near Aberdeen in the Grays Harbor area. In 1990 it was declared one of the ten most liveable "micropolitan" areas by Scott Thomas in his *Rating Guide to Life in America's Small Cities*.

## ―― ISSAQUAH ――

### Issaquah Library, King County Library System

120 East Sunset Way  
(206) 392-5430                                                                             Open every day

Issaquah is a pleasant town with clean, neat, restored shops and restaurants in old houses. It's nestled in rolling green fields that reach out to the foothills of the Cascade Mountains.

Rectangular, with high skylights, the library fits beautifully into this peaceful setting. It sits between a lovely, grassy playing field-playground complex and a restored train depot. A bronze and concrete sculpture of the salmon life cycle sets off the entrance, and windows open on the green fields of the playground and ball field.

## ―― KIRKLAND ――

### Kirkland Library

406 Kirkland Avenue  
(206) 822-2459                                                                             Open every day

Kirkland (across Lake Washington from Seattle) has more public waterfront than any other city in Washington, and the library is only two blocks from Marina Park and the docks. At the lake there is a small kiddie playground.

The library is plain and rectangular, with large light globes complementing the natural light that enters through large windows at each end. It's right across the street from a supermarket so you can stock up the car as well as the mind. And if you want to work on the body, the Peter Kirk Public Pool next door has a wading pool for children as well as a full-size adult pool. (The pool is open mid-June through Labor Day.)

# LACEY

## Lacey Branch Library, Timberland Regional Library System

| | |
|---|---|
| 500 College Street Southeast | A, E |
| (206) 491-3860 | Closed Sundays, summer |

There is really no obvious reason to visit Lacey (population 15,000), just outside of Olympia. But this fabulous 20,000-square-foot library is worth the visit by itself. Just a few minutes from Interstate 15, the Lacey Civic Center is a series of low-slung buildings tucked into the trees.

Around a corner at the edge of the woods is a glorious super-elongated library. From the outside you think that you are seeing a two-or three-story building. But that's not the case. The height simply supports the visual delight of high ceilings, clerestory windows and open space.

Picture a main room 250 feet long, 30 feet wide and 40 feet high. The major ceiling supports are 14 pairs of 40-foot-high fir poles, each about 2 feet in diameter. On these columns a spiderweb of wooden trusses supports a naturally finished wooden ceiling. Each end of the library is a glass wall. The main reading room is so high that lighting is accomplished by halogen fixtures hanging 20 to 25 feet down from the ceiling, and they are still 15 feet above the floor.

The builders cut down as few trees as necessary, leaving many right around the library. They've also planted some new ones, and as they grow the building will be surrounded. The library's windows show off

Lacey, WA
Lacey Branch Library

the greenery. The landscaping is very well done; even some old burned-out tree stumps are placed strategically next to the building.

The library is just two blocks from a major shopping center—typical suburban sprawl. The stunning contrast between the center and the library shows how people can build into the woods, not over them.

## —— LA CONNER ——

### La Conner Memorial Library

| | |
|---|---|
| 509 South First Street | T |
| (206) 466-3352 | Closed Sundays, Mondays, Tuesdays |

La Conner is a restored fishing port between Interstate 5 and Whidbey Island. Commercial fishing is long gone, although there still is a marina in town where you can charter sport fishing or sightseeing boats.

This is the Washington version of Carmel, California; Ouray, Colorado, or Bisbee, Arizona, towns that seem to exist because of loving care, restoration and shopping. Here you'll find more antique stores than you can figure out what to do with. Fancy restaurants and gift shops are all in restored, neatly painted Victorian houses—Skaggit Bay Book Sellers, La Conner Seafood & Prime Rib, La Conner Tavern, The Wood Merchant and many others.

The library is a tiny nondescript building on the main street, right in the middle of the shopping area. The library budget is minuscule ($30,000 per year) and the building shows it, but you can still come in here, rest your feet and find out what the residents think of all the tourist activity.

## —— LANGLEY ——

### Langley Branch Library, Sno-Isle Regional Library

| | |
|---|---|
| 105 Cascade Avenue | V |
| (206) 321-4383 | Closed Sundays |

This small wooden library looks out on Saratoga Passage and Possession Sound. It has the feeling of a home that has grown haphazardly as rooms filled up with books. Lots of windows and a little boardwalk around the building take advantage of the views. If you get here in the spring, you may actually see whales swimming past. To the east is the panorama of the Cascade Mountains.

The ferry ride from Mukilteo to Clinton, the small town on the south end of Whidbey Island, is a good choice if you want a one-way ferry trip. From here you can drive north on the island and take the Discovery Pass Bridge to get back to the mainland. Langley, with a surprising number of bed and breakfasts, is in a relaxed, pleasant country setting.

# —— LONGVIEW ——

## Longview Public Library

1600 Louisiana Street  
(206) 577-3380  

T, A  
Closed Sundays in summer

Some libraries are busy and exciting, others are calming. Longview's public library belongs in the latter category. Perhaps it's the size: The main reading room of the library is 150 feet long and 40 feet wide. Or perhaps it's the regularity of the tall, narrow, arched windows.

The building, in Georgian Revival style, was a gift from this planned city's founder. (A planned city has residential, commercial and industrial areas designated in a master plan before development starts.)

The library anchors one end of the Civic Center Park, near a number of other surviving buildings from the original plans of this 1920s city. The civic center is a National Historic District and most of its buildings are on the National Register of Historic Places. The city, while not prosperous at the moment, still reflects the care and planning that went into the City Beautiful movement and shows how preplanning can survive bad times.

## —— MARYHILL ——

### Maryhill Museum of Art Library

35 Maryhill Museum Drive
(509) 773-3733      Open every day, March 15 through November 15, or by appointment

After you get over the surprise of discovering a delightful museum of art in a solid Flemish-style château on the open bluffs overlooking the Columbia River 100 miles east of Portland, you can be surprised again by checking out the research library.

The museum has a permanent collection of Rodin sculptures, a Native American Collection, Russian icons, artifacts from Queen Marie of Romania and miniature theatre de la mode French fashion mannequins. The impressive 3,500-volume library has material on the collection, as well as historical information about Sam Hill, the library's founder, and his correspondence with both Queen Marie of Romania and Alma Spreckels, patron of the library.

This recently modernized museum along with its library and its coffee shop make a surprising (and pleasant) stop on this sparsely populated drive.

## —— MERCER ISLAND ——

### Mercer Island Library, King County Library System

4400 88th Avenue Southeast
(206) 236-3537      Open every day

The 15,000-square-foot Mercer Island Library, designed by Lewis/Nelson Architects, is located in a well-established upscale neighborhood on this 5-mile-long island in Lake Washington. The solid brick building is designed to blend with the wealthy community around it. Inside among its varied comforts is a reading room at one corner with lots of light flowing through.

## —— OCEAN PARK ——

### Ocean Park Branch Library, Timberland Regional Library System

256th and North Streets
(206) 665-4184                         Closed Thursdays, Fridays, Sundays

    The Ocean Park library is about midway up the Long Beach Peninsula on the Pacific Ocean and one block from the beach. This locally known tourist area has 28 miles of wide sandy beach (but no swimming). Long Beach is the main town, but there are other stops up and down the peninsula.
    The drive here is through sloughs, inlets, woods and backcountry so it's a bit of a shock to arrive in this well-established, beach-oriented tourist area.
    The building has gray wooden siding befitting a beach resort. It's set into a woodsy area and surrounded by orange and red plantings. This smallish library is as much an arboretum as a library. Skylights help ivy, potted plants and small trees grow inside and the library offers courses in low-maintenance gardening. The windows in the back wall open on green plantings so if you just glance up you're not sure if you're inside or outside. A convenient place if there's too much rain or too much sun.

## —— OLYMPIA ——

### Carnegie Antique Market and Espresso Bar

Corner of Franklin and 7th
(206) 357-5550                                              Open every day

    Just down the street from the rather undistinguished Olympia library at 8th and Franklin is an old Carnegie library that has been restored, but not as a library. It's now an espresso bar, antique shop and bookstore. It still has the basic design and hallmarks of the classic, early 20th century Carnegie libraries—it looks like a mansion that might have been built as a private residence in 1905. The coffee is great and the antiques numerous. The Washington Center for the Performing Arts is nearby between 5th and 6th Avenues.

## —— PUYALLUP ——

### South Hill Branch Library, Pierce County Rural Library District

15420 Meridian Avenue South
(206) 848-8686      Closed Sundays

    Southeast of Tacoma in Puyallup the red brick and concrete South Hill Library sits in the middle of a large expanse of lawn. Angled bay windows extend from the main structure like a ship's prow. When you enter you discover that these bays are open reading rooms that are amazingly quiet. Even though lots of cars speed by in this rapidly growing area, you don't hear a sound.

## —— RENTON ——

### Renton Public Library

100 Mill Avenue South
(206) 235-2610      Closed Sundays

    Renton, just southeast of Seattle, has a 1 1/2-mile shoreline on Lake Washington in Gene Coulton Memorial Park. The library, in Liberty Park about 2 miles away from the lake, is only a few blocks from the Renton Historical Museum. Three different architects and one local inhabitant claim the idea of building the library over a river, but in any case it's the only such library we know of.

    Librarians will give you a flyer describing the fish you can see swimming in the Cedar River under the library. This is home to the largest run of sockeye salmon in Washington state. You can watch them from the library's deck in June, July and August. Other fish migrate here during most of the year.

## —— RICHLAND ——

### Richland Public Library

| | |
|---|---|
| 955 Northgate | |
| (509) 943-7454 | Open every day |

Of all the libraries in the Richland, Pasco, Kennywyck tri-city area, the Richland library is by far the most useable. It is also the largest. The brick building with flat roof and narrow vertical windows is surrounded by a small but well-kept lawn.

The main room in this bright, 40,000-square-foot building is two stories high, and the reading areas under the set-backs are generous in height. There's a pleasant large mural of the local valley on a wall at the end of the main reading room and several open-air landscaped reading courts for summer use.

You are liable to meet some of the scientists from the Hanford Nuclear facility here, or some of their families, as Hanford and the Department of Energy facilities are the main attraction for the tri-city area. The staff say that they issue lots of library cards to foreigners because so many people from around the world come to work at Hanford.

## —— SEATTLE ——

### Seattle Public Library

| | |
|---|---|
| 1000 4th Avenue | T |
| (206) 386-4636 | Open every day |

As you would expect in a city so oriented to culture and arts, the multistoried main library takes up an entire block in the heart of the downtown area. The building is just across the street from the federal courthouse. From the windows of the upper floor reading rooms you can see downtown skyscrapers through the trees growing around the building. The architecture is a bit dated and the library is showing the wear of most big city main libraries, but it is busy and well-equipped.

The Terrace Cafe on the 5th Avenue side of the building is a welcoming touch—patrons can sit and have a cup of coffee or a bite

Seattle, WA
Seattle Public Library
View from the Terrace Cafe

to eat and admire the view. Bronze, iron and stone sculptures decorate the area.

Inside the library patterns of carpet mark different sections of the building. This is particularly useful in breaking up the large open spaces. Even the elevators have carpets specially designed in a book pattern. The directional signs in the library are very good; large easy-to-read graphics identify different parts of the collection.

Seattle's reference collections are huge. Separate reference desks serve business, humanities, technology, science, social services and even drama (there is a large selection of play scripts).

Video viewing stations accommodate up to three people per screen (with headphones). A card is not necessary. However, it may be necessary to reserve in advance. There are a limited number of VCRs.

## Fremont Branch Library

---

731 North 35th Street | T
(206) 684-4084 | Closed Fridays, Sundays

---

Fremont is the Left Bank/Greenwich Village of Seattle. It has coffee shops, a troll sculpture under a bridge, a chocolate factory and a mini-brewery—a relaxing change from downtown Seattle. Antique stores abound. Local store owners try to maintain a small-town feeling.

The library has a "magic cottage" air. The arched entryway has iron filigree at the top and along the sides, and is covered by deep orange-brown tile. Inside, the heavy dark beams and trusses impart an exceptionally solid feeling.

The library is down the street from the Still Life in Fremont coffee house, and it overlooks the Lake Union Ship Canal that transits from Lake Washington to Puget Sound. From the rear of the building you can watch the Fremont drawbridge go up and down, while in the background Highway 99 soars across the gorge on the George Washington Memorial Bridge.

## Queen Anne Branch Library

400 West Garfield Street
(206) 386-4227     Closed Sundays

This dignified, recently restored Carnegie is in the Queen Anne Hill neighborhood, northwest of downtown Seattle. It's replete with leaded windows high up in its walls. The roof of the building is made of beautiful multicolored slate of deep orange and other earth tones. With dignified brick all around, it looks like the formal library of an old country school.

The quiet, older neighborhood around the library is in the process of being gentrified. It's interesting to see such a quiet area fairly close to Pikes Market and the downtown business areas. Here you can find an intriguing mix of some houses that have not changed for many years, while others have been completely remodeled just recently. Queen Anne Avenue North, marked "20 MPH Residential" is a real twister of street, almost as scary as San Francisco's famous Lombard Street, with planters at each of the steep corners.

## Rainier Beach Branch Library

9125 Rainier Avenue South
(206) 386-1906     Closed Fridays, Sundays, summer

The building is yellow and off-white. The off-white is a vertical corrugated concrete surface; the yellow (a bright, bright yellow), the exterior frames and awnings over large windows. The front wall is a series of angular bays that let in lots of natural light. The library is on an ivied embankment with plantings in front of the windows.

This is a library that caters to families. A bronze sculpture of a family reading group welcomes residents of the neighborhood. Lots of children use this library, and love the children's collection almost as much as they love "Booker," the resident library cat.

# Public Libraries: Travel Treasures of the West

Seattle, WA
Rainier Beach Branch Library
Booker, the library cat

This is Seattle's most integrated neighborhood; one-third of the residents here are black, one-third Asian and one-third Caucasian. Directly across the street is Pho Van, a Vietnamese soup restaurant in a former Burger King. I like the new food a lot better.

*Also of Note:*

## Mountaineers Club

| | |
|---|---|
| 300 Third Avenue West | |
| (206) 284-6310 | Closed Saturdays, Sundays |

Organized in 1906, the Mountaineers Club is a private club with 13,000 members who are interested primarily in mountaineering, with a growing interest in other outdoor sports such as sailing.

The library, however, is open to the public for reference. It's small, with only 3,000 volumes, but most helpful in its specialized areas of hiking, conservation, and wildlife. There is an excellent map collection. Anyone who wants to discover hikes near Seattle can come, do research and then copy the appropriate map.

## Museum of Flight Library

| | |
|---|---|
| 9404 East Marginal Way South | T, V |
| (206) 764-5705 | Call about admission |

While there is a library at the Museum of Flight (one of Seattle's most popular tourist attractions), it is really more of a specialist's archive. The librarian insists that if you want to do research, you must make an advance appointment.

On the other hand they do have an enormous collection on the history of flight and aviation, including a large collection of prints and negatives. If you really want to get something specific, they might just get it out for you if you have called or written.

The views here are unique. From the door of the library (on a mezzanine) you can see down into the main exhibit hall of the Museum of Flight with dozens of aircraft both on the floor and hanging from the ceiling. When you enter the library you can see through it to planes landing and taking off on the runway of Boeing Field. You might not feel welcome here, but it's worth the effort.

## Seattle Art Museum

| | |
|---|---|
| 100 University Street (between 1st and 2nd Avenues) | T, V |
| (206) 654-3100 | Closed Mondays |

The research library (on the top floor of the building) is tiny with only 28 seats. It's only open in the afternoon.

On the other hand there are two educational resource rooms, mini-libraries with 50 to 100 books supplemented by reading lists, each referencing exhibits on their floor of the museum. In addition, there is a VCR in each room, with videotapes that expand on the artists and the works exhibited. If you become fascinated by an exhibit of African sculpture or the work of a particular artist, you can see more of it on tape.

Both of the rooms have expansive views of the harbor. These resource rooms are a fine way to spread out library services. While they are not formally called libraries, they are marvelous reference facilities and they are just a minor feature of a splendid new building. The Asian, African and Northwest sculpture collections are world famous. The main entrance to the museum on 1st Avenue opens into an imposing hall, with tall sculptures under orange arches. The museum itself is divided into many small rooms so you won't feel overwhelmed.

# SPOKANE

## Spokane Public Library

811 West Main Avenue (until 1994)
(509) 838-4288　　　　　　　　　　　　　　　　　　　　Closed Sundays

Spokane recently passed a bond issue to replace all of the existing branches and add one more. At this writing the main library was in temporary quarters. The new 80,000-square-foot main library, to be finished in 1994, will be at 906 West Main Avenue, home of the old main library. Like many of Spokane's public buildings, it will be connected to other buildings in the city by enclosed street overpasses.

Spokane is a good combination of old coming into new, with a nice sense of preservation. The new building will be brick and should fit very well into the downtown, which has a lot of successfully preserved older buildings.

## North Argonne Branch Library

4322 North Argonne Road
(509) 926-4334　　　　　　　　　　　　　　　　　　　　Closed Sundays

While the city of Spokane is just beginning to rebuild its public libraries, around it Spokane County has built a number of attractive new libraries, remarkable for their differences from each other.

About a mile and a half up Argonne Avenue from the freeway, on the north side of Spokane, the Argonne branch of the County Library System is a low building of wood and massive stone.

Inside, the library is large and functional. A strip of high windows around the top of the library both lights the interior and shows the surrounding trees and hills. This is a new, functional library, with a lot of well finished wooden furniture and a wooden ceiling, but the feeling is a little on the cold side—maybe there's too much formica on the counters and tables.

## North Spokane Branch Library

44 East Hawthorne Road
(509) 467-5250                                                    Closed Sundays

This branch of the Spokane County System is near a lot of malls if you want to go shopping and then take a break, or if you want to drop someone off at the library and then go malling. The building is gray wood with reddish-brown trim on the street side; on the other side there is an entrance of roughly cut granite blocks. The front walkway is lined with cut stone pillars.

The library is light and friendly. Rather than a high center going down to walls, there are two runs of skylights with a lowered center section. Copious light makes the library a friendly place. The furniture is cushioned, not deeply upholstered, but it is very comfortable. There is good use of carpet and tile to break up floor areas.

## Valley Branch Library

12004 East Main Avenue                                                         A
(509) 926-6283                                                    Closed Sundays

Here's a surprise—especially in a city known for its turn-of-the-century City Beautiful brick architecture. Way out on the east side of Spokane in a residential neighborhood is a remarkably modern two-story concrete structure with contrasting straight, angled and curved walls and a fabulous skylight ceiling.

Spokane, WA
Valley Branch Library

The windows are tall and narrow in an imposing monolithic concrete structure. You'll want to go inside and see what's going on. And when you enter, you'll find a startling expanse of angled translucent ceiling. This isn't a ceiling with a skylight, it's a ceiling that *is* a skylight. Translucent white panes are supported by a network of white braces. The natural light is aided by long strings of fluorescent lights attached to this great angled ceiling. Three or four different shades of carpet and upholstered seating contrast with the clear white light .

A mezzanine with groupings of reading tables looks down over the bright main library below.

## —— STEVENSON ——

### Stevenson Community Branch Library, Fort Vancouver Regional Library

Vancouver and Stevenson Streets
(509) 427-5471     Closed Sundays

There's a beautiful view across the Columbia River Gorge from this library, a pleasant, single-room structure with a white ceiling supported by dark arched beams. The whole east wall is windows, looking out at a deck, the river and the gorge.

Just across the parking lot is the Skamania County Museum, which wouldn't be at all remarkable if it weren't home to the world's largest collection of rosaries—almost 5,000 of them.

## —— TACOMA ——

### Tacoma Public Library

1102 Tacoma Avenue     A
(206) 591-5666     Closed Sundays

What you can't see here is almost as interesting as what you can. In the 1950s a completely unrelated addition was hung on a Carnegie library built in 1902. Then, in 1990 the Tsang Partnership did an

Tacoma, WA
Tacoma Public Library
Photo courtesy Tsang Partnership

award-winning redesign, with a restoration that connected the original building to the new, both visually and internally. The Roman arch of the new main entrance carries out the theme of the old building, while the more stolid and modern addition gives a massive anchor to the project. There's a good view of Mount Rainier from the upper floors.

In the old Carnegie section, columns, capitals, a rotunda, skylight and the original double-flight staircase have all been carefully restored.

## Martin Luther King Branch Library

1902 South Cedar Street
(206) 591-5088                    Closed Sundays, Mondays

This small new gray and blue library is just across the street from the 18-hole Allenmore Public Golf Course. The library has few windows but lots of light from skylights. It's light inside even on a typical gray day.

If golf is an interest of only part of your family, you can drop someone off here while you play a round. You can almost see the library from the golf course restaurant and club house.

## Anna E. McCormick Branch Library

| 3722 North 26th Street | A |
| (206) 591-5640 | Closed Sundays |

The 12,000-square-foot addition to a 60-year-old 3,000-square-foot Tudor style library is a well-done design by Messenger Associates. The new library is so large that most of the original Carnegie is simply used as a meeting/community room for the new structure.

The architects concentrated on picking up the line of the old building for the new building. This is similar to the recent rehabilitation that was done at the Tacoma Main Library—a new building reflecting and carrying out the direction of the older existing building. The archway entrance at the front of the new building echoes and enlarges the entrance to the 1920 Carnegie structure.

The library is in a quiet residential area, just a few miles from the delightful Point Defiance Park, whose 500 acres project into Puget Sound.

# —— VANCOUVER ——

## Fort Vancouver Regional Library

| 1007 East Mill Plain Boulevard | T |
| (206) 695-1561 | Open every day |

This library is on the edge of Vancouver's Central Park. In the park are Officers Row (a collection of restored officers homes), Grant House Folk Art Center, George C. Marshall House and Fort Vancouver National Historical site (run by the National Park Service). In addition there are the Pearson Air Museum and the Pearson Airpark, the oldest operating airport in the United States.

The non-history-lovers might prefer to stop off here while everyone else explores the restored West Coast home of the Hudson's Bay Company or the Pearson Air Museum.

## Vancouver Mall Library

5001 Northeast Thurston Way, Store 210
(206) 892-8256                                             Open every day

In a major shopping center on the edge of Vancouver is the only library in Washington in a shopping mall. It's a good place to stop if your feet get tired while you are stocking up for your trip, and it's a good example of libraries following people.

The rather plain library is in a store space on the mezzanine floor. It's only one store away from a Crown Books bookstore, with whom they do cooperative programs.

# ——— VASHON ISLAND ———

## Vashon Library at Ober Park, King County Library System

17210 Vashon Highway Southwest
(206) 463-2069                                             Closed Sundays

The Fauntleroy Ferry Terminal is in West Seattle. From here a lovely 15-minute ferry ride takes you to Vashon Island, a bucolic, agriculturally oriented community (one-fifth of the population commutes to Seattle or Tacoma for work).

Drive off the ferry onto Vashon Island SW, head north and go 3 1/2 miles to the library in downtown Vashon. It's hard to get lost as the entire population of the island is 9,300. This is an older, quiet residential area that doesn't look as though it's near a huge metropolis. Many homes here have splendid views of Puget Sound.

The library, a building of brick with a blue roof, is on the edge of Ober Park, separated from traffic by gently rolling grass-covered berms that are great for kids to roll on. It is also near a children's playground and sandbox. Inside, blond wood trusses support the skylighted ceiling, and high fans recirculate air. The blond wood contrasts with the royal blue formica of the modern wooden shelf fixtures.

The small community room is equipped with a videocassette player, and if the room is not being used, you can check out a tape and watch it there. This informality and friendliness is typical of both the library and its staff.

Vashon Island itself is a gentle delight. A number of stores sell local produce and preserves; others handle arts and crafts. The island, which is perfect for bike riding, has a dozen bed and breakfasts as well as a youth hostel. And as a further surprise, K2 skis are made here, and factory tours can be arranged in advance.

## —— WILKESON ——

### Wilkeson Branch Library, Pierce County Rural Library District

| | |
|---|---|
| 540 Church Avenue (Town Hall) | T |
| (206) 829-0513 | Closed Sundays, Mondays, Wednesdays, Fridays |

Wilkeson's main claim to fame is its location out in the boondocks. It's near the Carbon River entrance to the Mount Rainier National Park and Clearwater Wilderness Area. The library and town hall are in the same solid building built out of local gray stone—it looks like a pleasant jail.

This old backcountry town seems as though it has been here forever—without changing. If the weather's bad and you want a look at how an old town survives today, the library is part of the scene.

# · WYOMING ·

- Sheridan
- Buffalo
- Gillette
- Sundance
- Jackson
- Thermopolis
- Riverton
- Casper
- LaBarge
- Cokeville
- Evanston
- Green River
- Laramie
- Lyman
- Cheyenne

## —— BUFFALO ——

### Johnson County Library

| 171 North Adams | A |
| (307) 684-5546 | Closed Sundays |

One hundred thousand sheep grazing in this area are not surprising, nor is the fine collection of Western artifacts at the Jim Gatchell Museum in Buffalo. What is surprising is Buffalo's modern (1989) dark wood library. Its huge slanting roof seems to go on forever, its entryway has open trusses supported by stone columns, and a high bank of tinted clerestory windows reaches high over the entrance.

Inside, more stone columns support dark wooden trusses. The stone is from the nearby Hazelton Mountains, and has the original mountain moss still growing on it (in fact librarians spray the inside columns from time to time to keep the moss alive). Hanging pale blue signs with large black letters provide directions. The individual bookshelves have signs with the same letters, and the same pale blue material is used as a frieze around the library and serves as a background for Western paintings. Comfortably upholstered wooden furniture, mauve carpets, wood paneling and good lighting all add to the comfort of this Dehnert/Richardson (Lander, Wyoming) design.

## —— CASPER ——

### Natrona County Public Library

| 307 East Second Street | |
| (307) 237-4935 | Closed Sundays |

The highly polished bronze sculpture of Prometheus flying over a flower bed in front of a large expanse of curved glass windows makes this library hard to miss. Don't be surprised to see Prometheus wearing brightly colored shorts—local students like to dress him from time to time.

The library has been remodeled a number of times since it was built in 1972, and it's sometimes difficult to get from one section to another. There's a large earth science collection and a large collection of topographic maps aimed at supporting the local construction industry. The map collection is a good source if you're thinking of doing further explorations of the West. The exhibit of local gems and minerals on the second floor gives rock hounds an idea of what's available locally.

## —— CHEYENNE ——

### Laramie County Library

| 2800 Central Avenue | T |
| --- | --- |
| (307) 634-3561 | Closed Sundays in summer |

This large, low-slung brick building is home to the state's centralized collection of genealogical research materials, a specialized collection on North American elk and a unique Wyoming centennial stained glass window.

Only three blocks from the state capitol, this is the oldest county library in the United States. The first impression is an enormous open space covered with brown carpet. High racks and bookshelves are off to the side, leaving lots of study and reading space. The children's room is like the library as a whole, not fancy but with lots of space. This is a plain, serviceable, well-used facility.

You can use the public tennis courts across the street if they aren't being used by a local tennis team. See how well you do at an altitude of 6,000 feet (while your family studies resuscitation techniques in the library).

## —— COKEVILLE ——

### Cokeville Branch Library, Lincoln Valley Library

| 240 East Main Street | A, V |
| --- | --- |
| (307) 279-3213 | Closed Sundays |
| | Closed second and fourth Saturdays |

The Cokeville (population 493) Library is an absolute refutation to those who think that their home town is too small to have a good library or that small towns can't have blue-ribbon public buildings.

Public Libraries: Travel Treasures of the West

And it also suggests that you should explore libraries wherever you go—you may get a surprise like this.

This new (1989) blue-gray wooden library has a peaked black roof with skylights running most of its length. The skylights lead to a wall of windows at the back which in turn look out on a lovely view of the mountains. The interior of the library has exposed wooden beams and columns. Brass and glass light fixtures hang from the high ceilings.

Although small, and located between JR's Bar and a closed Western wear store, this delightful library, designed by Bruce Hawtin of Jackson, Wyoming, has become the center of community life in rural Cokeville.

## —— EVANSTON ——

### Uinta County Library

701 Main Street
(307) 789-2770                                               Closed Sundays

Evanston can be either a blip on your map, a huge number of truck stops and motels just off the freeway or a place to see what a small town in a boom and bust area can do to survive.

Historically, this is a railroad-oriented town. There's still an operating 27-bay railroad roundhouse here, and the old twin-turreted train station has been restored to its 1900 elegance.

You probably wouldn't guess that the library building was originally a supermarket. Broad brick columns support a white overhang

Evanston, WY
Uinta County Library

over a building front of large windows. Inside, sweeping wood laminated beams support the ceiling. The architects who did the original supermarket design (Holland and Pasker of Salt Lake City) did the conversion to library use. Interestingly, to save floor space for library purposes, they built a mezzanine in the high-arched ceiling for an art gallery, offices and conference rooms.

Even on gray days the glass front lets lots of light into this large building. For additional lighting, long, highly polished metal tubes go almost the length of the library, aiming fluorescent tubes at the white ceiling to provide gentle reflected light. There's also a lot of greenery in the building, which is cheery during the heavy local winters.

## —— GILLETTE ——

### Campbell County Public Library

2101 4-J Road  
(307) 682-3223

A, E  
Closed Sundays in summer

What a surprise in a town of 18,000 people! On the lawn in front of this large, sand-colored building are life-sized bronze statues of a mounted cowboy, a riderless horse and a sheepherder with his dog. They stand in front of a fieldstone chimney and doorway.

A tiled entry leads into a bright atrium, illuminated by clerestory windows in the upper level. There's a striking trellis-like structure of dark-stained wood suspended overhead that contrasts sharply with smooth finished beige concrete and grasscloth walls. The library is warm and friendly. The shelves are wooden and there's good regional art on the walls.

The library has solid comfortable chairs wherever you look, particularly in the 60-foot by 30-foot main reading room. Many of the chairs have individual reading lamps, others are near VCRs with headphones. One side of the library is all windows and windowed reading alcoves.

The children's room has a marvelous little amphitheater with padded steps for seating. The room is very bright, with lots of stuff hanging around and from walls, shelves and ceilings. There are both catalog and game computers for kids.

Near the entrance to the library is the formal and quiet George Amos room (George Amos is the cowboy benefactor of the library whose bronze sculpture sits outside), with a small collection of books on Wyoming. Some of the furniture is red leather, some fully upholstered. Paintings hang on fieldstone walls. The room has a glass-enclosed fireplace; it looks like the very large living room of a wealthy rancher. The library was designed by Rundquist and Hard of Gillette.

# —— GREEN RIVER ——

## Sweetwater County Library

| 300 North First Street East | T |
| --- | --- |
| (307) 875-3615 | Closed Sundays |

Fifteen or more eighteen-wheel trucks in a row on Interstate 80 near Green River are not uncommon—you sometimes feel like an ant on the highway. If you want a rest from traffic or want to visit the impressive scenery of the Flaming Gorge National Recreation Area, try this library. It's a good stop between Salt Lake City and Cheyenne.

You can find some dilapidated 1890s buildings down by the railroad tracks. They, and the town, are a bit run down, but the library is another surprise. It's an impressive building opposite Castle Rock, a huge rock across the freeway. You'll be struck by large expanses of stone, brick and glass and an angled roof. Inside, the expanse of slanted ceiling is most impressive. Reflecting fluorescent lights run the length of the library.

The librarians will be glad to share the library's secret with you: it is reputed to be haunted because it is built over a cemetery.

Green River, WY
Sweetwater County Library

Jackson, WY
Teton County Library

## —— JACKSON ——

### Teton County Library

| | |
|---|---|
| 320 South King Street | A, T |
| (307) 733-2164 | Open every day |

Jackson is in one of the most beautiful scenic areas in North America, if not the world. Add a highly eclectic collection of Western-oriented tourist attractions and fine skiing, and the popularity of this town is not surprising.

The library is a classic log cabin that looks like it belongs exactly where it is. Each end of the building is a peaked log section, with the middle room somewhat lower.

Inside, log trusses support plank ceilings and the walls are simply the inner side of the logs that make up the structure—no plaster or sheet rock here. Pictures hang all around, and the reading room has a collection of comfortable chairs and couches. The reading room is busy with tables, bookcases, a globe and even a large stuffed trumpeter swan. It's what many people would picture as the idyllic reading room for the mountain cabin they'd like to have.

This building (and it works), is the antithesis of the bright, modern Idaho Springs, Idaho, library, which also works. One is authentic Old West, the other, perhaps as authentic, New West. The library is also superbly located. It's only three blocks from the base of one of the ski lifts at the Snow King resort and three blocks in the other direction from Jackson's famous Town Square with its elk antler arches.

## ─── LA BARGE ───

### La Barge Branch Library, Lincoln County Library

| 262 Main Street | A |
|---|---|
| (307) 386-2571 | Closed Saturdays, Sundays |

Good (and surprising) things come in small packages. It's easy to drive past this small wooden building with a large stone chimney on the main (and almost only) street in this town of 800. But this small, modern library is worth a stop.

Inside, natural-color laminated wood beams and ceiling form inventive angles. Black metal plates highlight the knotty wood and bolt the sections together.

The building makes intensive use of solar heating with solar panels on the south side, carefully placed skylights, vents and large circulating fans.

## ─── LARAMIE ───

### Albany County Public Library

| 310 South Eighth Street | T |
|---|---|
| (307) 745-3365 | Closed Sundays in summer |

This library is a large low-slung brick building. Inside, the feeling of "lowness" continues because the 2-foot-deep beams over the entryway seem to reach down toward the floor. The children's section is separated from the main library by a set of low bookshelves.

The central reading area in front of a 45-foot-long set of windows is quite comfortable. Study carrels around the edges of the library are well lit from the windows, but lighting in other parts of the library is a bit of a problem and may be redone. If you wander through the high stack area you find a number of reading areas, like meadows in a forest. The library is only a block from the elaborate Laramie Plains Museum in the restored Ivinson Mansion.

While Laramie only has a population of 27,000, it is a multifaceted town. It has a number of historic sites, yet also caters to rock concerts and theatrical productions. The campus of the 10,000-student University of Wyoming is great fun to explore (with no less than four museums), and there are a surprising number of good art galleries in town.

Laramie's elevation is 7,171 feet and it gets snowed in from time to time. The library could be a handy "port in a storm." Ten miles southeast of here Interstate 80 reaches its highest point of 8,640 feet, near a newly finished rest stop and Lincoln Memorial.

## ——— LYMAN ———

### Lyman Branch Library, Uinta County Library

204 East Sage
(307) 787-6556                                Closed Saturdays, Sundays

If you decide to get off the interstate for a while and drive 2 miles to Lyman, don't be surprised if you have to slow down for some cattle being herded along the road by local cowboys on horses. Lyman is quiet. One can stand in the street for five minutes taking pictures without having to move for a car.

The library is a small brick building with a peaked roof. It's nothing out of the ordinary in the grand scale of things, but newish and it stands out from most of the plain older buildings in this small town. Somebody cares.

Inside, two small rooms shelve general books on one end, children's on the other. It's interesting to see how small rural areas can promote reading. Lyman's population is less than 2,000, but this county library is very useable.

## —— RIVERTON ——

### Riverton Branch Library, Fremont County Library

| | |
|---|---:|
| 1330 West Park Avenue | A, E |
| (307) 856-3556 | Closed Sundays |
| | Closed Saturdays in summer |

After travelling through mountains on the northwest or arid desert on the east it's startling to find the Riverton Branch Library, an amazingly massive brick structure with a globelike contemporary sculpture out front. Tall brick columns using specially cast rounded bricks support large laminated beams that pierce the sides of the building and then cross an entrance under a huge vaulted arch.

As you pass through the brick and tile entry you're impressed by a slanted ceiling sweeping up from your left. It starts at a height of 12 or 15 feet at the far wall, but by the time it reaches the center of the library it's almost 30 feet high. A barrel-vault of clear plastic, with huge adjustable shades below it, completes the roofline. Remarkably slender brick columns, again using rounded brick, reach up to support the structure. An elevator goes to a mezzanine used for exhibits and receptions.

The children's room is directly in front of the main entrance and has another flying ceiling, this one slanting up from right to left. Both the main and the children's rooms have lights aimed at the ceiling to reflect light downward.

A small Western Americana room carpeted in deep blue has comfortable red leather chairs, paneled wainscotting and a recessed (coffered) wooden ceiling that give it an incredibly rich and private feeling. The library's community room is a small theater with paneled walls, another coffered ceiling and a formal stage. All in all this is a library you might expect in a town of 50,000, not 10,000. The building was designed by Deines, Myrick, McLain and Associates in 1983.

## —— SHERIDAN ——

### Sheridan County Fulmer Public Library

| | |
|---|---|
| 335 West Alger Street | A |
| (307) 674-8585 | Closed Sundays |

Since Sheridan (population 15,000) is more than 100 miles from any major city, you'll probably find this stop quite a surprise. This inviting library is in a small parklike setting. There are two outdoor courtyards for reading and programs, a colorful wall of tiles made by local school children and a Richard Greeves sculpture just inside the Spanish style covered entryway.

You can enter either the main reading room with its gently arching ceiling or the children's section from the entry hall. Well-screened fluorescent lights illuminate a library in which paintings, artifacts, sculpture, Indian rugs and plants are combined to create a feeling of comfortable warmth. A spiral concrete staircase leads to a mezzanine used for art displays.

The children's room is high-ceilinged and bright with lots of room, lots of books and an aquarium. It has a significant collection of early editions of American children's books, including *Tom Swift*, *The X-Bar-X Boys*, *Bamba: The Jungle Boy* and *The Rover Boys*. The original 1973 building was designed by Adrian Malone & Associates, Architects, and a 1986 addition was done by Malone/Belton Associates in Sheridan.

Sheridan is the gateway to the nearby Big Horn Mountains. It's home to the beautifully preserved Trail End Historic Center, a Flemish style mansion of one of Wyoming's past governors and cattle barons. Also near the library is King's Saddlery, a traditional leather shop and saddle museum.

## —— SUNDANCE ——

### Crook County Public Library

| | |
|---|---|
| 122 North Fourth Street | T |
| (307) 283-1006 | Closed Saturdays, Sundays |

With a population of under 1,200, isolated Sundance is at the foot of Sundance Mountain. It's only 28 miles from here to the Devil's Tower National Monument and 18 miles to the Vore Buffalo Jump. This isn't a bad place for a rest stop if you've been driving across either northern Wyoming or South Dakota.

Newly remodeled, this plain but attractive library is a tribute to what a grassroots group of dedicated residents can create. It is an older school building that was remodeled and expanded in 1990 by Rundquist and Hard of Gillette, Wyoming. While it is still a plain building, the all-wooden bookcases salvaged from larger libraries undergoing modernization are most attractive in this setting.

Even this small library has an "Art Wall" featuring the works of Crook County artists of national prominence. It also has significant collections of the works of Wyoming authors and on the art of writing. The enthusiastic staff here will point out that library usage has boomed since the remodeling took place.

## —— THERMOPOLIS ——

### Hot Springs County Library

| 344 Arapahoe | T |
|---|---|
| (307) 864-3104 | Closed Sundays, Saturdays in summer |

Thermopolis, home to the world's largest mineral hot spring, is on the scenic route south of Yellowstone National Park and Cody. If you've been driving west through Nebraska and central Wyoming, this is a great place to rehumidify yourself after the arid, desolate drive through Douglas and Casper. Or, if it's wintertime, how about a soak in a hot pool—open year round.

A 10-minute walk from the free State Bath House, this plain brick library with white trim along its roof is next to a playground and public tennis courts. Narrow floor-to-ceiling windows and window corners let in lots of light. Plain wooden furniture makes the library useable, if not a place to lounge. Like the rest of the library, the children's room has lots of windows. Its brick walls and soft carpeting make it a pleasant place for children.

# — INDEX —

Abilene, 224
Abilene Public Library, 224
Aberdeen, 284
Aberdeen Branch Library, Timberland Regional Library System, 284
Air Force Academy Library, U.S.A.F. Academy, 114
Alamogordo, 184
Alamogordo Public Library, 184
Alaska, 1
Albany, 202
Albany County Public Library, 318
Albany Public Library, 202
Albuquerque, 185
Albuquerque Public Library, 185
Alpine, 224
Alpine Public Library, 224
Amanda Park, 284
Amanda Park Branch Library, Timberland Regional Library System, 284
Amarillo, 225
Amarillo Public Library, 225
American Numismatic Association Library, 115
American Productivity Library, 248
American Quarter Horse Foundation Museum and Library, 226
Anaconda, 156
Anacortes, 285
Anacortes Public Library, 285
Anaheim, 26
Anaheim Public Library, 26
Anchorage, 2
Anchorage Museum Library, 3
Anderson Branch Library, 275
Apache Junction, 8
Apache Junction Public Library, 8
Arabian Horse Trust Library, 130
Arcata, 26

Arcata Branch Library, Humboldt County Library, 26
Arizona, 7
Arizona Hall of Fame Museum and the Carnegie Library, 16
Arizona State Library, 16
Armijo Branch Library, 240
Ashland, 203
Ashland Branch Library, Jackson County Library System, 203
Aspen, 108
Astoria, 205
Astoria Public Library, 203
Atascadero, 27
Atascadero Public Library, 27
Athenaeum Music and Arts Library, Library Association of La Jolla, 52
Aurora, 109
Aurora Public Library, 109
Austin, 226
Austin History Center, 227
Austin Public Library, 226
Avenues Branch Library, 276

Bainbridge Island, 285
Bainbridge Island Branch Library, Kitsap Regional Library System, 285
Bakersfield, 27
Basalt, 109
Basalt Regional Library, 109
Beale Memorial Library, Kern County Library, 27
Bear Canyon Branch Library, 23
Beaumont, 230
Beaumont Public Library, 230
Bellevue, 286
Bellevue Branch Library, King County Library System, 286
Berkeley, 29

Berkeley Public Library, 29
Beverly Hills, 31
Beverly Hills Public Library, 31
Biblioteca Latino Americana, 88
Big Horn County Public Library, 163
Billings, 156
Bisbee, 9
Bernice P. Bishop Museum Library, 134
Blaksley Library, Santa Barbara Botanic Garden Library, 95
Boerne, 233
Boerne Public Library, 233
Boise, 146
Boise Public Library, 146
Bonham, 234
Bonney Lake, 287
Bonney Lake Branch Library, Pierce County Library System, 287
Bothell, 287
Bothell Branch Library, King County Library System, 287
Boulder, 110
Boulder City, 170
Boulder City Library, 170
Boulder Public Library, 110
Bozeman, 157
Bozeman Public Library, 157
Brand Library and Art Center, 46
Thomas Branigan Memorial Library, 190
Brigham City, 268
Brigham City Library, 268
Buffalo, 312
Burbank, 33
Burbank Public Library, 33
Burley, 147
Burley Public Library, 147
Butte, 157
Butte–Silver Bow Public Library, 157
Butt–Holdsworth Memorial Library, 249

California, 25
California Academy of Sciences Library/ Biodiversity Resource Center, 85
California State Library, 76
California State Railroad Museum Library, 77
Cambria, 34
Cambria Branch Library, San Luis Obispo City–County Library, 34
Campbell County Public Library, 315
Cannon Beach, 206
Cannon Beach Library, 204
Canon City, 112
Canon City Public Library, 112
Canyon, 235
Carlsbad, 187
Carlsbad Public Library, 187
Carmel, 34

Carnegie Antique Market and Espresso Bar, 297
Carnegie Public Library, 191
Carson City, 170
Carson City Library, 170
Casa Grande, 9
Casa Grande Public Library, 9
Casper, 312
Castle Rock, 112
Chandler, 10
Chandler Public Library, 10
Chapman Branch Library, 276
Cheyenne, 313
Chico, 36
Chico Branch Library, Butte County Library, 36
Chinatown Branch Library, 85
Cholla Branch Library, 14
Chula Vista, 36
Chula Vista Public Library, 36
Dr. Eugene Clark Library, 253
Clayton Library, Center for Genealogical Research, 246
Clovis, 188
Clovis–Carver Public Library, 188
Cochise County Library, 9
Coeur D'Alene, 148
Coeur D'Alene Public Library, 148
Cokeville, 313
Cokeville Branch Library, Lincoln Valley Library, 313
Colorado, 107
Colorado Springs, 113
Columbine Branch Library, Jefferson County Public Library, 124
Conrad, 158
Conrad Public Library, 158
Cooper Landing, 3
Cooper Landing Community Library, 3
Coos Bay, 204
Coos Bay Public Library, 204
Corona Del Mar, 37
Coronado, 38
Coronado Public Library, 38
Corrales, 188
Corrales Community Library, 188
Corrigan, 235
Corvallis, 205
Corvallis–Benton County Public Library, 205
Costa Mesa, 38
Costa Mesa Branch Library, Orange County Public Library, 39
Coupeville, 288
Coupeville Branch Library, Sno-Isle Regional Library System, 288
Cowboy Artists of America Museum Library, 250
Crook County Public Library, 321
Crow Agency, 158
Cut Bank, 159

Dallas, 236
Danville, 39
Danville Branch, Contra Costa Public Library, 39
Daughters of the Republic of Texas Library, 259
Lorenzo de Zavala State Archives and Library, 230
Deer Lodge, 160
Denver, 116
Denver Public Library, 116
Desert Botanical Garden, Richter Library, 17
Dillon, 161
Dillon City Library, 161
Dobson Ranch Branch Library, 13
Douglas County Public Library, 177
Downtown (Albany, Oregon) Branch Library, 202

East Bonner County Library, 152
East Library and Information Center, Pikes Library District, 113
El Paso, 239
El Paso Public Library, 239
Elbert County Library, 122
Elko, 172
Elko County Library, 172
Ellensburg, 288
Ellensburg Public Library, 288
Estes Park, 118
Estes Park Public Library, 118
Eugene, 206
Eugene Public Library, 206
Eureka Valley–Harvey Milk Memorial Branch Library, 84
Evanston, 314
Everett, 289
Everett Public Library, 289

Fairfax, 40
Fairfax Branch Library, Marin County Library System, 40
Fairfield, 41
Fairfield–Suisun Community Branch Library, Solano County Library, 41
Family History Library, 277
Fayette Public Library, 252
Norman F. Feldheym Central Library, 79
Octavia Fellin Public Library, 190
Ferndale, 41
Ferndale Public Library, 41
Fine Arts Center Library, 115
Flagstaff, 10
Flagstaff City–Coconino County Public Library, 10
Florence, 207
Fort Bragg, 42
Fort Bragg Branch Library, Mendocino County Library, 42
Fort Collins, 118
Fort Collins Public Library, 118
Fort Stockton, 240

Fort Stockton Public Library, 240
Fort Vancouver Regional Library, 308
Fort Worth, 241
Fort Worth Public Library, 241
Fountain Valley, 43
Fountain Valley Branch Library, Orange County Library, 43
Helen Fowler Library at the Denver Botanic Garden, 117
Frankston, 242
Frankston Depot Library, 242
Fremont Branch Library, 300
Fremont, 43
Fremont Main Branch Library, Mesa County Public Library, 43
Fretz Park Branch Library, 237
Frisco, 119
Fruita, 119
Fruita Branch Library, Mesa County Public Library, 119
Fullerton, 44
Fullerton Public Library, 44

Gallup, 190
Galveston, 243
George Memorial Library, Fort Bend County Library System, 257
Gillette, 315
Glacier County Library, 159
Glendale, Arizona, 11
Glendale, Arizona, Public Library, 11
Glendale, California, 45
Glendale, California, Public Library, 45
Glendora, 47
Glendora Public Library, 47
Glenwood Springs, 120
Glenwood Springs Branch Library, Garfield County Public Library, 120
Golden Gate Branch Library, 64
Goldendale, 290
Goldendale Community Library, Fort Vancouver Regional Library System, 290
Frances Howard Goldwyn Hollywood Branch Library, 56
Grand Junction, 120
Great Falls, 162
Great Falls Public Library, 162
Green River, 316
Green Valley Library, Las Vegas–Clark County Library District, 172
Gresham, 208
Gresham Branch Library, Library Association of Portland, 208

Half Moon Bay, 48
Half Moon Bay Branch Library, San Mateo County Library, 48

Hardin, 163
Harrison Memorial Library, Park Branch, 35
Harwood Public Library, 198
Hatfield Marine Science Center Library, 213
Hawaii, 131
Hawaii Kai, 132
Hawaii Kai Public Library, 132
Hawaii State Library, 132
Healdsburg, 48
Healdsburg Branch Library and Sonoma County Wine Library, Sonoma County Library, 48
Hearst Free Library, 156
Heber City, 268
Heginbotham Library, 121
Helena, 164
Henderson, 172
Henderson District Public Library, 173
O. Henry Museum and (sort of) Library, 228
Hertzberg Circus Collection Museum and Library, 260
Hilo, 140
Hilo Public Library, 140
Holualoa, 141
Holualoa Public Library, 141
Holyoke, 121
Honokaa, 142
Honokaa Public Library, 142
Honolulu, 132
Hood River, 209
Hood River County Library, 209
Hoopa, 49
Hoquiam, 291
Hoquiam Branch Library, Timberland Regional Library System, 291
Hot Springs County Library, 322
Houston, 245
Houston Public Library, 245
Sam Houston Regional Library and Research Center, 252
Humboldt County Library, 181
Huntington Beach, 50
Huntington Beach Library, 50
Huntington Library, Art Collections and Botanical Gardens, 91

Idaho, 145
Idaho Falls, 148
Idaho Falls Public Library, 148
Idaho Springs, 122
Idaho Springs Public Library, 122
Idaho State Library, 147
Julia B. Ideson Building—Archives and Texas Room, 246
Incline Branch Library, Washoe County Library System, 173
Incline Village, 173
International Fly Fishing Federation Library, 168

Ironwood Branch Library, 15
Irvine, 52
Island of Hawaii, 140
Island of Maui, 138
Island of Oahu, 132
Issaquah, 292
Issaquah Library, King County Library System, 292

Jackson, 317
Johnson County Library, 312
Lyndon Baines Johnson Library and Museum, 228
A. Holmes Johnson Memorial Library, 5
J. Erik Jonsson Central Library, 236
Juneau, 4
Juneau Public Library, 4

Kailua, 135
Kailua–Kona, 142
Kailua–Kona Public Library, 142
Kailua Public Library, 135
Kaiser Permanente Health Education Center, 65
Kaneohe, 136
Kaneohe Public Library, 136
Karpeles Manuscript Library, The, 95
Kaysville, 269
Kaysville City Library, 269
Kealakekua, 143
Kerrville, 249
Ketchikan, 5
Ketchikan Public Library, 5
Ketchum (Sun Valley), 150
Ketchum Community Library, 150
Kilgore, 250
Kilgore Public Library, 250
Martin Luther King Branch Library, 307
Kingman, 12
Kiowa, 122
Kirkland, 294
Kirkland Library, 292
Klamath County Library, 210
Klamath Falls, 210
Kodiak, 5
Koelbel Public Library, Arapahoe Library District, 123
William K. Kohrs Memorial Library, 160

La Barge, 318
La Barge Branch Library, Lincoln County Library, 318
La Conner, 294
La Conner Memorial Library, 294
La Grange, 252
La Jolla, 52
Laboratory of Anthropology Library, 196
Lacey, 293
Lacey Branch Library, Timberland Regional Library System, 293

# Index

Lahaina, 138
Lahaina Public Library, 138
Lake County Library, 53
Lake Oswego, 210
Lake Oswego Public Library, 210
Lake Tahoe Branch Library, Douglas County Library, 182
Lakeport, 53
Landa Branch Library, 258
Langley, 294
Langley Branch Library, Sno-Isle Regional Library, 294
Laramie, 318
Laramie County Library, 313
Larkspur, 54
Larkspur Public Library, 54
Las Cruces, 190
Las Vegas Library and Lied Discovery Children's Museum, 174
Las Vegas, Nevada, 174
Las Vegas, New Mexico, 191
Lewis and Clark Library, 164
Liberty, 252
Library Bookstop, The, 197
Linda Vista Branch Library, 81
Little Big Horn College Archives and Library, 158
Littleton, 123
Livingston, 166
Livingston Public Library, 166
Lockhart, 253
Logan, 269
Logan Library, 269
Long Beach, 54
Long Beach Public Library, 54
Longview, 295
Longview Public Library, 295
Los Angeles, 55
Los Angeles Public Library, 55
Los Gatos, 57
Los Gatos Memorial Library, 57
Z. J. Loussac Public Library, 2
Loveland, 125
Loveland Public Library, 125
Lovington, 192
Lovington Public Library, 192
Lubbock, 253
Lubbock City–County Library, 253
Lyman, 319
Lyman Branch Library, Uinta County Library, 319

George and Helen Mahon Library, 255
Manhattan Beach, 58
Manhattan Beach Branch Library, Los Angeles County Library, 58
Manzanita, 211
Manzanita Branch Library, Tillamook County Library System, 211

Marin County Free Library, 92
Marion Koogler McNay Museum Library, 261
Maryhill, 296
Maryhill Museum of Art Library, 296
Marysville, 58
McClelland Public Library, 127
Anna E. McCormick Branch Library, 308
McGinley Memorial Library, 254
McGregor, 254
McMinnville, 211
McMinnville Public Library, 211
Mendocino, 59
Mendocino Community Library, 59
Mendocino County Library, 102
Merced, 60
Merced County Library, 60
Mercer Island, 296
Mercer Island Library, King County Library System, 296
Mesa, 12
Mesa County Public Library, 120
Mesa Public Library, 12
Mesquite Branch Library, 16
Mililani, 136
Mililani Public Library, 136
Mill Valley, 60
Mill Valley Public Library, 60
Philip S. Miller Library, 112
Minden, 177
Mission Branch Library–Biblioteca de la Mision, 84
Missoula, 166
Missoula Public Library, 166
Missouri City, 255
Missouri City Branch Library, Fort Bend County Library System, 255
Moapa Valley Branch Library, Las Vegas–Clark County Library System, 178
Modesto, 62
Mohave County Library, 12
Montana, 155
Montana Historical Society Library, 165
Monterey, 62
Monterey Public Library, 62
Montrose, 125
Montrose Branch Library, 247
Montrose Public Library, 125
Moscow, 150
Moscow–Latah County Library, 150
Mount Angel, 212
Mount Angel Abbey Library, 212
Mount Charleston, 178
Mount Charleston Branch Library, Las Vegas–Clark County Library System, 178
Mount Shasta Branch Library, Siskiyou County Public Library, 63
Mount Shasta City, 63
Mountaineers Club Library, 302

Multnomah County Library, 215
Museum of Flight Library, 303
Museum of International Folk Art Library, 197
Mustang Library, 18

Nampa, 151
Nampa Public Library, 151
Napa Valley Wine Library, 78
Natrona County Public Library, 312
Nevada, 169
Nevada State Library and Archives, 171
New Mexico, 183
New Mexico State Library, 198
Newport, 213
Newport Public Library, 213
Elisabet Ney Museum and Library, 229
Richard Nixon Library and Birthplace, 106
Nogales, 13
Nogales City–Santa Cruz County Public Library, 13
North Argonne Branch Library, 304
North Bend, 214
North Bend Public Library, 214
North Berkeley Branch Library, 30
North Oak Cliff Branch Library, 238
North Portland Branch Library, 216
North Spokane Branch Library, 305
Northside Branch Library, 241

Oakland, 63
Oakland Public Library, 63
Ocean Park, 297
Ocean Park Branch Library, Timberland Regional Library System, 297
Oceanside, 65
Oceanside Public Library, 65
Ogden, 270
Old Colorado City Branch Library, 114
Olympia, 297
Oregon, 201
Oregon Historical Society Library, 217
Oregon State Library, 219
Orem, 271
Orem Public Library, 271
Otay Mesa Branch Library, 82
Ouray, 126
Ouray Public Library, 126
Overton, 178
Oxnard, 66
Oxnard Public Library, 66

Pacific Grove, 67
Pacific Grove Public Library, 67
Palestine, 255
Palestine Public Library, 255
Palm Springs, 68
Palm Springs Public Library, 68

Palo Alto, 69
Palo Alto Children's Library, 69
Palo Alto City Library, 69
Panhandle–Plains Historical Museum Library, 235
Park Branch Library, 35
Park City, 272
Park City Library, 272
Thelma Parker Memorial Public and School Library, 143
Parmly Billings Library, 156
Pasadena, 70
Pasadena, City of, Department of Information Services Library, 70
Patagonia, 13
Patagonia Public Library, 13
Pearl City, 137
Pearl City Public Library, 137
Phoenix, 14
Phoenix Art Museum Library, 17
Phoenix Public Library, 14
Pitkin County Library, 108
Polson, 166
Polson City Library, 166
Pomona, 71
Pomona Public Library, 71
Portland, 215
Provo, 273
Provo City Public Library, 273
Pueblo, 127
Puyallup, 298

Queen Anne Branch Library, 301

Rainier Beach Branch Library, 301
Sam Rayburn Foundation Library and Museum, 234
Ronald Reagan Presidential Library, 101
Redding, 72
Redlands, 72
Redwood City, 74
Redwood City Public Library, 74
Mickey Reily Public Library, 235
Reno, 179
Renton, 298
Renton Public Library, 298
Richland, 299
Richland Public Library, 299
Richmond Branch Library, 84
Richmond, California, 74
Richmond Public Library, 74
Richmond, Texas, 257
River Center Branch Library, 23
Riverton, 320
Riverton Branch Library, Fremont County Library, 320
Judson W. Robinson, Jr. Westchase Branch Library, 248

Rockrimmon Branch Library, 114
Rosenberg Library and Museum, 243
Ross–Cherry Creek Branch Library, 117
Roswell, 193
Roswell Public Library, 193
Ruidoso, 194
Ruidoso Public Library, 194
Helen Crocker Russell Library of Horticulture, 86
Charles M. Russell Museum Library, 163

Sacramento, 75
Sacramento Public Library, 75
Saint Helena, 78
Salem, 218
Salem Public Library, 218
Salinas, 79
Salt Lake City, 274
Salt Lake City Public Library, 274
San Antonio, 258
San Antonio Conservation Foundation Society Library, 261
San Antonio Public Library, 258
San Bernardino, 79
San Diego, 81
San Diego Public Library, 81
San Francisco, 83
San Francisco Public Library, 83
San Jose, 88
San Jose Dr. Martin Luther King, Jr. Main Library, 88
San Juan Capistrano, 89
San Juan Capistrano Branch Library, Orange County Public Library, 89
San Luis Obispo, 90
San Luis Obispo City–County Library, 90
San Marino, 91
San Pedro Branch Library, 185
San Rafael, 92
San Ramon, 93
San Ramon Valley Branch Library, Contra Costa County Library System, 93
Sandpoint, 152
Sandy, 279
Sandy Branch Library, Salt Lake County Library System, 279
Santa Barbara, 94
Santa Barbara Museum of Natural History Library, 96
Santa Barbara Public Library, 94
Santa Fe, 194
Santa Fe History Library/Photo Archives, 196
Santa Fe Public Library, 194
Santa Monica, 97
Santa Monica Public Library, 97
Santa Rosa, 98
Sausalito, 99
Sausalito Public Library, 99

Kenneth Schlientz Memorial Library, 200
Scottsdale, 18
Scottsdale Public Library, 18
Seattle, 299
Seattle Art Museum Library, 303
Seattle Public Library, 299
Sedona, 20
Sedona Public Library, 20
Shasta County Library, 72
J. Porter Shaw Library at the National Maritime Museum, 87
Shelby, 167
Sheridan, 321
Sheridan County Fulmer Public Library, 321
Sherman Research Library and Gardens, 37
Allan Shivers Library and Museum, 266
Sierra Madre, 99
Sierra Madre Public Library, 99
Sierra View Branch Library, Washoe County Library System, 180
Sierra Vista, 20
Sierra Vista Public Library, 20
Simi Valley, 100
Simi Valley Branch Library, Ventura County Library System, 100
Nicholas P. Sims Library, 264
Sisters, 220
Sisters Public Library, Deschutes County Library System, 220
Siuslaw Public Library, 207
Skyline Branch Library, 238
Slavonic Benevolent Order of Texas Museum and Library, 262
A.K. Smiley Public Library, 72
Sonoma County Library, 98
Sonoma County Wine Library, 48
South Hill Branch Library, Pierce County Rural Library District, 298
South Valley Branch Library, 185
Southwest Branch Library, Kern County Library, 29
Southwest Regional Library, 242
Sparks, 181
Sparks Branch Library, Washoe County Library System, 181
Special Collections Branch Library, 186
Spokane, 304
Spokane Public Library, 304
Sprague Branch Library, 276
Springville, 282
Springville Museum of Art Library and Archives, 280
Springville Public Library, 280
Stanislaus County Free Library, 62
Steamboat Springs, 127
John Steinbeck Library, 79
Stevenson, 306

Stevenson Community Branch Library, Fort Vancouver Regional Library, 306
Summit County Library, 119
Sun Valley see Ketchum
Sundance, 321
Sunnyvale, 102
Sunnyvale Public Library, 102
Sunrise Branch Library, 177
Sweetwater County Library, 316

Tacoma, 306
Tacoma Public Library, 306
Taos, 198
Telluride, 128
Tempe, 21
Tempe Public Library, 21
Temple, 262
Teton County Library, 317
Texas, 223
Texas Ranger Museum and Hall of Fame Library, 264
Texas State Library, 230
The Dalles, 221
The Dalles City–Wasco County Library, 221
Thermopolis, 322
Tombstone, 22
Tombstone Reading Station, 22
Tooele, 281
Tooele Public Library, 281
Tool Lending Library, 31
Toole County Free Library, 167
Trinity County Free Library, 104
Truth or Consequences, 199
Truth or Consequences Public Library, 199
Tucson, 22
Tucson Public Library, 22
Tucumcari, 200
Twin Falls, 152
Twin Falls Public Library, 152
Tyler, 262
Tyler Public Library, 262
Tyrrell Historical Branch Library, 232

Uinta County Library, 314
Ukiah, 102
University Park Branch Library, 52
Utah, 267
Utah State Historical Society Library, 278

Vail, 129
Vail Public Library, 129
Vallejo, 103
Vallejo Naval and Historical Museum Library, 103
Valley Branch Library, 305
Vancouver, 308

Vancouver Mall Library, 309
Vashon Island, 309
Vashon Library at Ober Park, King County Library System, 309

Waco, 263
Waco–McLennan Public Library, 263
Waialua, 138
Waialua Public Library, 138
Waikiki–Kapahulu Library, 134
Wailuku, 139
Wailuku Public Library, 139
Waimea, 143
Warner Research Library, 33
Wasatch County Library, 268
Washington, 283
Washoe County Library, 179
Waxahachie, 264
Weatherford, 265
Weatherford Public Library, 265
Weaverville, 104
Weber County Library, 270
Weiser, 154
Weiser Public Library, 154
Bud Werner Memorial Library, 127
West Jordan, 282
West Jordan Branch, Salt Lake County Library System, 282
West Las Vegas Branch Library, 176
West Yellowstone, 168
West Yellowstone Public Library, 168
Westminster, 130
Wilkeson, 310
Wilkeson Branch Library, Pierce County Rural Library District, 310
Wilkinson Public Library, 128
Willits, 104
Willits Branch Library, Mendocino County Library, 104
Wilsonville, 222
Wilsonville Public Library, 222
Winnemucca, 181
George and Elsie Wood Public Library, 78
Woodville, 266
Wyoming, 311

Kim Yerton Memorial Library, 49
Yorba Linda, 105
Yorba Linda Public Library, 105
Yuba County Library, 58
Yuma, 24
Yuma County Public Library, 24

Zephyr Cove, 182

# — LIST OF ARCHITECTS —

Aalto, Alvar; 212
Adrian Malone & Associates, Architects; 321
Alvidrez and Associates; 240
Anderson, Mason, Dale; 124
Anthony & Langford; 50
Aotani and Associates; 132
Architectural Alliance, Inc.; 105
Architronics; 176
Arturo Cambeiro and Associates; 177
Balles, Jerry; 167
Barker/Rinker/Seacat; 125
Belluschi, Pietro; 206
Bruder, William; 14
Bull, Field, Volkman, Stockwell; 40
Callan & Willison; 290
Cardwell/ Thomas Associates; 206, 289
Clifford Moles, Associates; 93
CRSS; 242
De La Torre, Jorge; 186
Dehnert/Richardson; 312
Deines, Myrick, McLain and Associates; 320
DeLorenzo-Sticha; 171
Dickey, C. W.; 139
Edwards and Daniels; 268, 274, 276
Environmental Concern, Inc.; 2
Flammang, Barbara; 173
Flesher and Foster; 35
Fraser, Bruce; 90
Gehry, Frank O.; 56
George Wheeler & Associates; 37
Gibson and Reno; 129
Good, Hass and Felton; 238
Goodhue, Bertram; 55
Gould, Carl; 289
Graves, Michael; 116
Guinn, Leland; 251
Hall/Merriman; 255
Hardy, Holzman, Pfieffer Associates; 56

Hawtin, Bruce; 314
Holcomb and Lusso; 49
Holland and Pasker; 315
Huckabee and Donham; 240
Hunt, Myron; 70, 72
Iwasaki, George; 142
Kaplan, McLaughlin and Diaz with Simon,
    Martin-Vegue Winkelstein; 76
Klipp, Colussy Jenks DuBois, Architects; 116
Lewis/Nelson Architects; 288, 296
Malazzo, David; 29
Malmstrom, Cathleen (Architectural Resources);
    74
Malone/Belton Associates; 321
Marble, George N.; 251
Mattson and Prugh Lenon; 157
Maybeck, Bernard; 34
McCarthy, Francis Joseph; 99
McIntyre, Ken; 27
Messenger Associates; 308
Michael Brendle Architects; 117
Minch, Ritter, Voelckers; 4–5
Moore, Charles; 66
Morgan, O'Neal, Hill and Sutton; 256
Neal Huston Architectural; 220–221
Neutra, Richard; 50
Page-Werner Architects; 163
Parsons, Brinckerhoff; 28
Peckham, Bill; 104
Pherson, Clint; 284
Plachek, James; 30
Predock, Antoine; 174
Quigley, Rob Wellington; 82
Ray Bailey Architects; 247
Reed, John; 184
Richardson Design Partnership; 152, 282
Ripley Associates; 74
Rundquist and Hard; 316, 322

Scott, Louie and Browning; 271, 279
Seieroe, Vern; 110
SERA Architects; 208
Settecase, Smith, Doss; 219
Simon, Martin-Vegue Winkelstein; 44
Snowdon and Hopkins; 11, 129
Spenser Associates; 69
Stevens, Malory, Pearl and Campbell; 185
Stone, Edward D.; 69
Sundberg and Associates; 148
Swanson and Associates; 54
Thorp, Roger; 118
Tonkin/Storch Architects; 291
Tsang Partnership; 308
Turi, Richard; 207, 214
Villanueva, Gregory and Oscar Arnoni; 80
Waggoner, Dick; 193
Wagner and Klein; 233
Walker, Tom; 3
Warner/Burns/Toan/Lunde; 109
Wells, Hewitt; 179
Welton Becket & Associates; 71
Wheeler, John; 108
The White Budd Van Ness Partnership; 248
Wright, Frank Lloyd; 92
Wurster, Bernardi and Emmons; 60–61
Wurster, William; 62
Zimmer Gunsul Frasca Partnership; 286